COUPLE ON THE RUN

Eight Marathons,
Eight Countries,
Eight Weeks,
One Couple – Every Step Together

**The extraordinary story of how running together helped
a couple take their relationship to the next level**

Andrew and Sue O'Brien

Foreword by **Ron Clarke MBE** Running Legend

Afterword by **Jeff Galloway** Best Selling Running Author

Notice

The information in this book is meant to supplement, not replace proper exercise training. All forms of exercise pose some inherent risk and you should consult your medical doctor before commencing any exercise and dietary program. Exercise should be undertaken in recognition of your level of experience, aptitude, training and fitness.

Mention of specific individuals, companies, organisations or authorities in this book does not imply endorsement by the authors or publisher, nor does mention of specific individuals, companies, organisations or authorities imply they endorse this book, its authors or the publisher.

PARTNERUNNING™

First published 2011 by Publishing That Matters
www.publishingthatmatters.com
email: support@publishingthatmatters.com
Brighton, Victoria, Australia

National Library of Australia
Cataloguing-in-Publication data:

O'Brien, Andrew and Sue
Couple on the run /Andrew and Sue O'Brien.

ISBN 9780646546896 (pbk.)

Running, Marathon running, Australia, Biography

796.4260924

Designed by Russell Jeffery, Emigraph
International Edition

Inspiring powerful partnerships

About Couple on the Run

In 2008 Sue and Andrew O'Brien became known as the 'Couple on the Run' when, side by side, they ran 8 marathons in 8 countries in 8 weeks together. They live by the philosophy that by harnessing the principles of exercising with a partner and applying these to other areas of our everyday lives we can achieve more. With more than 100 marathons under their belts, overcoming a case of Chronic Fatigue Syndrome, the early detection of their son's life-threatening condition, and personal and professional successes all attributed to their running partnership, who are we to argue?

They claim fitness is one part of the equation, but it plays only a small part. The greater benefits include sharing the motivation to get things started, the commitment to regular exercise and enjoying quality time with one another. All of which leads to greater understandings, shared goals and ultimately lessons in life.

The O'Briens combine a diverse yet complementary experience base. Sue is a fitness expert and former Australian Triathlon representative, while Andrew is an award winning CEO, expert in creating Desired Futures, corporate adviser and talented facilitator.

COUPLE ON THE RUN

Dedication

'Cooperation is the thorough conviction that nobody can get there unless everybody gets there.'
Virginia Burden

Some people like to run alone, others like to run with a partner.

Some people like to go as fast as they can, others are happy just to go.

Some like to race, some to cruise along and for others strolling is the way to go.

Fast or slow, competitor or participant, alone or together, we think you are all wonderful and hope this book encourages you to start or continue your fitness journey.

Couple on the Run is dedicated to:

- individuals, couples and friends contemplating going further in life by going together
- the wonderful volunteers who every weekend make it possible for others to participate in fitness events
- all the weekend runners who regardless of size, shape, age and ability train and participate and by doing so inspire and encourage the rest of us
- Jack Clarke for showing us the value of always looking forward
- Ron Clarke MBE for reminding us that by having a go you just might succeed
- Paul Ramler AM for teaching us not to be afraid to name the outcome we seek.

Contents

'No road is long with good company.'

Authors' notes

*'Collaboration on a book is the
ultimate unnatural act.'*

Tom Clancy

Distances

One of the challenges of running in different countries is the shift
between miles and kilometres. Often in the big races both are
displayed, but this is rare. We have chosen to refer to markers in
keeping with the way distance was measured in the various places
we ran.

For the record, 1 mile equals 1.609344 kilometres and 1 kilometre
equals 0.621371192237 of a mile. A marathon is 42.195 kilometres
or 26.2 miles.

Funding, fundraising and sponsors

All costs associated with training and running 8 marathons in
8 countries in 8 weeks, including travel, accommodation, food,
medical expenses, entry fees, websites, promotion and clothing –
i.e. everything! – was paid for by us.

We promoted Oxfam as much as possible and encouraged
people to donate to Oxfam via a weblink. All money was paid direct
to Oxfam; we did not administer or transfer any of the funds as this
was 100 % the role of Oxfam.

We were sponsored by Injinji towards the end of our 8 marathon
trip and this involved receiving a discount on the retail price for
Injinji socks, caps and running gear.

Foreword

When my niece Sue first told me about her intention to run eight marathons including the Comrades in eight successive weeks, I told her she was out of her mind. I admired her concept and optimism, but up until then she had only run a few marathons in her entire life. If anything, she was a triathlete, having successfully taken the event up when her father (my brother Jack) decided he should try it at the tender age of 50.

Jack was the inspiration for everything I did. When we were kids he was the leader of the pack, constantly coming up with new ways to exercise and new challenges to conquer. My earliest running memories are of him, just three years my senior, telling me to concentrate on the pit of his back while he paced me up and down the hilly streets for the 4 kilometres between our house and our maternal grandmother's. We would visit her each week, getting faster and faster, and it wasn't until years later I found our mother had been giving him, as the oldest and more responsible brother, a couple of shillings for the fares there and back. Jack decided we could get there quicker by running, and the couple of bob gave him some extra pocket money.

For a good decade, I spent every non-school hour competing or training with Jack over a huge variety of sports and activities. He was training for football every day at a time when the wise old pundits were advising us youngsters that training more than twice weekly would make you 'go stale'. Some 20 years later the same 'wise pundits' were telling me I was 'over-training', even though I was setting world distance-running records.

'Look at the Europeans,' they said. 'Their training programs are the result of generations of experience.'

'But I'm beating them,' I'd protest.

'Ah,' came the reply, 'but think of how much better you could become if you copied their approach.'

Certainly both experience and reality must be considered and appreciated, but you must also have the self-belief and confidence to do it 'your way'.

And obviously these are the genes Sue has inherited. Married life and children restricted her in her 20s, but now, in her late 40s, she was free to follow her own star.

To run the 80-odd kilometres of the Comrades Marathon in South Africa – the toughest challenge that exists in athletics – and then to contemplate running another marathon the next weekend is ambitious enough. But to continue travelling and running another seven marathons for another seven weeks is something I just could not envisage having done – or thought was possible to do – and I'm up for most challenges that come my way.

But then I had some second thoughts. Sue is small and light – all muscle and sinew. She had been a top performer in a variety of sports all her life, excelling at tennis and squash, swimming and athletics, as well as being academically brilliant. She had the build, the mind, the determination and the ambition, so who was I to doubt she could realise her dream? Consequently, after my initial reaction of sheer disbelief that anyone would attempt such a feat, I became enthusiastic.

'What a challenge!' I said to her. 'Go for it, and the best of luck.'

Then she told me her husband Andrew was going along as well. Fine, I thought. It's a wise gesture to support your wife in her endeavours, look after arrangements, drive her back-up vehicle, massage the legs, and so on. His help would be invaluable.

'No, you don't understand,' she said. 'Andrew is going to run it as well.'

They explained how they wanted to write a book about partnering, and how training – and running – with a close partner assists enormously.

Now Andrew is a nice bloke. He's an above average sportsman, but essentially he is a businessman with no great background in any type of athletic endeavour. He is not a giant but neither is he small, muscular and petite like his wife. For him to run alongside Sue for the length of the Comrades Marathon would be an extraordinary achievement. All the runners that I knew who have been crazy enough to try it took two to three months to recover. And they were all lifetime runners, far fitter than Andrew.

'Andrew will do well to finish the Comrades, amazingly well,' I said to Sue. 'But to expect him to front up the next week to run a marathon is entering the miracle status.'

But Sue, being Sue, politely shrugged her shoulders and said, 'It's worth the try.'

Who could argue with that?

As you'll read in these pages, it was hardly a smooth passage, but no-one should underestimate the enormity of the feat this suburban, middle-aged couple have been able to achieve.

If this is what partnering – and Partnerunning – is all about, then I say, 'Bring it on!'

Ron Clarke
August 2010

Preface

*'A race is just a race, but a friend who
paces you is a friend for life.'*
Joseph Franko

This is not a book on how to be the best, fastest or longest runner in the world. It is about the power of partnership, and using health and fitness as the foundation for working towards individual and shared desired futures. It is also a story of personal and professional growth and development, taking a chance, leaving our comfort zone behind and getting things done in small achievable steps so as to bring a hoped for goal to reality. It tells of inspiration and achievement, of overcoming hardships, setbacks and limitations, of fun and learning.

In our experience, regardless of age, sex, nationality, country of residence, language, profession or social status we all benefit from:

- being fit and healthy so as to be able to enjoy life and accomplish the things we need and choose to
- positive and supportive relationships in the private, social and professional aspects of our lives
- clarifying our desired future and then working hard to bring it to fruition
- completing a multitude of tasks on a daily, weekly, monthly and annual basis to give us the success we desire.

Along the way to fulfilling our goals, many of us seek a sense of adventure, achievement and belonging while enjoying the satisfaction that comes from growing, learning and sharing the ups and downs of life with our family and friends.

The circle of life dictates that the separate parts of our lives are connected. We achieve our best results when we consider the impact of our actions on what matters to us. As an example, by maintaining fitness we can be more successful in our careers and better able to contribute to our relationships. At the same time, successful careers can provide skills and options to assist us with our fitness and relationships. To complete the circle, successful relationships tend to help with both fitness and career success. The reverse is also true; if we let our fitness suffer it has a negative impact on everything else we do, and so on.

In *Couple on the Run* we tell the story of setting out to run 8 marathons in 8 countries in 8 weeks. We also explain how we discovered Partnerunning and the many challenges and obstacles we encountered along the way to find each other, run together and complete our round the world running challenge.

In 2000 we ran our first marathon together. Although we did not realise it at the time, it changed our lives forever in ways we could never have imagined. As we strolled (hobbled!) from the finish line in Grant Park, Chicago we stopped to join other marathoners enjoying a bite to eat and a cold post race beer. As we waited for a post race photo to be taken, a fellow runner asked if we'd run the whole marathon together. When we told him we had, he seemed genuinely impressed.

'Yeah, all right! That is great! You are so lucky. I wish my partner and I ran together.'

We didn't think much of it at the time, putting it down to a runner's post marathon euphoria. But in the following months and years conversations just like that one were to happen at least every time we ran an event together – and often on our training runs as well. It did not seem to matter whether we were in Australia, Northern America, Europe, Asia or elsewhere, the response was the same: 'I wish my partner and I could run together.' The only variation on the theme was: 'I wish I had someone to run with.' We concluded there were a lot of people who sounded keen to run or exercise with someone else, and not necessarily with life or romantic partners but also with friends and training buddies of all types and persuasions.

We also noticed that many people seemed to give the same reasons why they thought they could not run or exercise with their partner: 'She/he is too fast', 'He/she is much fitter than me', 'Running is something you do alone', 'We have kids', 'She/he is too busy' and 'He/she is not interested'.

A common theme emerged among non-runners as well, and this related to the reasons people give for being unable to run: 'I am not fit enough to run', 'I tried to run but my knee/leg/foot hurt', 'I don't have time' and 'I used to run a bit but it hurt and I had to stop'.

We started to research material on running with a partner and groups but quickly discovered it was not a subject that had received a lot of attention. Most of the information we came across suggested that group runs and training with a running partner were good things to do, but aside from the occasional comment on drills there was not much we could find to assist people wanting to form and sustain successful running partnerships. We figured that with so many people expressing an interest in running together, we'd do some more research, develop a few ideas and maybe in time write a few articles.

We focused on the two themes we kept encountering – 'I wish I had a partner to run with' and 'I can't run because …' – and set about combining our backgrounds in fitness training, athletics, teaching, management, personal development, relationship skills, leadership and communication to develop a series of tips and tools to assist people to run together and overcome the obstacles to getting started.

After a few years our ideas had grown. We were well advanced in the preparation of a book on 'Partnerunning' when the idea to undertake the 8–8–8 challenge came along. What a great way to further test drive our material, we figured, and maybe we could provide some inspiration for people to start or return to running – and to do so with a partner.

When it comes to our philosophy, we agree with Aristotle: 'The whole is more than the sum of its parts.' For us, running together is a strategy that enables us to achieve the important things in our lives. In years to come we may replace running with walking, cycling, golf, stamp collecting or any number of pursuits. But the key principles of Partnerunning will remain. Focusing on what is important will guide the rest of our journey together until we find a better way.

We are confident that our approach can help you achieve your goals, not only for general fitness and running, but for life. For the technical aspects of marathon and other event running, and advice that will assist you in going faster and longer, there are many wonderful books, magazines, websites and other resources that focus solely on running and we encourage you to make use of them.

We are not going to pretend that our way of Partnerunning is the best and only way, but we hope it outlines a proven and effective approach from which you can adopt those strategies that work best for you. Most of all we hope the story of our round the world running tour encourages you to think, dream, learn and take action to seek out the life you desire.

Sue and Andrew O'Brien
September 2010

'Only those who will risk going too far can possibly find out how far they can go.'
T.S. Eliot

How about we take a trip?

'To be pleased with one's limits
is a wretched state.'

Goethe

It all began on a cold, wet and rather gloomy Melbourne morning in August 2007. I had been in my home office, toiling for several hours on a chapter for a book I was working on and was taking a break. Sue was buzzing around getting ready for work and daughter Shelley was looking for a lift to school. Our son Anthony, who when I started the day had yet to turn off his light, still hadn't surfaced.

As Sue and Shelley zipped in and out of range I chatted about our end of year family holiday. Planning our trips 12 months in advance had been working very well for us. As well as paying the fares well ahead of time, the year of planning gave us something to look forward to. With my current workload, a few weeks in Florida, running the Disney Marathon with Sue, and hanging out with Anthony and Shelley was just the sort of thing I needed to focus on.

'With Shelley and Anthony both at university next year we'll need to plan our 2008 trip around their study and work schedules,' I said as Sue came back into hearing range.

From that moment on our lives took an exciting turn.

'I thought just the two of us might take a trip next year, which means we can be more flexible about when we go.'

I was a bit slow on the uptake. 'What do you mean?'

Sue appeared from around the corner, put her hand on my shoulder, gave me the look (no, not that one, the other one, the one that a woman gives her man and he just has to say yes, as opposed to other one when he is scared to say no).

'Well I thought it would be nice if you and I went somewhere new, somewhere warm, somewhere without work or family. After all it will be our tenth wedding anniversary.'

Silly me! With 6 months to go I clearly should have been planning something. It sounded great – in theory. But I wasn't sure it was possible to take a holiday without the family, and I was certain it wasn't possible to travel without working. A few days off maybe, but not a whole trip. Edward Lorenz once suggested that when a butterfly flaps its wings in Brazil it sets off a tornado in Texas. I was soon to discover that when my lovely wife flutters her eyes events unfold very rapidly. So with Sue's hand on my shoulder and her giving me the look, it never occurred to me that we weren't going somewhere.

My mind raced to the practicalities. We already had plans in place for a big overseas holiday at the end of the year to celebrate Shelley completing high school, and the prospect of two lengthy overseas running trips in one year presented a number of challenges, least of all the cost. But within moments, the planning for our trip of a lifetime was underway.

Ever since my first marathon I had dreamed of one day running the famous 89 kilometre Comrades Marathon in South Africa. And for almost as long I'd had my eye on the Rio De Janeiro Marathon in Brazil. Both were in June, and I knew Sue was keen on Brazil. Perhaps a round the world trip was the way to go?

The next few weeks were full of excitement as we began planning our romantic getaway. After years of focusing on getting the kids through school, and O'B completing a couple of masters degrees and a doctorate and taking on a very demanding CEO assignment, the past 10 years had flashed past. We certainly had run in a lot of places and had some great family holidays, but I liked the idea of a real holiday with my man.

When my father Jack passed away unexpectedly in 2001 after being struck down with a rare form of cancer, I had changed my attitude to life. The loss of my dad, great friend and training partner had shaken me up a lot. Dad was working hard until he died, still saving for his retirement, but like a number of our friends he passed away just before being able to enjoy other activities after working full time all his life. The 2001 AFL Grand Final was one of the saddest yet proudest days of my life as Jack had the honour of presenting the premiership medals at the end of the game in front of 100,000 fans and a huge television audience. O'B and I took Dad and Mum to the game and few people realised how tough it was for Jack to make it through the day but he harnessed the last of his strength to present the medals. With his beloved Essendon Bombers beaten on the day by Brisbane no-one was more disappointed than Jack and our worst fears were realised when he passed away several weeks later.

I was determined to strike a balance between saving for retirement and enjoying life along the way. This meant seeing certain parts of the world and doing some of the running events I was keen to experience while I was fit and healthy enough to enjoy them. Fortunately, with O'B and I both working, we'd been able to invest almost all of his salary and live off mine. And since running is a pretty inexpensive pastime, we were able to find a healthy balance between investing for the future and having our annual vacations. Now I was mindful that completing the two races O'B had longed to participate in would add South Africa and South America to the continents where we have run, giving us at least one marathon in six of the seven continents – a challenge that had been on our list of things to do as partner runners for a while. Comrades 2008 was scheduled for 15 June 2008, Rio for 29 June. The cost of a round the world airfare was not much different to going to South Africa and back. A plan was beginning to unfold.

Quality time and other benefits of Partnerunning

A mutual interest in fitness had drawn us together in the first place. Over several years of running together 3 or 4 hours per week, we discovered the benefits of this to our relationship by accident. Most of our running is done at a pace where you can still carry on a conversation. And no phones, emails, TV, family or other distractions means it's quality time together.

Sometimes we see couples running and one or both are listening to iPods. What a lost opportunity! Over the years we've talked over many important issues while running – from deciding to get married to the children's schooling to our various career changes. We've resolved major problems about our future, discussed buying houses, and brainstormed about dealing with difficult people. The list goes on.

We also run together to mark special occasions and reflect on the year gone by and the year ahead. Each year, birthdays, Christmas and New Year are special running days for us. We've also discovered that running together is a great way to explore new areas; you can see more of a city in a 1 or 2 hour run than you can in a whole day as a tourist. For property investors or those seeking to buy a home, there is no better way to get to know a neighbourhood. In fact, one of our favourite running stories involves a property purchase. Since getting married we have lived in a house built by Sue's father on a block of land he bought while out for a run one day.

'How was your run, dear?' Sue's mum asked when Jack returned.

'Ah, not bad … Just need to grab my cheque book, I've just bought the house at the 9 kilometre mark.'

Running together provides the basis for making the effort so that you keep your commitment to the other person rather than skipping your exercise and training. This shared goal is a great way of focusing on the satisfaction that comes from achievement. Running with the person you live with has other advantages. You tend to eat similar foods, get out of bed at the same time, rest at the same time, and share in life's pleasures, pains and rewards. A mutual interest in something like running also makes it easy to buy each other useful presents. You can share magazines and books – and you have someone to talk to about your interest.

Aside from developing the 'yes we can' attitude, for us probably the biggest result of running together is that it has opened doors and taken us to places we never would have gone. At one end, this relates to the physical travel, seeing new cultures, meeting people, having new experiences, and always having something to plan and look forward to. Somewhere in the middle are the wonderful friendships that have formed. At the other end of the scale is personal development – as individuals and as a couple. We never know what will happen next in terms of our learning and have been amazed at the insights that have flowed since we've been running together. Certainly we never would have guessed that we would discover so much about ourselves and our relationship.

A couple of other things are important: the physical fitness benefits that flow from running together and simply doing something together that you are both passionate about. Almost all the lessons we have learned can be applied to other activities – walking, cycling, stamp collecting, surfing, wine appreciation, dancing, book clubs and so on.

Running together

Running is often seen as an individual pursuit – and one that belongs to elite athletes and those who are super fit. The running cause is also often at the mercy of comedians who reinforce the stereotype with a range of gags, many of them questioning the connection between 'fun' and 'run'. It took us a while to discover the pleasures that come with Partnerunning. But after our first marathon together we continued training together. With our newfound confidence in sticking together, we soon stumbled across a whole range of benefits that come from running with a partner.

After Sue completed her first marathon and I completed my third, we both focused on going faster rather than going together. We did our long runs side by side but when we went to the track for our weekly speed sessions we ran mile repeats at different paces. We also did a lot of 10 kilometre races to improve our marathon times, and although we started together we soon split up as we ran our own races.

At 189 centimetres/6 feet 2 inches, I was faster than Sue over short distances (up to 10 metres) but beyond 5 kilometres Sue was able to maintain a much faster speed. She was particularly strong in the second half of a 10,000 metre race. Watching her run down opponents in triathlon was great fun, but in our first few races against each other it was rather frustrating; I became one of those opponents she loved to chase down. I rather enjoyed chasing her tail for a short spurt, but the enjoyment soon passed as it disappeared over the horizon.

At first I despaired at not being able to run as fast as I would have liked. But I began to realise that for some of us the speed at which we run is far less significant than the fact we run at all. Certainly my height and build are not those of a long distance runner but as a teenager I loved to run. During my 20s, however, I lived on coffee, cigarettes, beer and junk food. Running was to play an important role in regaining my health and fitness; the speed at which I ran did not matter so much when I came to losing weight and teaching my lungs to function again.

I regained peak fitness, but in 1997 was struck down with Chronic Fatigue Syndrome (CFS). Even walking 100 metres was a major challenge. Once again I turned to running, first of all just thinking about being able to run, then walking, then jogging. In time I trained for and completed my first marathon. The speed at which I ran that race (4 hours and 1 minute) was not as important; the fact that I could run at all when a few years earlier I had struggled to walk 100 steps was what really mattered. Little did I realise that within a few years I would make the journey from smoking 100 cigarettes in a day to running 100 kilometres in less than a day.

In 2002 O'B and I headed to the Canberra Marathon, each intent on running personal bests. While we planned to start together, we had no intention of running the 42 kilometres side by side. It turned out to be a cruel day, with freezing cold temperatures and heavy rain. After finishing just 5 minutes apart, we questioned the value of running alone. We started to think seriously about running all our marathons together, yet were still lured by the 'go faster' thinking that dominates the mindset of many runners.

During 2003 I suffered a stress fracture while winning a quarter marathon in Chicago. The idea of running together became even more attractive. Any thoughts of continuing to work on our individual speed were finally dismissed later that year when, after battling hip and groin pain, O'B was diagnosed with arthritis in the right hip and advised to never run again. The night he returned from the sports medicine specialist was depressing, but by the next morning he had decided he would continue running. He'd do what he could to strengthen the hip, he said, mumbling something about anything being better than retiring to the couch and dying of a heart attack. Nonetheless, he needed to avoid track work and we agreed to run all our events together from that point on. We figured it was better to run together at a reasonable pace than to try for speed, continue to get injured and not run at all.

Exploring Partnerunning

Free from the pressure to always run as fast as we could, we made the most of our time together and opened ourselves up to experiencing the places we ran and enjoying each other's company. The more we ran together, the more we discovered the unexpected benefits for all aspects of our lives. When more and more people kept telling us how lucky we were to run together, we started to develop a keen interest in the idea of running and exercising with a partner.

O'B is a prolific reader and loves to research topics of interest. Before long he had filled a bookcase and a hard drive with books, magazines and research papers on running. With each one, he noted the lack of material on running with a partner, and before long we dedicated some of our long runs to discussing the merits of writing an article about Partnerunning, as we'd come to call it. Perhaps later on we'd write a book on the subject, combining my fitness and athletic experience and training with O'B's management skills and research into shared vision, teams, relationships, leadership, strategy and communication. Meanwhile, the only material we could find on running with a partner or group amounted to occasional magazine articles or a brief section in a book about the motivational benefits of running with someone else. We didn't come across a single article on the dynamics of running with a partner, and began to develop the simple hypothesis that most people run alone. Indeed, most running events reinforce the individual nature of running and the romance of the long distance runner. It follows from this that those who are great and/or keen runners enjoy this aspect and if they write about it they tend to focus accordingly.

But our accidental discovery of running with a partner had opened our eyes to benefits beyond the individual. And as well as improving our own Partnerunning experience, we liked the idea of encouraging others.

Developing Partnerunning

By 2007, I'd been working as a CEO in service industries including retail, fitness, hospitality, facility management and higher education for more than 20 years, and had decided to take some time out of the full time corporate world to pursue a few other interests. As well as wanting to regain peak fitness after years of long hours and part time postgraduate studies, I was also keen to pursue a number of writing projects and take on some consulting assignments. In my doctorate I'd focused on creating desired futures through the practical application of corporate and personal vision, strategy and teams and was now keen to make some major progress with Sue on our Partnerunning ideas. By the time we started planning the 8 marathons in 8 countries in 8 weeks we had developed a set of tools for assisting people to establish, maintain and succeed in running with a partner. We quickly realised the 8 marathon challenge would be a great opportunity to give our techniques a serious test. At the same time we could capture some great Partnerunning stories to encourage others.

One exciting aspect of developing the Partnerunning model was, with the exception of the technical components, our whole approach is based on developing successful professional and personal relationships. In fact, Partnerunning techniques can be applied at work and at home, not just when running. Apart from the many health and fitness benefits, regularly exercising with a partner can provide a super boost for your relationship. At first, the ease with which Sue and I found we could talk about anything while running together caught me by surprise. A lot of people, men in particular, find sitting around chatting with your partner, especially about relationships, not that easy. But when running or walking together, the sometimes difficult conversations don't seem so hard, in fact become easy and natural.

'You can't' and the challenge of planning

'You can't be serious! You can't run a marathon on consecutive weekends!'

'You certainly can't run a marathon every week for 8 weeks!'

'You can't take 2 months away from home and work when you are in your mid 40s!'

'No way can you spend that much time alone with your husband/ wife! You must be crazy.'

'Can I carry your bags?'

These are just some of the things people said when we told them we'd decided to embark on what would become known as our 8–8–8 challenge. But we were undeterred. When we realised we'd be returning home on the 8th day of the 8th month in 2008 a friend pointed out that the number 8 was connected with prosperity and seen as a lucky number for both the Chinese and Japanese. We hoped it would be lucky for us too.

There'd be many challenges running 8 marathons in 8 countries in 8 weeks, we knew, but one that occupied much of our attention at this early stage was the travel logistics. We weren't helped by the timing; there are fewer events to choose from during the northern summer. However, since we were in the advanced stages of preparing a Partnerunning travel module to assist individuals, couples and families plan and complete destination fitness events, it was a good time to put this also to the ultimate test.

A key aspect of one of our Partnerunning modules was identifying options, scenarios and the potential for problems and disasters to derail the best laid plans. For our own challenge, we were keen to minimise costs while maximising safety, security, reliability of transport and accommodation, health and recovery. We had to take into account:

- flight and other travel schedules, including allowances for cancellations
- ticket restrictions, including stops and direction of our ticket
- hotel availability and costs as well as locations, amenities and meals
- travel savings available by flying overnight
- fluctuations in exchange rates and variations around the world
- personal safety and luggage security.

With our preferred airline, we opted for around the world tickets which were the best fit for what we wanted to do. We combined this with a reliable global business traveller focused chain of hotels as our chosen accommodation. Both were known for their reliability, facilities, business support and service, and were to provide both savings and much convenience throughout our hectic schedule.

Ideas and false starts

Then it was a matter of where exactly to run. Finding events to participate in each weekend, while following the terms of our round the world ticket and starting in South Africa, was a major task in itself. After spending several months searching the internet and changing our minds several times about when and where to run, we finally came up with an itinerary:

15 June	Comrades Marathon (87 kilometres), Durban, South Africa
22 June	Flic-en-Flac to Port Louis return (45 kilometres), Mauritius
29 June	Rio de Janeiro Marathon (42.2 kilometres), Brazil
6 July	Calgary Marathon (42.2 kilometres), Alberta, Canada
13 July	Missoula Marathon (42.2 kilometres), Montana, USA
20 July	Pattaya Marathon (42.2 kilometres), Thailand
26 July	Swiss Alpine Marathon (42.2 kilometres), Davos, Switzerland
3 August	Townsville Marathon (42.2 kilometres), Queensland, Australia

Initially we decided not to run the week after Comrades as we didn't know how our bodies would react. But 7 marathons in 7 countries in 8 weeks or 7 marathons in 6 continents in 8 weeks didn't sound as exciting as 8 marathons in 8 countries in 8 weeks. Moreover, the idea of taking a week off seemed to detract from our adventure so we decided to combine our desire to visit Mauritius with organising our own run. While not an official marathon, the challenge of plotting our own course and measuring the distance with the assistance of locals, added another dimension to our expedition and definitely provided a challenge neither of us had undertaken previously. Running in Mauritius would be a great way to see the island – and running without race support would only add to our experience.

So much for a work free final itinerary

As we finalised our itinerary we recalled our initial conversation regarding the trip. The idea was to travel alone, without family, friends or work. However, in the 60 days away we'd be catching up with friends in South Africa, Canada and the US. And we'd share the last marathon with family and friends in Townsville.

As for a trip without work, this was an entirely different matter. While still looking forward to our exciting adventure, we had somehow managed to turn the whole gruelling exercise into a chance to promote Partnerunning. We planned to pack our schedule with daily blog writing, taking photos and video footage, gathering information and stories, writing diary entries and media releases, promoting and fundraising for Oxfam, and doing a constant stream of media interviews.

Creating a desired future

At the heart of Partnerunning is agreement about a desired future which enables genuine commitment to desired behaviours. Personal and shared vision has been a long term passion of mine and I was critical of much of the goal setting hype promoted by some experts. Too often, in my opinion, people focus on short or medium term goals that are not grounded in their true vision. And once those goals are achieved, the individual or team involved is left asking what is next.

For instance, we often see someone complete a 10 kilometre event, a triathlon or a marathon and then lose all interest in fitness and end up in worse condition than before they started training for the event. In this context, completing the event is more akin to ticking a box rather than marking a milestone to a long term destination that matters.

In deciding to take on our 8 marathons in 8 countries in 8 weeks challenge, Sue and I were very clear about how this trip of a lifetime could help us create the kind of future we wanted for ourselves. And as events unfolded, we were more and more certain Partnerunning was the key ingredient to our success.

Using the Desired Futures and Partnerunning approaches, we created a clear link between our short, medium and long term objectives.

Long-term vision	Be fit and healthy so we can live the life we choose. Do the work we want to do, where we want to do it, when we want to do it and with whom we want to do it
Medium-term strategies	Develop our concept of Partnerunning and inspire people to improve their health, fitness and relationships and create their own desired futures and success. Promote our ideas via books, seminars, speaking to corporate and community groups, and an online community.
Short-term actions	Complete the 8 marathons and capture the story of our shared challenge. Use our challenge to further test our Partnerunning methodology and promote healthy relationships. Be supportive partners, never give up, have fun and enjoy ourselves, learn at every opportunity and do what we can to encourage others to take action and be successful in their own lives.

Partnerunning Tip

COMMON GOALS

Making sure you are working to the same outcome and that your goals are genuinely shared rather than dictated by one partner, or non existent, is fundamental for commitment, motivation and focus.

Common Goals are	
Enhanced by	**Hindered by**
• Personal vision	• Lack of personal vision
• Consideration of common goals	• Failing to discuss common goals
• Linking goals to a desired future	• False agreements
• Asking questions about the future we want to create	• Goals without vision

Ground rules and behaviours

Ray Maclean is widely recognised as one of the world's leading experts on leadership and team behaviour, and from the early 2000s his approach made a significant contribution to the success of the Sydney Swans and Geelong Cats in the Australian Football League (AFL) – so much so, that his approach is followed by most AFL teams.

In the late 1990s I was the first corporate CEO in Australia to engage Ray to work with an executive team. His principles help overcome the political and politeness games most corporate teams play in order to feel safe but which ensure they fail to perform anywhere near their peak.

Sue and I have incorporated many of Ray's ideas into the development of Partnerunning. The most vital have been those which allow us to focus on what we must do in order to be successful and what we must avoid doing so as to not undermine our desired performance. This approach was also an important aspect of mentally preparing for the 8–8–8 challenge.

We work hard to incorporate the following guidelines into Partnerunning, and indeed everything else we do:

- Stick to our race plan
- Stay within 3 metres of each other
- Continually encourage each other
- Stay positive with no 'put downs'
- Share problems early
- Use run time for conversation, planning and reflection
- Have fun
- Encourage other runners and thank volunteers, supporters and organisers
- Learn together
- Use our Partnerunning techniques and tools for success
- Finish together – holding hands if possible!

We've discovered that it's important to not only identify your desired behaviours but also to pin down those negative behaviours that could undermine performance. In other words, if you do all the positives but continue with the negatives you are wasting your time. Negative behaviour needs to be eliminated to achieve the positives – a principle that applies to individuals, couples, teams and organisations.

In Partnerunning we work hard to avoid:

- false commitments
- ignoring or changing ground rules or goals
- failing to review all aspects of our performance
- ignoring problems
- blaming others and 'bagging' each other
- going faster than our race plan
- failing to eat and drink
- not listening
- failing to respect others
- giving up.

Injury scenarios

From the moment we began preparing for the marathons, injury was a major concern. We figured as long as we could avoid major injuries we could continue to train and reach the starting line. But injuries gathered along the way once we left home were another thing altogether.

Our worst fear was being unable to complete the journey, which would be made worse by having had to incur expenses without the satisfaction of completing the 8 runs. We hoped like crazy that injuries would not occur but if they did we were very clear on what we would do.

Our plan was:

- In the event of injuries where we could keep running, albeit slower, we would stick together no matter what.
- If an injury was incurred during a race we would withdraw together unless 100% certain the other person was safe and able to make it to the finish where they could get medical attention.

- If one of us was unable to start a race the other would run and the injured party would act as the support crew.

With this plan firmly in mind we felt confident. We crossed our fingers that neither of us became ill in the weeks leading up to the trip. There was always the chance of an accident but we were extra careful during our taper period, O'B having rolled an ankle the day before a half marathon a few years back and been unable to compete.

Pre-departure thoughts

The 'legwork' of making arrangements complete and our run plans firmly in mind, the last few weeks seemed to fly past very quickly indeed. From the time we finalised our itinerary and completed the vast majority of our training we worked flat out on preparing posters, t-shirts, website information for www.partnerunning.com and media releases to promote our Oxfam fundraising.

It was hard work but certainly stopped us thinking too much about what we were about to do. With less time devoted to training and more time on our hands, we'd started to realise the difficulty of our undertaking. I for one felt rather daunted by the whole adventure when, a few weeks before leaving, we received an email from a member of the Australian group of Comrades runners who had run the previous year's race. It included this statement:

> I remember our guide on the bus trip explaining the course last year telling us to be careful on race day during the early stages when it is dark if you go off to the bushes for a toilet stop that you don't get your shoes or watch stolen! I thought not only is it going to be hard but with NO shoes, what a journey ... However, I did cross the line with my shoes and watch!!!!

Well, that certainly helped us refocus! What have we let ourselves in for, I wondered. But it also alerted us to the need to be vigilant.

As the months and now weeks flew by, slowly but steadily we'd ticked off our training runs. We felt confident we'd identified the main obstacles and used our planning, risk and scenario techniques to prepare ourselves well. There were so many things that could go wrong, some we could manage and some we could only plan to deal with if they eventuated. At this stage the main things we were worried about were:

- pre-existing injuries and niggles
- new injuries and the potential of stress fractures
- illness
- fatigue
- slow recovery and soreness
- weight gain for O'B and weight loss for me
- travel problems and cancellations
- security and safety
- food poisoning
- weather and natural disasters.

On the plus side, we were looking forward to some beach and pool time as part of our rest and recovery strategy and had our fingers crossed for good weather. We were also taking advantage of the low tourist season in some places to stay in good locations at bargain prices. A little bit of luxury now and then couldn't hurt!

As the day of departure got closer, it began to dawn on me that it was actually going to happen. All our training and the organising of the trip behind us, my fears about what we had to overcome to make the trip a success were dominating my thoughts. My mind was racing. But somehow I knew that we were ready to run.

REST AND RECOVERY

Status report

O'B was injury free and running as well as he ever had over long distances. As always, he could be a few kilos lighter but when it came to running he specialised in carbo loading and it was always a challenge for him to run at his lightest. Sue was super fit but we were both worried about her foot (plantar fasciitis). She was so tough it was always a worry that the injury might be much worse that she realised.

PROGRESS

Lesson for life

Have a go.
Be prepared to have a go; you might win.

When we decided to turn Partnerunning from an idea into a reality by setting out on the 8 marathon challenge we convinced ourselves to think about what might happen if we succeeded rather than worrying about what would happen if we failed. Too often we have not taken action as we worried about failure and missed out on what might have been.

The first time

*'Running is the greatest metaphor for life
because you get out of it what you put into it.'*
Oprah Winfrey

They'd talked about it for some time but did not feel ready. He was keen. She said she wanted to but didn't think she could. She'd never done it before; he claimed he had a few times.

He said he would tell his mates they went all the way even if they didn't. She thought they should keep it to themselves – it might be a one-time thing. While he wondered if she would run off and leave him, she worried it would hurt. He said she could control the pace.

She almost did it with friends at university, but he'd never been asked by anyone else before. She told him she'd talked to her parents about it, whereas he'd never discussed it with anyone.

They had been building up to it and had been part of the way many times. Was it a good thing to do at their age, she asked. They were both well above the legal age, he reminded her. They read books that told them how to do it. They became aware that doing it well would take time, patience, trust, talking, listening and practice. They watched movies that really made them want to do it!

She felt anxious and hoped she could relax. He worried about measuring up to her expectations. They'd considered doing it before they were married but decided to wait. Now she thought they should start and finish in a park, but he hoped for a big crowd to watch and encourage them.

She liked it that he was a younger man; he liked it that she was an older woman. She wondered if he would hold her afterwards. He just hoped he did not fall asleep as soon as he finished. When they finally gave it a go, they could not wait to do it again, and again, and again.

Grant Park, Chicago
22 October 2000

The first time O'B and I ran a marathon together was with 33,171 other runners in the 2000 Chicago Marathon. O'B had previously run marathons in Los Angeles and Sydney, but despite being the athlete of the two of us I was yet to cover the 42.2 kilometre distance. As a young, enthusiastic but inexperienced university student I had attempted the 1981 Melbourne Marathon. Despite high hopes of a brilliant run, knee problems prevented me from finishing. Despite my hard training, constant dedication to my fitness and going on to represent Australia in Olympic distance triathlons, for more than two decades I remained convinced that after my demoralising attempt at the Melbourne Marathon I was incapable of covering 26 miles in one event.

I inherited my competitive spirit and athletic ability from my father, Jack Clarke. He and his brother Ron Clarke are among Australia's most successful sporting brothers. Jack was a legendary Australian Rules footballer with the Essendon Football Club and Ron is one of the all time distance running greats, setting numerous world records.

A year and a half earlier I watched O'B run his first marathon in LA and admitted to a strong preference for competing rather than watching. However, as I discovered then, it can be a long day watching a middle of the pack marathoner like O'B. Depending on the layout of the course and the number of people, you might completely miss seeing your runner at any stage of the race.

O'B loves live music and for 30 minutes after the LA finish we sat on the grass in the warm Californian sun watching the band Sixpence None the Richer which was entertaining the weary marathoners and their supporters. When O'B tried to stand up and couldn't without my assistance, I knew at once that if he changed his mind after swearing 'never again' I would attempt my second marathon. Despite his post race suffering, I also wanted to feel that good, hard earned pain that comes from giving your all to a competition.

In April 2000, O'B ran the Host City Marathon, a test event for the Sydney Olympics. At the same time as he was running in Sydney, I was competing for my country in the World Triathlon Championships in Perth. And while each of us enjoyed our events, we both came to the same conclusion: it was just not as good when we were not together. I was pretty sure I would only compete in future events when O'B was with me. So, 18 months after watching O'B in LA and 6 months after our racing weekend apart, when O'B decided to enter the Chicago Marathon I decided I would not be left on the sidelines again. I was convinced my knee would not carry me the whole 42.2 kilometres but figured by running at least the first half with him I would experience the start, be able to share some of the experience with him, and at the same time enjoy a decent workout. I would return to the hotel for a shower and make it back to the finish to see O'B cross the line.

Often when men talk of chasing their wives they mean the initial stages of their relationship, when they were first dating. But for me back in 2000 it was about doing all I could not to fall too far behind Sue on our regular 10 kilometre runs along the bayside trail near our home in Melbourne. Of the two of us, Sue is definitely the athlete; my interest in running was purely for my health and fitness. Even though she'd said she'd not run the whole race, I was so happy that she'd decided to join me for a marathon and was harbouring a secret plan to make sure we crossed the finish line together.

The streets of Chicago were cool and quiet early on the Sunday morning as we walked the 2 kilometres from the hotel to the start. Once again our conversation turned to how far Sue would run. She was still determined to run halfway, make her way back to the hotel, shower and meet me at the finish line. She was convinced of the merit of her plan and I played along. But I had other plans for how the day might unfold.

I knew Sue was much fitter and stronger than me so was keen to keep our options open. Planting the seeds for her to go a bit further than halfway, I pointed out that train stations were located near miles 17 and 21. She could run to either and then catch the train back. As we entered the starting zone we agreed Sue would consider going as far as she could. Deep down, we both hoped the energy and excitement would carry us to the finish line together.

The Chicago Marathon started and finished in Grant Park between Lake Michigan and the majestic buildings of downtown Chicago. The first half of the race would head north for a little over 7 miles, then just before halfway, the course would head west before turning south, with about 3 miles or 5 kilometres to go before it returned to the finish. We'd been warned the weather could be very cold or very hot but were blessed with ideal running conditions. With more than 30,000 runners packed into the starting corrals we were able to keep warm. Once the gun went off, it took us 7 minutes and 4 seconds to walk, shuffle, stand still, shuffle, stop, shuffle, walk and finally cross the start line. By the time we started running, we estimated the leaders would be about 2.2 kilometres or 1.4 miles ahead of us. From this position I knew it might be difficult for Sue to win, not that it was part of the plan, but I did wonder as she is a fierce competitor.

The crowds on the streets were 10 and 12 people deep in the downtown area. We crossed the river three times before heading north towards Old Town, Lincoln Park and Lake View East, and were blown away by the enthusiasm of the crowds who held signs, waved, cheered and screamed encouragement. Sue said it felt like everyone was cheering for her. How could that be possible? I was convinced I was the focus of their attention! Then another runner suggested we were both wrong– they crowd was cheering him. Whatever, the atmosphere was electrifing and we all felt very special, as if the entire crowd had turned out to barrack for us personally. If this was what running a marathon in the US was about then we were all for it.

As we left downtown, the hair on the back of our necks was still standing up. How come we hadn't been told how good this was? Now we began to understand why increasing numbers of people love marathon running as much as they do.

The first half of the Chicago Marathon was very picturesque, and I was fascinated by the Chicago skyline and magnificent buildings. O'B was crowd watching and soaking up the atmosphere. Running through the park next to Lake Michigan, we wondered why Chicago was known as the windy city. We could feel a breeze coming off the lake but for us it was far less windy than running around Port Phillip Bay back in Melbourne.

Before I realised it, we had been running for almost 2 hours and were back in the downtown area. We were both doing well, loving every minute of it, and I was only just starting to show signs of knee soreness. At the pace we were running we were right in the middle of the field, with the road densely packed with runners. I wondered if it would be like this the whole way.

The crowds had lost none of their enthusiasm and we talked about how hard it would be to describe the atmosphere to the people back at home. We had no doubt that anyone who knew what an amazing experience this was would want to give it a try at least once in their life. As we approached the turn that would take us west and away from the point where I planned on leaving O'B, he suggested I keep going.

'You never know,' he said, 'maybe you'll make it to the end.'

Confident I could catch the train back and still see him at the finish line, I decided to run with him for another few miles. We were heading along West Adams Street, having passed the halfway mark, and were about to cross the I94 and head through Greektown out towards West Loop when I began to notice the small niggling pain in my knee had increased hugely. After seeing me wince, O'B asked if I was okay. By now the run was notably quieter than the first half of the course and the going was getting tougher with each step. As we passed empty factories and office blocks, my mood and energy dropped dramatically and I started planning my return to the hotel.

In hindsight, it was startling the way I went from being on top of the world to doom and gloom within a few blocks. As the pain in my knee increased, I reminded O'B that I'd said I couldn't run more than 20 kilometres with my knees. Walking through a drink stop provided a little relief but I was becoming increasingly convinced it was time to let O'B continue on his own.

'I don't want to hold you up,' I told him.

But O'B kept talking about looking for a baseball field up ahead. Part of me felt he was ignoring my suffering, but another part of me figured maybe he was trying to get me to focus on something other than my knee.

Just after mile 14 I was done.

'That's enough, honey,' I said. 'I can't keep going.'

O'B suggested we walk a few minutes. We'd already been walking through the drink stations to make sure we drank more than we spilled but these only involved 15 seconds. I couldn't see how more walking would help but decided to give it a try. I didn't really have a choice. According to O'B, I was about 3 miles from the hotel and 3 miles from a train station – the same distance for me to go forward as it was backwards. And if I returned alone there was a good chance I'd get lost and have to go even further.

Basically I was not in a happy place, either physically or mentally. Memories of my Melbourne Marathon attempt of many years back returned. I reminded myself that I was not a marathoner.

Sue didn't think taking a walk break would help her sore knee but I said I was not going to leave her alone.

'We can walk together, go back to the hotel together or finish together,' I told her.

With more than 10 miles to go, deep down I realised sticking together was our best chance of us both finishing, although it would have been much easier for Sue to return to the hotel and for me to run on ahead. Still unconvinced about a walk, Sue agreed to give it a go.

'Can we make it to the turnaround at mile 15?' I asked her.

'Yes, we can!'

By then we'd be on Jackson Boulevard heading back towards the city and the station that was located between mile 16 and 17.

A 200 metre walk was followed by a run to the next drink station. The walk had provided some relief for Sue from the pain in her knee and by the time we reached the rail line she was doing okay. We agreed to keep going to the next drink stop and encouraged each other; together we could do it.

When it comes to marathon running, my best work is done at the carbo load the night before the run and I must draw on my business and life experience to make my way around the course as it is planning, strategy, risk management and determination that enables me to finish rather than any natural running or athletic ability. In my 20s I was rather partial to a cold beer and devoted myself to developing my beer consumption skills. One thing I knew from those days was that if you were in a bar with your friends and it was quitting time you had to play your cards carefully. Suggesting you stay for another 10 beers would never work. But by suggesting 'just one more for the road', more often than not you could wear at least some of your friends down with 10 more 'last drinks'. I decided this was the best approach to help Sue reach the finish line. Rather than telling her there were only 10 miles to go, I adopted the one more drink stop technique and we made steady progress.

With slightly longer walk breaks at the next few drink stations, Sue picked up the run pace. Before long her knee pain was a thing of the past and we zoomed past the rail line near mile 21 without a mention of stopping to take the train home, just a focus on reaching the next drink station. Unfortunately, the second half of the Chicago Marathon lacks the scenery of the first and soon we were both looking forward to the finish. I found the going particularly tough after mile 21 and as we turned on to Michigan Avenue with about 2 miles to go I was struggling to put one foot in front of the other. I found time for a quiet chuckle though, as I was amused by the situation we'd found ourselves in as we pushed towards the finish. Yet again I was chasing Sue who by now was bouncing along as if she'd just started the race. Whereas I was barely moving, a far cry from an hour or so earlier when she was ready to call it quits and I felt like I could run all day.

At mile 14 I'd been ready to drop out. I was concerned that I'd hurt my knee, upset my forthcoming triathlon season and slowed O'B down. Amazingly, 8 miles later I was fresh as a daisy, almost bounding along towards the finish while O'B was really struggling, crawling towards the finish. Somehow I had broken through 'the wall', but it wouldn't have happened without O'B's encouragement. The 2½ miles up Michigan Avenue to reach the finish on Columbus Drive in Grant Park seemed to take forever, but we both knew we were going to make it. I got quite teary during the final stretch, an experience not uncommon for first time marathoners who often become overcome with emotion.

As we approached the line, we instinctively held hands, a gesture we have since repeated more than 50 times in marathon and ultra marathon finishes since. The rest of the finish was a blur, however, and we hobbled past the beer tent unable to stomach the sponsor's normally enticing product. We proudly had our photo taken together with our medals and slowly made our way out of the finishing area to enjoy the celebrations and soak up the post race atmosphere which was every bit as good as the buzz before and during the race.

Only in the days after we left Chicago did we begin to realise the significance of what had occurred, particularly our 'moment of truth' just past the 14 mile mark when we decided to stick together rather than go it alone. It would have been so easy for me to run on ahead and Sue to pull out. Certainly me slowing down and Sue trying a walk break to ease her pain were not what you are meant to do in a running event! But in the moment when Sue said she was going to stop and told me to go on alone, instinctively we made the best decision of our lives. It was a choice to stay together, no matter what – and it would become another critical turning point in our relationship and our lives.

We'd both messed up our first marriages and the decision we made in Chicago was a sign we were on the right track this time. In our former relationships, at the first sign of tough going I would have said something like, 'Oh well, if you don't want to do it I will do it by myself.' Sue had a similar approach but rather than running away from a difficult situation by chasing a quiet beer or going to work, her solution was to head out for a 3 hour bike ride or a long solitary swim. Rather than facing our problems and finding solutions, for each of us the easy way had been to go it alone and do our own thing. It felt good to discover an alternative. We realised we could go much further together than we could alone.

In 2008, the US Presidential campaign provided a timely reminder of our 2000 Chicago Marathon lesson. As we watched rallies across the US embrace the 'Yes we can' mantra, it took us back to the day when we learned to say the same thing. It was a day that changed our lives forever. When we went to Chicago we had been married 2½ years. Everything was going well but we were spending a lot of time talking about what we wanted to do and not much time doing it. Staying together in that race was tough for both of us, but the benefits have proven to be dramatic. In that moment we discovered that by sticking together and helping each other we could achieve anything we put our minds to.

In the years following Chicago, not only did we discover the benefits and pleasures of running together, but we also went on to use our newfound self-belief and partnership approach to push beyond our comfort zone to pursue a range of successes in the work, investment, education and health arenas of our lives. And as well as going after the future we wanted together, we became much better at helping each other through the day-to-day challenges in our lives. When you're running together, you can't hide or deny problems. If you slow or stop there is no pretending; it is obvious something is wrong. This valuable lesson has helped us share problems and challenges in everything else we do.

For the record, in the 2000 Chicago Marathon Sue was the 4,956th woman to finish and 16,688th overall. O'B was the 11,732nd man and 16,687th overall. We both crossed the line in 4 hours 28 minutes 49 seconds – and so began the mystery of 'who finishes first when we cross the line together', or 'how come your time is a second faster when we crossed the line together holding hands'.

In 2003 we returned to Chicago to run the marathon again and enjoyed every minute of it. Once again we crossed the line together, 42 minutes – that's 1 minute per kilometre – faster than our first attempt.

Partnerunning Tip

COMMUNICATION

Exercising together is a great opportunity to talk about what matters. Encouraging each other, learning to improve, solving problems, clarifying your desired future or just passing the time are all great options when you are on the run or exercising with a partner..

Communication is:	
Enhanced by	**Hindered by**
• Listening	• Talking 'at' rather than 'with' each other
• Planning conversations in advance	• Failing to listen
• Regular reviews	• Not planning review times
• Talking openly	• Ignoring goals and ground rules
• Personal reflection	• Blaming and 'bagging'
• Focusing on ground rules and goals	• Putting others on the spot

Lesson for life

Go further together.
Embrace the brilliance and potential of true collaboration.

This was the day we discovered the value of sticking together. When we pushed beyond the point where you normally go it on your own, we found out that with the power of partnership we could go further together and achieve far more than we ever could alone.

Couple on the Run
Reader bonus number 1

Bonus Download Offer from www.coupleontherun.com

Check out the latest news from Couple on the Run and Partnerunning and receive these exclusive bonuses.

- The extra chapter: Training for the 8-8-8-1 Challenge (pdf)

- Sue and Andrew talk about Partnerunning and their book
  Couple on the Run (audio)

A popular question from readers is 'how did you train to run 8 marathons in 8 countries in 8 weeks?'. The bonus chapter could have been a stand alone book and contains a fascinating insight into the required training including a midnight family run in Central Park New York and Andrew's near demise running in New Zealand.

Select: www.coupleontheun.com and go to Book Bonuses
Download password: Partnerunning

Becoming a Comrade: South Africa

'If you are going through hell, keep going.'
Winston Churchill

Cumulative flying distance:	**12,243 kilometres**
Cumulative flying time:	**16 hours and 35 minutes**
Cumulative total travel time:	**36 hours and 35 minutes**

Once in the air, there was no turning back. From here on, the challenges would be real. Now all we had to do was eat, run, recover and fly – 8 times in 8 weeks in 8 countries – while doing our best to have fun, document our journey, promote Oxfam and healthy relationships, and stay safe. It was the first time either of us had really stopped in we didn't know how long and it was rather daunting now we had time to think about it. In retrospect, it was helpful that the past few weeks had been so busy.

Even once abroad, we still had two main concerns. First, about how Sue would cope if her plantar fascia caused problems; second, what we'd do if I couldn't run all the way with her. Sue's the toughest person I know and always achieves what she sets out to do, so I also wasn't sure how she'd cope if her foot let her down. She'd carried many minor injuries over the years but nothing that had ever slowed her pace. It would be hard on her if she couldn't continue at any point, and I knew she was worried about letting me down too.

On the other hand I am much more prone to injury. Whenever I ring Peter, my physiotherapist, for an appointment and say I have a leg injury, they always ask for more information as it could be any one of several pre-existing problems. But I'd run strongly in our practice events and was hoping this form would continue. Nevertheless, the pain I'd experienced running up Mt Buller during a training run in January had been severe and I doubted I could keep going week after week if that was to recur.

The biggest thing we were worried about seemed to be letting each other down but we'd already talked about this a lot. If it happened we'd know how to deal with it, but I still wasn't convinced we'd be prepared for disappointment if one of us couldn't continue.

You look like a runner

On the plane I was again reminded of what might be my biggest challenge – my size. Often when we've mentioned the marathon to people their response to Sue has been, 'Oh yes, you look like a runner.' Then I get the look that says, 'But you don't!'

'We always run together,' Sue explains.

To which the surprised response is usually, 'Oh, so you run too, do you?'

Unlike Sue, who is built for both speed and endurance, for me carrying the extra size is another part of the challenge. At 189 centimetres, I am 24 centimetres taller than world record holder Haile Gebrselassie. Called the 'Big Fella from Black Rock' by one journalist, my best running weight is 85 kilograms, but more often than not I run at 88 to 90 kilograms, 32 kilograms heavier than Haile, the 'Emperor of Ethiopia'.

People's responses used to bother me but nowadays I take them as a compliment. After all, I run as far and as fast as Sue and we almost always finish in the first half of the field. I might not look the part but I sure feel like it – especially in the 48 hours after a race. Besides, marathoners are defined by determination and the ability to have a go, regardless of bodyweight and running speed. So, as we flew over the South Pole, I reminded myself yet again that while I may be tall for a runner, and slower than most, I can't give up until I succeed – a trait that I hoped would stand us in good stead in the coming weeks.

What if we fail?

While those around me snoozed, I was struggling. What if we don't make it? Imagine the embarrassment in telling sponsors, Oxfam, family, friends and the media that we'd failed. But fear of failing generally didn't stop me trying new things. In fact, part of our decision to embark on this trip had been to challenge negative thinking. Over and again, Sue and I had drawn on her uncle Ron when it came to thinking differently. While most of us don't have a go in case we fail, Ron always gives things his best. The way he sees it, he might win but so what if he doesn't?

As we stepped off the plane at last I realised that we were having a go – and we just might make it.

We left Sydney late, so things in Johannesburg were pretty stressful as we were catching the last plane for the day to Durban. The passport control line was long and slow, and with only an hour to transfer we were concerned we would miss our 6pm connection and be stranded for the night.

In the passport queue we met up with three fellow Comrades runners – Jane, Mari-Mar and Michael. In what seemed like a scene from the television show *The Amazing Race*, it took five of us to find the 'clues' (well-hidden sign posts) to make our way through passport control and customs and 500 metres down the road to the domestic terminal where our frantic search for check in, security and the departure gate continued – a serious workout which saw us walking down the air bridge on to the plane drenched in sweat with just a couple of minutes to spare.

Then the boarding staff insisted the plane was not equipped to handle Australian size cabin baggage. Having lost luggage on numerous occasions, this was no simple matter. Our carry on bags contained all our travel documents, laptops, iPods, cash, credit cards and cameras. Our most prized possessions – running shoes and orthotics, run shorts and race singlets – were in our small backpacks. A quick stuffing of valuables into the backpack while carrying the laptops finally saw us on the plane. We were relieved to finally settle in our seats for takeoff, although a little disappointed we would be landing in Durban in darkness which would deny us the chance to see the landscape we'd be running between there and Pietermaritzburg.

After a short flight we arrived in Durban where our transfer driver was waiting for us. We were pretty keen for some sleep by this stage but still had to deal with the hotel check in and a few booking problems, having been allocated a room with two single beds. After some shuffling of rooms, we called it quits for the day. One of us slept very well, the other did not.

Registration and expo
Thursday 12 June

After an early breakfast with members of the Travelling Fit group from Australia we headed off to walk the 20 minutes to the expo and race registration. It was a lovely sunny morning and there was a real sense of excitement among us. As a bunch of first timers we walked as a tight group, sharing stories of our running adventures and travel challenges, and swapping tips we had been given to avoid being robbed or mugged. We'd been told to bring our registration cards with us but most of us had left Australia before we received them so the first half hour involved moving from one official table to another before we could actually register.

The Comrades Marathon Expo provides a lounge area for international runners and this became our base for the next 5 hours as we toured the expo and took advantage of the free massage service. The expo was huge, with many local stallholders and some very well priced goods for Australian shoppers. I bought a new pair of the Brooks shoes I run in for AU$80, and was very happy as they're normally $200 at home.

Sure this would be our one and only Comrades, we bought as many souvenirs as possible – beach towels, gym towels, t-shirts, race singlets and shorts, bottle openers, caps and teddy bears. The Comrades red wine was very popular, and many Australians purchased a bottle or so for the post race celebration.

After lunch we jumped into a taxi and headed back to the hotel for a rest before dinner with a few other runners. With all the walking already, we felt we needed some time off our feet. A check of emails found some encouragement from back home including the comment, 'Love the new website! I'm getting my way round it!

Congratulations and enjoy every second of the experience together'. A nice boost!

By 9pm we turned off the lights, hoping for a decent sleep. Once again, one of us slept well and the other did not.

The Comrades theme

Having taken a melatonin tablet, I felt no signs of jet lag and was looking forward to exploring Durban and getting some fresh air. We were in awe of the character of the Comrades Marathon – and well aware of the challenge we'd taken on. The following, from the Comrades Marathon Association website, gives some insight into the race's history:

> The Comrades Marathon is not just a race, it is a definition of who you are. It dictates your lifestyle, your eating habits, and your self esteem. It tests your body, your endurance, your will power. And every year it defines thousands of runners as they cover an 87 kilometre journey which makes or breaks them.

We spent several hours at the expo enthralled in the stories of marathons gone by. It was easy to understand why this was such a famous race. We felt privileged to be able to take part in this incredible event, yet still found it hard to believe we were about to run it and become part of its history.

Ever since I ran my first marathon and heard people talk of the Comrades I'd wanted to run it 'one day'. For many years 'one day' and 'some day' were safely in the distance. But no longer. What makes long distance running unique is that middle of the pack runners like me can participate in the same event as the world's best.

International runners were made very welcome in Durban and I was surprised that there weren't as many as we'd expected, with just 518 in the field of 11,140. The field also included 17.8% first time Comrades runners and 17% women, very low compared to most of the marathons we'd run.

The Good Oil and a tour of the course
Friday 13 June

Friday started with a Skype catch up with Anthony and Shelley back in Melbourne, followed by an interview with Mark Doran on his show *The Good Oil* on SEN 1116 radio in Melbourne. Mark had done his research and he explored a wide range of issues, which was good as we got some great feedback from listeners. Afterwards, however, I was a bit worried about extra pressure we now had, given the interest from the Australian media.

A bus tour of the course and a visit to Comrades House in Pietermaritzburg was available to novices and we looked forward to finally seeing those famous hills. Not being a marvellous hill runner I was very anxious they'd turn out to be mountains and I shivered with nervousness contemplating running up these 'monsters'. Our experience was that running courses always look harder from a vehicle so we were hoping that once again this would prove to be the case.

A team of volunteers had been constructing the finishing area for the past 3 weeks and had turned a beautiful cricket stadium into a mass of tents, stands and a giant finishers chute with Comrades signs everywhere. In 'down' years they repeat the process at Kingsmead

Oval, the ground for international test cricket. We could only imagine the atmosphere as the 12 hour cut off for the finish approached and those missing the time limit were not recognised as completing the race. Now it really dawned on us. What if we don't make it?

It was hot and I worried about O'B who is not built for running in the heat. The race day temperature was expected to be 25 degrees Celsius – nice on the beach but for O'B an extra challenge, and one we'd hoped to avoid. But as we walked down the finishers chute, we just wanted to get on with it and wished we could run the race that day. There'd been enough waiting.

A story from the previous year's Comrades

During dinner the night before the conversation had turned to race tactics. Tory, who had completed the 2007 run in a very respectable time of 8½ hours said he found the second half tough going as running alone for so long was mentally gruelling. His challenge was that he couldn't find any other runners to pass the time with as everyone he tried to strike up a conversation with spoke a language other than English. Tory's story was good blog content and Jock Macneish back in Melbourne soon sent us a cartoon for our website capturing Tory's adventure of the previous year.

One of the types of Partnerunning relationships our research has identified is the 'One Night Stand'. This involves two people (usually complete strangers but not always) passing the time during a race or training run by engaging in conversation. Running conversations are great for dealing with the mental challenge of long distance running and, with a common goal, it's amazing how even complete strangers can discover so much about each, often without even knowing the other's name. More often than not they never meet again.

Tory also told us that people who run back-to-back Comrades receive a special medal. We were yet to run our first Comrades but already were thinking about coming back in 2009!

The day before
Saturday 14 June

This was one of the most difficult pre-race days I have ever experienced. The excitement of being in Durban, sharing the experience with some great Aussie runners and waiting for the race to start was both enjoyment and nervous torture. O'B is normally very relaxed before a marathon but I could tell he'd had enough of the waiting. For the first time ever, he even hinted that he was feeling a little apprehensive.

After a quick meal, uncertain if we ate the right food and the right amount, we retreated to our room to prepare. We rechecked our clothing, experimented with the best way to attach our timing chip to our race shoes, packed our bag for after the race and set as many alarms on phones and watches as we could to make sure we were awake in plenty of time. Lights out at 10pm.

Early to rise
Sunday 15 June

The day started at 2.50am with quick showers and some serious application of anti-chafe balm to every part of our bodies that had the remotest chance of chafing. Feet, underarms and between the legs were the main targets for both of us. I paid extra attention to where my nipples used to be before a number of extra humid races as good as erased them, leaving only enough skin to still chafe at the most inopportune times. We checked and packed our bag before heading down for breakfast, taking everything with us ready to race, not wanting to risk getting locked out of our room.

By 3.30am Sue was eating porridge and I tried some muesli and toast. While we ate conservatively in case we upset our stomachs, we watched in awe as the African runners tucked into huge serves of bacon, eggs, beans and sausages. Had we inadvertently stumbled across the real reason for the African/Ethiopian/Kenyan runners' dominance of long distance events?

At 4.15am about ten of us Australian runners met in the lobby and set off to walk the 3 kilometres to the start, not something you would do on any other day of the year but we'd been assured it was probably safe on the morning of Comrades Marathon. There was a tremendous feeling of excitement and trepidation and more than one anxious runner was heard to say, 'I wish we could just start.'

As we progressed, our group grew in size as more and more people came out of hotels and apartments to join the procession to the start. It was not long before we tagged along with a large group singing as they walked, and soon there were cars and people everywhere as we entered the starting compound.

Not long to go now and the mix of nerves and excited tension meant we all kept up the humorous banter so as to pass the time. Once inside the compound we joined the queue to check in our bags which were traded for stickers applied to the back of our race numbers. Several trucks were lined up to take all the bags to Pietermaritzburg while we ran the course.

Our attention then turned to the portable toilets and the massive queues. The town hall bushes seemed more inviting to most in our group and after waiting for the girls to emerge we broke up as each runner headed to their corral. We were joined by Michael and

Mari-mar from our touring party and headed for the C corral. It was 20 minutes to the race start.

The start

The countdown was spectacular. The crowd sang the South African national anthem, then an unofficial South African sports anthem, a moving song called' Shosholoza' which is Zula for 'to push forward'. Then 'Chariots of Fire' poured out of the speakers. As the clock ticked down to 5.30am we waited nervously for the cock to crow twice. In years gone by one of the locals used to crow just before the start, a tradition that has continued, only these days the crow comes through the speakers. Once the gun fires, runners shuffle towards the starting line for an event that the Comrades Marathon program promises will 'entertain and inspire while being an accessible, affordable, inspirational and extraordinary challenge, attainable by ordinary individuals prepared to make an exceptional commitment'.

As we made our way across the starting line it was clear that the 2008 Comrades was well on the way to delivering on its promise! Along with 11,000 others we were soon to find out just how much of an extraordinary challenge was ahead of us. It was hot and, lacking in air, we waited with a mixture of nervous energy and apprehension. What have we got ourselves into, I wondered. Wouldn't it be nice to be at home in bed?

It took us 1 minute and 30 seconds to cross the starting line. Later in the day we'd discover this was significant when included in our overall time. Unlike most big races, Comrades only recognises gun time not chip time. This means your time is recorded from when the gun goes – not from when you cross the line. Interestingly, at Comrades this packs a double penalty for the slower runners as they are seeded further back from the start and can take up to 7 minutes to cross the starting line. These same slower runners who battle the 12 hour time limit can least afford to give away important minutes. Despite this, a change is not practical. A huge part of Comrades is the cut off points along the way and the closing of the course after 12 hours. Until recently, the time limit was 11 hours and we were soon to discover the extra hour would make a big difference to many of the runners.

The early stages

Once across the line it was difficult not to get caught in the hype and run too fast. Going too fast too early can prove costly in the second half of any marathon but we'd been warned that going too fast too early in the Comrades was likely to result in not finishing at all. After a long straight section through the downtown shopping district we turned right and plunged into darkness as we ran alongside a cemetery and some outdoor markets.

No streetlights were on and we heard many shouted warnings to watch out for potholes, something I'm extra nervous of on crowded courses. When running the 2006 New York Marathon, I stepped in one and tore a hamstring. If not for a great catch by O'B, I'd have hit the deck and been trampled by the pack. The thought of falling in the dark just 1 kilometre after the start quickly made me focus until we'd made our way onto the freeway. You really do need to concentrate on where you run early in the race. With so many people, discarded clothing and drink bottles on the road – and often dark conditions – it is prudent to look for the spaces even if it means running a little wider than the mass.

Distances in a big race are difficult to recall with accuracy, especially if it's a foreign course. The next section seemed to go on for 4 to 5 kilometres and it was constantly uphill. Our climb was broken when we reached the 'Jesus Dome' where the sound of footfalls on the road was shattered by the smash of metal on metal. An Audi sedan driving alongside the freeway on a service road had missed the turn and ploughed into a street sign and tree.

No-one was hurt, though many runners were startled. It provided a welcome distraction as we speculated on whether the driver was watching the race rather than the road, and if it was a friend or family member driving a runner's car to the end of the race. Regardless, we refocused and set our sights on following our race plan of 30 minutes running and 5 minutes walking, with adjustments to allow for walking through drink stations and on the tough hills early on. Our plan was for early and frequent breaks to stop the build up of lactic acid in our muscles, which can cause both fatigue and cramp. We looked forward, albeit nervously, to reaching the first of the notorious 'Big Five' and reminded ourselves of our ground rules for working together. Especially we needed to encourage each other, and on the crowded course had to stay mindful of our 3 metre rule, which meant always staying close no matter who else we were talking to.

The 'Big Five'

Preparing for Comrades, one of the first things we came across was the 'Big Five'. At first we thought it was 'The Big Five Marathon' which draws its name from Africa's most powerful and prestigious animals – the lion, elephant, leopard, buffalo and rhinoceros. The Comrades Marathon however has its own 'Big Five', which are also as dangerous, intriguing, noble in stature and an inspiration for all who travel to see them. Energy draining and cramp provoking on the up run, and quadriceps destroying on the down run, the 'Big

Five' are in fact hills which stand out on the course. Daunting, but by taking centre stage they divert runners' attention from the rest of the course which, being full of ups and downs, is punishing in its own right. The way it felt to us, whoever settled on the big five could easily have chosen a big six, seven or more! As we approached the first of the 'hills' we recalled one of our first briefings with Jane, our friend and Comrades adviser. She'd suggested in no uncertain terms that mountains was a more appropriate description.

Partnerunning Tip

RULES

GROUND RULES

Agreeing how you will behave helps clarify expectations and sets you up to behave in a positive way and avoid negative behaviour. It also makes it easier to evaluate performance and discuss what is working and what is working against you achieving your desired results. After all, none of us are perfect.

Ground Rules are:	
Enhanced by	**Hindered by**
• Upfront determination of ground rules	• Lack of ground rules
• Written ground rules	• Not using ground rules
• Simple behaviours	• Not writing ground rules down
• Including pluses & minuses	• Failing to regularly discuss ground rules
• Regular review	• Failing to implement ground rules

No report on Comrades would be complete without describing the Big Five. Here are the descriptions as we found them at www. comrades.com the day before the race – plus our own thoughts on each of them:

COWIES HILL
The Comrades website says:
Cowies is a moderately difficult climb rising about 137 m in the space of 1.5 kilometres. Although this does not sound too difficult an obstacle so early in the race, the preceding 14 kilometres is a relentless ascent, to an altitude of nearly 300 m at Westville, which warrants its inclusion in the 'Big Five'.

We say:
In most marathons you run a hill like Cowies easily. In Comrades we ran most of it but mindful of what was to come we scheduled a walk break on the way up. We found other hills tougher and Cowies' danger is marked by the fact it can lure you into a false sense of security by encouraging you to think the rest of the 'Big Five' are as friendly.

FIELDS HILL
The Comrades website says:
After the descent from Cowies Hill and the easy flat section of Pinetown's Old Main Road, this hill … rises some 213 m over a distance of 3 kilometres. It offers a foretaste of things to come.

We say:
Tough going and a relentless climb, especially in the early stages where it seemed particularly steep. We combined running and walking but felt confident as we reached the top.

BOTHA'S HILL

The Comrades website says:

Botha's Hill offers another challenge with a somewhat lesser altitude rise of some ± 150 m, and covering a distance of 2.4 kilometres, but is nevertheless taxing. At the top of this hill lies a landmark well known to all veteran Comrades runners in the form of the boys of Kearsney College who have gathered in numbers outside the famous school's gates since the beginning of Comrades' long history, providing much appreciated support to the weary runners. Their vociferous and enthusiastic support together with refreshments and any other assistance needed has helped lift the flagging spirit of many a runner and encapsulates the school motto Carpe Diem.

We say:

A tough hill requiring a combination of running and walking but also a confidence booster as it marked three of the big five behind us and the approach of the halfway mark. The boys from the school were of great support but after experiencing the women of Wellesley College on the Boston Marathon course and their enthusiastic squealing and dancing with runners we could not help but think the South African schoolboys, despite being incredibly enthusiastic and supportive, could learn a thing or two, although to be fair the boys have a much tougher job due to the longer race distance and the longer period in which runners pass their cheering station.

INCHANGA

The Comrades website says:

Immediately after reaching the welcome milestone of the halfway mark, runners are confronted with this monster. It winds relentlessly for 2.5 kilometres and also rises some 150 m in altitude, but at this stage of the race seems far more difficult than the preceding hills.

We say:
Yes, a relentless monster seeming more difficult and requiring us to walk more than run with rising concerns of cramping. A huge relief to reach the top and look down on the people still to make the climb. Only one of the Big Five between us and the finish.

POLLY SHORTTS

The Comrades website says:
On the up run, shortly before the notorious Polly Shortts, there lies a climb of far gentler proportions of about 1.5 kilometres. This is reached after a welcome stretch of about 7 kilometres of downhill running from the highest point at Umlaas Road. This little climb sometimes confuses unknowing runners into believing that this is the Polly Shortts. Local runners refer to this as 'Little Pollys'.

This is the ultimate in heartbreak hills. It lies in wait 80 kilometres away from Durban and is often the make or break point for even the top contenders. The climb is 1.8 kilometres in length with the summit at an altitude of 737 metres, (a rise of nearly 100 metres) and while this is 133 metres less than the highest point on the course, it is a formidable obstacle to any runner with two back-to-back standard marathons behind him/her.

We say:
If this is *%^^$ Little Polly we are not looking forward to the real Polly!

Little Polly was tough and promoted a lengthy walk with the heat of the day taking its toll. The level of encouragement among runners appeared to grow even more on this section of the course. From the top of Polly Shortts there were only 7.5 kilometres to the end. Depending on how we coped with this particular hill, a 10 hour finish was going to be close.

We walked most of Polly Shortts, although there was nothing short about it. But we welcomed the opportunity for some guilt free power walking and convinced ourselves the walking was good for our recovery and next weekend's run in Mauritius. Pre-planning possible run conversation topics is something we encourage and one we like to explore with new running partners is to name the toughest and most challenging parts of a race we have experienced. For us, Polly Shortts wins hands down due to its timing in the race, its location and the degree of difficulty – to say nothing of the fact you have to run 80 kilometres before you tackle it. It really does lay in wait. The Boston Marathon has Heartbreak Hill which in comparison is like breaking up with your first love after a 2 week romance when you are 16, whereas Polly Shortts is more like the pain of losing your partner in a tragic accident the day after you propose marriage. One is forgotten almost instantly, the other stays with you forever.

As we made our way up Polly Shortts we wondered why only these five hills were so much talked about. Little Polly and numerous other hills had taken their toll; surely all were worthy of a mention. Then again, 'Big Five' sounds so much better than 'Big Seventeen'.

At last over Polly Shortts, the words from the Comrades Marathon Association website that had sent a chill down our spines before the race were now taking on new meaning as we gained in confidence and settled in to enjoy the run home.

It's a life changing event. One, in which everyone will dig deep into their human reserves, in order to overcome some of the biggest obstacles and challenges that each and every one will ever face in their lives. And on that day, whether they are running against the clock or running to their own beat, each one is a giant, giants among men.

There are those that will make us laugh, and those that'll make us cry, and some that'll make us blush and so many that'll make us proud.

The Comrades crowds

Despite it being a 5.30am start, crowds of people already lined the course yelling support and encouragement. There are several categories denoted on the race bibs of Comrades runners: green club (10 or more Comrades); back-to-back (consecutive); international runners; and the runners' first name. We never tired of hearing the cheers for Susan and Andrew. A common shout from the crowd was 'go lady' and with women making up just 17% of the runners it often felt like I had my own special fan club cheering me along the road to Pietermaritzburg.

Many of the Australians we saw on the course had Australian flags on their running singlets and these prompted many cheers from the crowd and fellow runners. As one Aussie commented the next day, 'It was almost too much.'

As the race moved into the second half she was concerned about the energy she was using responding to the well-wishers as opposed to focusing on running. Still, it is difficult to imagine Australians cheering for South Africans (or any other nationality) with anything like the passion that the South African crowd supported the Australian runners in the Comrades. All along the course people stood cheering by the side of the freeway or road, bands performed, families held picnics and barbeques. In some neighbourhoods elaborate set-ups saw crowds of people holding dinner parties, watching the race on flat screen televisions with power leads coming out into the street from their houses.

As the day went on the number of spectators grew, as did those showing the signs of significant alcohol consumption. We're sure the hot sun added to their enjoyment. Having been offered beer, champagne and even marihuana in other races, it was surprising we were not offered any liquid refreshments along the way. But then it was a long day and maybe the spectators felt they didn't have any spare.

Other more appropriate supplies were offered to us in addition to what was available at the official assistance tables. Biscuits, oranges and sandwiches were among the most popular. In several parts of the course the crowds pushed further and further out on to the road, as they do in the Tour de France, leaving only a small gap for us to pass through.

Crowd numbers were almost non-existent though on the section just before halfway, near the wall of honour and Arthur's Seat. The wall was created as a permanent landmark to honour the achievements of runners who have completed the epic journey, while Arthur's Seat is a niche cut into the wall. Legend tells us this is the spot where the famous Arthur Newton, five times winner of the Comrades during the 1920s, used to sit for a breather while out running.

These days runners are urged to pay homage to Mr Newton with a greeting and a flower. Supposedly this ensures a great second half of the race. We picked flowers from the roadside as we approached and placed them on the ground. I wished Mr Newton a pleasant day while much to my dismay O'B said, 'G'day Arthur, old mate.'

I'm superstitious and the legend stipulates that the greeting should be to Mr Newton not Arthur. No doubt O'B missed this information during our guided bus tour but I was concerned his casual greeting might undermine our performance.

Food and energy

For some unknown reason we both struggled with our normal energy supply and were only able to stomach six of the 12 energy gels we planned to use during the race. As a result we relied even more on the food and drinks provided by the race organisers. We were pleased to discover water and electrolyte drinks were provided in plastic sachets, and Coca Cola and a green creamy soda in small plastic bottles. Drink stations were frequent throughout and well stocked, with the friendly, hardworking volunteers ensuring runners never missed out. Sue survived on electrolyte drink and, after avoiding it until 40 kilometres into the race, I used Coca Cola as my main source of energy.

Official food supplies consisted of oranges, chocolates, bananas, small potatoes and biscuits. Sue made use of the first three oranges, bananas and chocolates but my body rejected anything bar the spuds. Unfortunately the next two potato stands were empty, although the last couple provided valuable energy for the run home. There were numerous other food stands along the way, with friendly spectators handing out oranges, chocolates, sandwiches and jelly beans, but other than the jelly beans we tended to avoid these unofficial supplies.

We both had good and not so good energy periods but were continually troubled by upset stomachs and difficulty consuming food and drink. It was not until afterwards that we fully realised how our food problems were affecting us.

Getting it done at last

From the top of Polly Shortts, there are only 7.5 kilometres to the finish. We'd been led to believe (or deluded ourselves!) that it would all be flat. This was not the case. We took off, unaware of the hills ahead, in the hope that we might just sneak under the 10 hour mark. We remained firm about our race plan and reaffirmed our view that sticking to it – not only to finish Comrades but also to set ourselves up for the next 7 weeks of marathons – was most important.

We ran well for the last 7.5 kilometres and reached the point where with 2 kilometres to go we estimated we had about 11 minutes to beat the 10 hour gun time and 12½ minutes to beat the actual run time of 10 hours. Picking up the pace, we ran home strongly, enjoying the flat surface as we approached the stadium grounds. All our agony seemed forgotten as we entered the grounds and huge crowds cheered us along. We passed a large number of runners walking towards the finish line. Finally we made the stadium, just before the 10 hour mark. As we ran around the track to the finish the crowd noise was awesome and we dashed across the line in 10:00:18 or 10:00:20 (we have seen both published).

As the officials tried to move us out of the way of our fellow finishing runners, we were both in shock. All of a sudden it was over, gone, done, no more. Part of me wanted to be back out there still running, but I just stood there stunned. As we received our medals we found ourselves reflecting on what we'd read on the Comrades website:

> Whether fleet or heavy footed this is not just a race or marathon, it is a journey. A journey of discovery, one in search of one's inner self, of one's self worth. A day in your life that you can proudly say, that you have taken part in one of the most gruelling challenges known to man … the Ultimate Human Race.

Our official time reminded us of O'B's 4 hours and 1 minute in his first marathon when the extra minute provided him with the motivation to return and beat the 4 hour mark. Amid the pleasure and pain as we finished the Comrades, we were unaware that our 20 seconds over would contribute to our decision to return for a back-to-back Comrades attempt.

The last few kilometres of Comrades are very difficult to

describe. Each of us recalled the sense of disbelief and relief that we'd felt as we headed towards the finish of our very first marathons. In a marathon you want the first 42 kilometres to pass as quickly as possible and the last 200 metres to last forever so you can savour the moment. Unfortunately, at Comrades it happens the other way around. The last 400 metres seemed to be over in an instant, and we both would have loved to experience the high and the crowd encouragement for another 10 hours. But we congratulated and thanked each other, reminding ourselves that we'd actually done it, as if we somehow needed to convince ourselves. We were given our medals, quickly photographed and ushered away. Never had we felt this good and this bad at the same time!

Honey, I don't feel so good

In the euphoria of the moment we began to contemplate a return in 2009. We picked up our bags and headed to the international tent to enjoy the next 2 hours as the 12 hour cut off approached. By the time we caught up with the few Australians already celebrating we'd cooled down significantly and both of us were feeling nauseous. We knew that our recovery would be enhanced by eating and drinking as soon as we could, so went looking for a drink and something to eat. We settled on a glass of Sprite (lemonade) each. After a couple of sips Sue began feeling even worse. She leant over a rubbish bin and began dry retching. Magnus Michelson, one of Australia's best ultra marathon runners, came by to see if she was okay and he, Michael and I all agreed she needed medical attention. We hastily grabbed our gear; by now both of us were struggling not to vomit.

I was soon feeling even worse and was dry retching myself. With no bin in sight I 'parked the tiger on the grass' and runners who moments before had been lying on the ground unable to move quickly found new life, giving me a wide berth.

Inside the medical tent

We soon discovered there were three medical tents, and Sue would eventually spend time in each one. After being told we were in the public medical area not the runners' one, we were taken to the main runners' tent staffed by St John's Ambulance and run by a team of nurses. We were among the few people walking in, as many were being carried in on stretchers. Sue had her blood pressure taken (80 over 50) and was then put on a blanket on the ground with her feet raised. After a few minutes and only a slight improvement she became distressed. The head nurse said she should be taken to the next tent where the doctors were in action. But there was no room in there for observers. My suggestion that I was also a doctor (my doctorate is in business, vision, strategy and relationships) was met with a look that said I should sit down, shut up and do as I was told.

As Sue was taken away I was finally assessed. With a blood pressure of 122 over 78, I was declared all clear and served cold Coca Cola. I spent an hour in the medical tent waiting for Sue. In addition to worrying about her, cut off from her as I was, I watched an endless procession of runners being carried in on stretchers. About 90% seemed to be suffering cramp or sore legs; the rest were mostly presenting with nausea. One particularly unfortunate patient was brought in. We'd passed this woman on the course and, seeing the brown stuff running down her legs, had joked about how she had saved time on toilet stops along the route.

Now the medical staff raced around looking for an area to wash their latest patient. As if there was ever any doubt, the head nurse decided the best place was next to where they had parked me. Let's just say the smell was enough to start me dry retching again. Thankfully Sue returned after a few minutes of this and we quickly left the medical centre, hoping to catch the end of the marathon.

Sue had been given a series of tests, including for blood sugar, potassium and sodium levels, and had her blood pressure monitored. Once it had been established she was okay, she was given Maxolon to settle her stomach. Later she confessed to losing the plot a bit once away from me, and said she'd blubbered like a baby, having suddenly become emotional and lacking the energy to keep her feelings under control.

By now she was feeling much better, but I was feeling worse than before and was to continue to struggle with nausea for the next 24 hours. Comrades diehards say you need to run an 'Up' and a 'Down' course to be a real Comrade. Traditionalists say you need to finish under 11 hours. We have not heard anyone say you need to spend time in the medical tent after crossing the finish line but no-one can claim it's not a fascinating experience.

On the buses

One feature of the Comrades is the size and approach of the 'buses'. Elsewhere, these are referred to as pace groups, and an experienced runner runs with others to finish the race in a specific time. But the South Africans have developed this approach so well that the bus metaphor fits perfectly.

We ran close to the 9 hour bus for the first 30 kilometres and looked forward to watching the last few buses enter the stadium. We'd heard stories of the 12 hour bus and the skill of the 'driver' in bringing home a large number of runners about 10 minutes before the cut off. Sure enough, with about 10 minutes to go, the 12 hour bus approached the stadium much to the pleasure of the crowd, but we suspect even more so to the runners. The bus burst onto the track with 350 metres to run to the finish. We watched in amazement, yelling and screaming as the big screen camera followed several hundred runners around the track as they rode the bus to the end.

Later we were intrigued to learn of the similarities between the way the buses worked and our own Partnerunning. Sharing the work, encouraging each other so as not to leave one another behind, sticking to a race plan, reminding each other of the need to drink, eat and take strategic walk breaks, as well as entertaining each other along the way were some of the tactics used on the buses – the very same approaches we use to complete both our training and our races.

The 12 hour cut-off

Definitely one of the most exciting and unique sporting events we have ever witnessed, the 12 hour cut off was everything we had been led to believe it would be plus more. A number of people left the viewing area with 10 minutes to spare as they didn't want to see the pain and heartache of those who did not cross the line before the deadline. But we wanted to see the countdown and enjoy the celebrations of those who finished just before the cut-off. With just minutes and then seconds to go we expected to see some spectacular human efforts as runners – both individuals and in groups – surged towards the line. Perhaps the most spectacular was a bloke around 60 years of age. The cameras picked him up with about 150 metres to go and less than 2 minutes on the clock.

Our hero was bent at the waist, with his head and upper body parallel to the ground. Miraculously, from the waist down he remained upright and moving towards the finish – but only just. As the crowd cheered, he stumbled and fell. We urged him on as the clock ticked on closer to the 12 hour mark. Up he got and, resuming his bizarre running position, stumbled closer to the finish. Then the unthinkable happened. Our man wobbled, changed direction, shifted to the left and ran head first into the fence with some 15 metres and 20 seconds to go. The crowd erupted as the runner looked doomed to finish short of the line. But our bent over hero 'rose from the dead', literally put his head down and bottom up, and stumbled across with the clock showing 5 seconds to spare before the gun went off and no more medals were awarded for the day. The crowd went absolutely ballistic.

The mood quickly shifted from elation to despair as those left realised they had missed the cut off. The announcer reminded those coming towards the finish that they had still run the distance and it was a great achievement, but nothing could change the fact that they were not going home with a medal and would not be included in the race finishers book.

We were so very glad we were able to see the finish. Watching the final runners crawl across the line, looks of sheer relief on their faces, then the pain and anguish of those who did not make it on time, and the closing ceremony including the sounding of the bugle and lowering of the flag were among the most memorable moments of our lives.

Some people we met along the way

As its name suggests, comrades are what you find along the way in this race. This was the first time we spent time with an organised group at a marathon and it was a lot of fun to hang out with our fellow runners. And with everyone concerned about safety it was an advantage to be able to walk to and from activities as part of a group. Some of those we enjoyed spending time with were Mari-Mar, our effervescent Travelling Fit tour leader, and Jane, our Comrades guru who was completing her 3rd Comrades. Michael had run marathons all over the world, while David from Victoria was famous for adding another 15 kilometres to the Great Ocean Road Marathon to make it a Comrades workout. The boys – Rene, Robert and Tim – were a mix of Dane and Brit and all very good runners; Rene ran his first marathon in Copenhagen at age 11. Kaye and Karen from Cobram in regional Victoria were a runner and supporter team, with Kaye finishing in around 11 hours. Tory, a personal trainer from Melbourne, was completing his second Comrades in as many years.

We also met some wonderful people on the course and ran with them for various amounts of time. They included Maureen and Kevin who we came across at a drink fountain along the cliff tops on our very last training run at home. They motored past us just before the halfway mark looking very strong. Joe, a South African veteran of 13 Comrades, has family living in Australia and made us very welcome as we chatted running up Field's Hill. And, Estelle running her 9th Comrades, struck up a conversation when she noticed our international numbers. This Comrades was especially poignant for her as her running partner had emigrated to Melbourne the previous month and she was missing her badly.

Later that evening

After the closing ceremony first stop was the lost and found tent. Our friend Mari-Mar had lost her mobile phone and wanted to check one last time to see if it had been found. We all laughed and told her she was 'dreamin' only to be lost for words to hear some wonderful person had handed it in. The following day a local wrote to the paper: 'Why can't we treat each other the way we treat each other during the Comrades on the other 364 days of the year?' We all agreed that on any other occasion Mari-Mar would have been looking to buy a new phone.

Soon we were on our way back to Durban, showers and dinner. We sat next to a fellow who finished the race in 11 hours, 59 minutes and 55 seconds and gave him a ribbing over not taking the extra 4 seconds available to complete the course! Back at the hotel I could not believe how steep the bus steps were. More than one Comrade commented that we were lucky to be dropped right at the front door. But our aching muscles would be nothing compared to the pain that awaited us the next day.

The hotel restaurant was packed. Sue ate a hearty meal but I made a quick departure from the dinner table, unable to keep any food in my stomach for long. For some the finishing celebrations continued long into the night, but Sue and I retired around 9.30pm, tired but not exhausted, sore but not in agony, satisfied but more relieved than thrilled, and hoping for a sound night's sleep. Before turning out the light we answered the question a number of people had asked us in recent months and one we had wondered about ourselves. Was it possible after running 87 kilometres together?

The next day and recovery
Monday 16 June

Our sleep was interrupted with great news coming in during the night. First of all, Injinji socks indicated they were keen to support us. And US Olympian, author, Runners World columnist and running mentor Jeff Galloway sent us an email wishing us the best and agreeing to write the afterword for our book.

O'B had been up at 4am and working for several hours before I woke. We headed down for breakfast, both hungry, but nothing much appealed, which was especially tough for O'B who had lost everything he had eaten for the past 24 hours. Luckily breakfast stayed where it belonged and after grabbing the papers we headed to the rooftop pool. The water was icy cold, thanks to the staff putting ice blocks in the previous evening to assist with runner recovery. Even in the warm sun it was difficult to spend too long in the water. We were not complaining though; the colder the better to reduce the bleeding in our muscles due to the micro-tears. We later discovered that the hotel had provided large garbage bins with wheels for runners to ice their legs in. Rene, Robert and Tim had taken advantage of this and told us about one poor runner who was unable to climb out and had to endure extra icing until rescued.

A quick check of our emails reminded us of the different meanings words can have from one country to another. 'Hi Sue and O'B,' one started. 'Safe travel and hope all is well. No Bonking!' We'd been amazed – and amused – a few years back to visit the marathon expo in Chicago where one of the sponsors was handing out 'Keep going: No bonking' signs for spectators to hold up. At that stage we didn't know in the US to 'bonk' means to hit the wall or experience advanced fatigue – a very different use of the term to in Australia where to bonk means to have sex.

We spent another few hours by the pool reading the local papers and discovered that in separate incidents two Comrades participants had been robbed at gun point and had their runners stolen while stopping by the roadside to meet a call of nature. One continued on and completed the run in bare feet; the other called it a day.

Later we went for a long walk along the beach promenade, took photos of the sand carvings and called in for a beer at a bar called

'Joe Cools' with the West Coast running club from Cape Town. These Comrades runners and their supporters were all partying pretty hard and had a huge start on us. After one beer and watching them dance on the bar and play a series of drinking games, we figured they were beyond catching and we headed on our way.

Returning to the local paper after dinner, we discovered that 8613 runners finished the Comrades and 1738 did not. We realised how fortunate we were to have participated in this great event, which may well be the world's greatest ultra marathon. Would it change our lives?

REST AND RECOVERY

Status report

As we prepared to leave South Africa we were very pleased. We had zero injuries to our feet and although our legs were sore they could have been much worse. O'B reported a painful left knee which was unexpected and minor Achilles soreness which was not. Sue had a swollen right ankle which was causing considerable pain as well as a very painful right iliotibial band (with knee soreness). Much to our relief, her chronic heel injury was in good shape; however, she was suffering a lack of feeling in her left foot. O'B was feeling some slight chest heaviness and coughing, as often occurs the day after long races. Also of note was our general tiredness but it was not the massive fatigue we experienced after the Oxfam Trailwalker in April (then again, it was only day 1).

In the coming days Sue continued to have right knee and right ankle pain and left toe numbness, but O'B was recovering well with minimal leg soreness. We were confident of avoiding major post Comrades fatigue and of being ready for our next run.

PROGRESS

Lesson for life

Keep moving.
Regardless of speed always progress towards your target.

At the Comrades they say keep moving until you reach the finish line
or the sun sets. No matter how slowly you feel you are moving, if you
continue to make progress you will reach your target. But if you stop
moving and sit by the side of the road, nothing ever happens.

For us keeping moving applies to mortgages, studying for degrees,
weight loss, recovering from chronic illness, raising children, writing this
book, developing Partnerunning and all those other life challenges that
seem like they will take forever yet with continual movement the time
passes quickly.

Mayhem in Mauritius

*'It is what we think we know already that
often prevents us from learning.'*
Claude Bernard

Cumulative flying distance:	**15,816 kilometres**
Cumulative flying time:	**21 hours and 40 minutes**
Cumulative total travel time:	**68 hours and 40 minutes**

After a single night stopover at a Johannesburg airport hotel, we were about to board our flight to Mauritius with British Airways. The plane was parked well away from the terminal, requiring a 2 kilometre bus ride. Just as O'B was about to step on to the plane I realised I had left my wheel-on hand luggage (including our new laptop) at the departure gate. We quickly jumped back on the bus and retraced our route to the terminal, hoping that the bag was still there – and that it would be quicker and easier for them to delay the plane than find our luggage in the meantime and fly without us. Ever the pessimist, I was hysterical, sure the bag would be gone and that we'd miss our flight.

The drive back seemed to take forever and the boarding staff gave us some very strange looks when we returned to the gate. But luckily the bag was right where I had left it and everything was still intact. If we'd been in the UK or US an unattended bag may have resulted in all sorts of security problems, including closing the airport. We quickly grabbed the bag and headed back to the plane where we were relieved to see the doors still open and the stairs in position.

After giving a big tip to the bus driver and copping a stern talking to from one of the boarding staff, we took our seats. But we didn't escape quite that easily. Before takeoff the Captain commented on our mysterious return to the terminal. Sue cringed with embarrassment but I just shrugged my shoulders. If only he knew!

The flight was a bit of an eye-opener for us. The cockpit door was constantly open and many of our fellow passengers were visiting the pilot to see how the plane was flown. Then our meal came with real knives, and towards the end of the flight we watched the flight attendants fill their friends' bags with wine and other goodies. Not something you see flying in most parts of the world these days!

Unseasonal conditions
Thursday 19 June

We arrived to an overcast and wet day, not the glorious sunny skies of the brochures. There was a distinctive chill in the air, although not nearly as cold as the icy winter breeze in Johannesburg. Somehow we'd forgotten that French was the primary language, although just about everyone seemed to speak English as well, but the accents were so thick we had to really concentrate.

Apart from the freeway, all the roads on the island are single lane. As we weaved our way through back streets and along narrow roads our driver took any half opportunity to overtake. Thankfully we arrived at La Pirogue in one piece.

An air of decay hung about most of the buildings, as if exposure to the baking sun and monsoonal rains had taken a heavy toll on both the paintwork and the wooden structures of the balconies and verandahs. The shops were crammed full of long lasting products, and fruit and vegetables sold from outdoor stalls. It seemed like a cross between Fiji and Thailand, but with all the signs in French and the population of Indian descent. Indeed the majority of the population is Hindu.

On every horizon there were massive eruptions of sharp cliffs surrounded by sugarcane fields. Once we crossed the central plateau a glistening grey ribbon of sea appeared in the distance.

Resorts on the island offered either half or full board. We'd opted for full as it seemed the easy option for a couple of resting marathoners but we were frustrated by what we saw as late dining times – 7.30am to 10.30am for breakfast and 7.30pm to 10.30pm for dinner. With our early to rise and early to bed lifestyle this would be a nuisance. The first night, O'B rocked up to the outdoor buffet dinner in his best Ralph Lauren shorts only to be told that full-length trousers were a pre-requisite for gentlemen in the evening. This was a big problem. Trying to minimise our luggage, he hadn't brought any long pants with him. The only solution was for him to swap his expensive dress shorts for a pair of track pants.

We were very relieved to wake up to a glorious sunny morning, although scattered showers continued to appear. Both of us really enjoy a little bit of time in the sun and feel it helps with our recovery, so it was nice just to lie back and read a book and relax after the tumultuous effort of Comrades and the wheelie bag incident. After a few hours it was time to again focus on our recovery by walking in the sea. We booked a massage too, confident our legs would be able to handle a gentle rub. At last we both thought Saturday's marathon run might be achievable – and even enjoyable.

It was really exciting receiving emails of encouragement from friends at home and people who'd begun following us along the way.

Included among them was one from a friend who we'd not seen since our wedding. 'G'day to my old mate O'B and Sue,' it said. 'Was driving my car listening to SEN the other day when I heard your interview … Nearly drove off the road!!!! Congratulations on what you are setting out to achieve. I've been telling as many of our mates as I can. Hope all goes well.'

We were hopeful that Saturday would bring more delicious weather for Mauritius. The locals were telling us that the showers and cold temperatures were unusual, but sometimes it seems that we attract atypical weather. Over the last 12 months Phuket, Koh Samui, Honolulu and Miami were all supposed to be warm and dry when we were there but we found them cooler than expected and wet!

Before turning in we studied the map of the island and plotted our run course. Our plan for the next day was to hire a taxi to drive us over our intended route so we could scout possible drink stops and reconnoitre the landscape for markers to denote distances.

REST AND RECOVERY

Status report

Four days after our Comrades run we were both walking okay but neither of us felt ready to run. Sue was worried about her foot and swollen ankle and O'B was tired but injury free.

The lay of the land
Friday 20 June

The hotel concierge had informed us that private taxis could be hired at a predetermined price and the amount charged to our rooms. However, when we arranged our taxi pick-up we were told by another of the hotel staff, 'No, your driver must be paid in cash.' Not to worry, we could stop at an ATM along the journey.

In an immaculately clean taxi, finally we set off to mark the 42 kilometre return journey we'd be running the next day. We were in t-shirts and shorts but our driver wore long pants and a woollen jumper – and had the heating on. But after all, this was winter! We'd been advised to head south to Tamarin instead of north to Port Louis as was our original plan for two main reasons: first, the scenery was more interesting to the south; and second, the traffic was less congested. The scenery was indeed spectacular with those majestic, craggy mountains standing alone like sentinels among seemingly endless fields of sugarcane, and glimpses down to the glistening Baie de Tamarin. We took notes as to where our various drink stops might be. This was not a supported race so having a sense of where we could purchase drinks was very important. We could carry gels and food but had not brought special hydration backpacks.

Having marked out our run we headed into Port Louis, very relieved that we'd decided to go with the taxi driver instead of hiring a car ourselves. The local drivers were daredevils extraordinaire, overtaking without care or consideration for oncoming traffic or seemingly more than a few metres of road visible in front of them. We were both holding our breaths when a procession of two minibuses, one car and our taxi began to overtake a slow truck at the base of a slight hill. It was as if the changing gears of the truck were the starting gun for all vehicles behind to charge! We were very thankful to arrive in Port Louis in one piece.

Our driver dropped us at the popular tourist destination of the Caudan waterfront, an old shipping office and storage area that now boasts restaurants and shops galore – duty free, of course! I like to collect a small charm for my silver bracelet from every country we visit in our travels, a habit that began back in 1972 when I travelled around Europe with my family in the quintessential 'Kombi' van. I had over 25 charms now that I'd bought a small silver dodo in Mauritius, with one more yet to come on this trip from Brazil.

The shops were spilling with dodo merchandise, from tiny painted wooden statues to t-shirts to large ceramic wall decorations. This plump white bird, only ever found on the island of Mauritius, has been extinct since the late 1800s. Unable to fly, it made for easy sport for the European settlers. And sport it was, the bird being basically inedible due to the taste and texture of its flesh.

Charms, being tiny, don't lead to luggage problems. That's my justification, anyway! O'B, however, collects concert and race t-shirts, CDs and books aplenty, all of which take up space on the road – and at home. He says he likes to understand the 'why' of people and organisations, and it annoys him that I don't understand why he collects these things. I had a laugh not long ago when he came home from a function and told me he'd been talking to a psychologist about why he collects the things he does. The psychologist said that maybe it's because he likes them. Full stop, end of sentence. Not the deep and meaningful answer he was searching for!

It was hard to believe we were running another marathon the next day and needed to pay attention to hydrating properly and carbo loading to give our legs the energy they need. I'd brought my container of electrolyte powder along from home for mixing drinks and was very thankful that I did as we found no shop in Flic-en-Flac that sold electrolyte drink. The buffet at the hotel was extremely extensive, so at least no problem there to get pasta and rice, although not, sadly, our favourite pancakes, which only seemed to be available at breakfast.

After dinner we headed back to the room for an early night. Beforehand, Sue had laid out her run gear, a habit that we've developed to avoid that early morning panic of trying to find bits and pieces that may be scattered throughout our luggage. But the hotel turn down staff had been at work again. Not only had the bed been turned down, but a lot of our clothes had disappeared. It was time for another round of hide and seek. On previous occasions when this had happened, we'd finally found our belongings in drawers under the bed, top shelves of cupboards, and folded and placed on the bedhead. This evening, however, we were stumped. Eventually we discovered our clothing on a line in the bathroom, our shoes in the wardrobe, and our hats and glasses on the work desk. They'd almost won!

REST AND RECOVERY

Status report

O'B was feeling ready to run. His muscles were good, and there were no joint problems. Sue continued to feel concerned about the front of her right ankle. It was still swollen and very sore to walk on and to touch. In preparation for the run tomorrow she'd begun taking anti-inflammatories and had been massaging her calf and applying pressure point work to the painful area. Fingers crossed!

Our Mauritius run
Saturday 21 June

We headed out at 5.30am to run what we hoped would be about a 4 hour marathon, taking us along the beach at Flic-en-Flac, up the hill through the canefields to the main road, then along the main road through more canefields to Tamarin, and then on to our turnaround point near Black River. We were in for a number of surprises that made the run more challenging than we had expected but as we headed off in the dark we were blissfully unaware of the challenges ahead.

Apart from some very short 100 metre jogging, this was our first run since Comrades 6 days before. Although we'd done lot of walking since and felt our muscles had recovered well, we were in uncharted territory. We felt anxious about the task ahead and more than a little concerned about the ongoing soreness in Sue's right foot.

We planned to leave early and beat the morning traffic. However, only a few hundred metres down the road, we encountered a vehicle, the first of many cars and buses that were on the road early transporting hotel and other workers. The first 2 kilometres were along the flat between the shops and beach at Flic-en-Flac. We ran through the town and embarked on a 4 kilometre rise through the canefields to the main road. We had planned to run along a gravel road between the main road and the canefield but encountered two unforeseen problems. First, in the dark the gravel was too dangerous; we could not see the ruts and rocks along the path. Second, we'd not anticipated that the farmers would be watering their cane so early;

as well as being difficult to see, the gravel had turned to mud in many sections.

This left us to run along the shoulder of the road which was pretty scary. The amount of traffic increased and soon running along the narrow, single lane roadway became downright hair raising with drivers overtaking each other constantly. On more major roads they have 'crawler lanes' (known in other countries as slow vehicle or overtaking lanes) so slower vehicles can move to the left and allow others to pass. But these are rare and most overtaking takes place with little notice and seemingly scant recognition of oncoming traffic or vehicle acceleration power. Several times we saw four or five vehicles attempting to overtake at once where there was only space for one.

It was tough enough keeping an eye on the traffic coming towards us but a major problem was the traffic heading in the same direction as us. We wondered what the Mauritian road toll was, and who had right of way when overtaking. It was a great relief when, an hour later, the sun began to rise. Now we could run on the gravel road between the main road and the cane, which was very comfortable, and our second hour of running was rather enjoyable.

We felt strong and were very pleased with the feeling in our legs. Our only concern was the lack of drink stops. We had planned three possible ones in the first two hours at petrol stations, but had not expected that they'd be closed. We didn't feel thirsty yet, but were mindful of the guiding principle that once you feel dehydrated it is too late.

We'd thought running through endless kilometres of canefields a month before harvest might be a challenge, but in the early Mauritian sun and with picturesque mountains to our left and occasional ocean glimpses to our right, the second half of the run was a pleasure. We'd seen enough in the taxi to map our route but the view from a speeding car makes it impossible to suss out the detail that running puts you in touch with. We were able to read the signs along the way, say good morning to people waiting at bus stops, check out the grounds of the houses we passed, and study several roadside religious monuments.

On more than one occasion we heard rustling amid the cane, and each time picked up our pace not knowing what creatures might be lurking there. Past some construction workers at a golf and real estate development, we came upon a man standing beside his motor scooter and praying. Candles were burning brightly in the little niche and the man looked at us with a smile as if to say, 'I will pray for you too. You must be crazy running out here among the canefields.'

The big mountain that designated our turnaround point loomed in the distance as we approached the 2 hour mark. As is often the case with distance markers, it had appeared close for so long and it was good to finally reach the foothills and the township. About a mile before the turnaround we found a baker open and ran in to buy a much-needed drink, only to discover they only sold milk, which was the last thing we needed. O'B easily jumped the 2 feet wide ditch between the roadside and the shopping strip car park, but when I followed I landed on my sore foot. Ouch! Hopefully it was just the force of the landing that caused the sharp pain and not a new injury.

Finally we found a small petrol station that had opened early and bought a bottle of Coca Cola, the only drink available. Not ideal as we were looking for electrolyte but we were still very grateful for the drink. After the Coke and some energy gel, relieved the latter went down well after our digestive problems with it the previous week at Comrades, we headed off in search of the turnaround. About 500 metres before the halfway mark I had shooting pains in my foot and called for a walk break. The carry over soreness from Comrades hadn't been bothering me until now but jumping the ditch must have aggravated my still undiagnosed foot injury. We walked a little, then ran to the turnaround, but the pain was too great for me to continue running.

As we turned for home and the long, slow walk back to our hotel, we wondered if this meant the end of our Mauritian Marathon. After just 10 minutes it was obvious I was in great physical pain, but even more upsetting was that I couldn't run at all. I was concerned that the injury may be serious, with a stress fracture being the scariest of possibilities. O'B took the view that the swelling during the week had been a good sign and the pain was just post Comrades soreness; with further rest this week it would recover. Besides, you can't expect to run a marathon the week after Comrades and not experience some pain. Once again, his voice of reason calmed my bubbling hysteria.

I took an anti-inflammatory tablet and we decided to run for a while or until the shooting foot pains returned. After more than 20 minutes without any severe pain we took a short walk, then continued to run. Soon we were back on the canefield gravel road with about 15 kilometres to go. Despite it being constantly uphill, the running was good and my confidence grew as the pain failed to return. Being back on a flat running surface, combined with the anti-inflammatory, seemed to have resolved the problem. Phew!

Another 5 kilometres down the road we stopped for another drink. I worked the camera while Sue carefully crossed the ditch to buy a drink from a roadside stall. By this time it was after 8.30am and we had been running for more than 3 hours, although it seemed like only 30 minutes, no doubt in the light of last Sunday's 10 hour effort. It was still relatively early so we had plenty of daylight and beach time ahead of us. Sue returned with drink in hand and told me that the shopkeeper had been sitting on the counter, beer in hand and several empties beside him. I pointed out that it was mid Saturday afternoon in Australia – a perfectly respectable time for a beer – and clearly the bloke was working on Australian time.

Our pre-planned drink stop at a petrol station shop was open this time and after another drink we headed for home. By now the streets were crowded, and shops and restaurants open, and we hit the peaceful foreshore, running under the trees between the beach and the road.

Across the line in just over 4 hours, we were relieved to have this challenging run out of the way and determined to focus on Sue's injured foot before tackling the Rio de Janeiro Marathon the following weekend. We estimated that we ran 70% of our time on soft surface and we were optimistic this would make a huge difference to our recovery. During our training for Comrades we'd been able to run 6 or more hours on soft surfaces, experience almost no soreness and return to running 2 days later. But anymore than 3 hours on hard roads left our legs sore and often in need of several days of recovery before running again. With a London stopover in a few days' time, we were keen to run Hyde Park and see a few of the sights, but were mindful of not injuring ourselves.

Some r and r

Finally back at La Pirogue and it was time for a celebratory breakfast and a chance to refuel. We have discovered it's important to get both carbohydrate and protein to assist our muscle recovery and the cereal, yoghurt, eggs and toast on offer really ticked all the boxes. That morning we were lucky to also have entertainment – in the form of a wandering band.

The rest of the day was spent soaking our legs in cold water, taking walks along the beach and generally resting in the sun. As the sun set and we headed to dinner we felt very satisfied with our efforts and thankful that our muscles felt no sorer than after a long training run.

Ouch!
Sunday 22 June

My ankle had swollen up again and was causing me a fair degree of pain so I decided to try the acupuncture needles our physio had given us (along with instructions on how to use!). I was quite nervous but they did not hurt and if they helped, then why not? Aimed at releasing tension in the targeted muscles fibres, apparently this sort of self-treatment is becoming increasingly popular among professional athletes, including some of our Australian Rules footballers. Peter had told us that he expected to see many athletes at the Beijing Olympics using this form of therapy.

We slept in our compression tights again to aid muscle recovery and woke to glorious sunshine for our last morning in Mauritius before heading to the airport for the long trek to London via Johannesburg.

Good lounge facilities at the airport gave us the opportunity to plug in our laptops for some writing time, but the monster child had other ideas! We have all been in the situation where a quiet meal, cinema session or whatever is disturbed by a crying child or baby but this toddler gave new meaning to the 'terrible twos'. He moved throughout the lounge like a whirling dervish, screaming, yelling and crying at the top of his voice as his hapless parents tried unsuccessfully to calm him. One by one the lounge guests evacuated, and it was not long before we too beat a path to the gate. Not even complimentary drinks, food and comfortable seating could tempt any of us to remain in the lounge.

Once seated on the plane, we began to feel nervous again. Where was the toddler from the lounge? Was he on our flight? Sure enough, our worst fears were realised as he and his parents took the seats directly in front of ours. Around us collective groans filled the cabin and passengers began to request earplugs from the bemused flight attendant who clearly had no idea of the horror that lay in front of her. We'd like to say that our fears were groundless, but apart from a 30 minute respite as the child took a drug induced nap, the flight was one of the most unpleasant we've ever experienced.

Arriving in Johannesburg, we went straight to the departure gate for our connecting flight to London. But there was a slight delay. Unbeknownst to us, a very special passenger would be on the same flight.

You never know who you might meet
Monday 23 June

We realised something was up when the cabin crew closed the front left door to our British Airways jumbo and then opened the front right door, the one without the airbridge. When you are waiting to take off for a long haul flight the slightest delay seems to take forever. We must have been waiting about 20 minutes before we knew what was going on. Word went around the plane that someone famous was boarding. We were trying to focus on some work and I grumbled to Sue that I hoped it was not some movie celebrity. I was prepared to wait for Nelson Mandela, I said, but he was the only person I felt deserved this type of treatment.

It was a miracle the plane did not tip over with everyone looking out one side, trying to see who was worth waiting for. Being a dark night, all we could see was airport staff piled on trucks trying to get a better view. But our special guest finally arrived. And it was indeed Nelson Mandela – on his way to London for a special concert to celebrate his 90th birthday. After years of being too busy with work and my doctoral studies to read much, I'd used my rest time in Mauritus to finally read Mandela's autobiography *A Long Walk to Freedom* – and here I was about to share a plane with the great man himself.

It then dawned on me that it was likely he'd pass by my seat. And so I met Nelson Mandela! Not just a smile as he passed, but he stopped and spoke to this broken down marathon runner from the back blocks of Melbourne before continuing on his way to seat 1A. What a journey we were on! An observation shared a few days later by an emailer who wrote, 'You are having the experience of your lives. All the different cultures and expectations of life. Incidentally, Nelson Mandela lived in the same street as I did. He often went for walks in the neighbourhood with his bodyguards. Also in the nearby shopping malls shaking hands with one and all. A truly great man.'

36 hours in London

Cumulative flying distance:	27,951 kilometres
Cumulative flying time:	37 hours and 55 minutes
Cumulative total travel time:	87 hours and 55 minutes

Our whirlwind visit to London was really just a stopover on our way to Rio rather than the destination in itself as it often is for travellers. Arriving before 6am left us with a long day ahead. We spent a few hours working in the BA Business Lounge before taking a 9am tube

(London Underground) train to the city where O'B had a really good workout carrying our heavy cases up and down the numerous flights of stairs to get us in and out of the stations, across roads and into the hotel.

Straightaway London assaulted our senses. The bustling crowds, the traffic noise and the smoke! It wasn't long before I started sneezing; it seemed that many more people were smoking here than we were used to. It all seemed far more hectic than I remembered too. The hotel staff explained it was Wimbledon fortnight and virtually every hotel in the city was full. Combined with the tennis and a number of tube disruptions, road traffic had increased and cars and buses were reduced to a halt.

There are many jokes about the dismal English weather but during our 36 hours in London we saw sunny skies with only scattered cloud. The temperature was about 23 Celsius, which for us felt mild and pleasant, but was obviously hot enough for placards to be placed outside tube stations announcing that giant fans on platforms would keep patrons cool. There were also announcements on the tube warning travellers to take bottles of water with them to keep hydrated during the hot conditions. Indeed we did notice the stuffiness and lack of air-conditioning in many shops and buildings as we wandered about during the day. It was quite oppressive, actually, and there were stories in the news that night of people fainting.

We spent our first afternoon wandering around the Covent Garden redevelopment looking at shops and checking out the many bookstores along Charing Cross Road. Booklovers could spend hours along this one stretch of road and it was difficult for Sue to drag me away, but I escaped with only five extra books to add to our luggage.

We love catching live theatre shows and try to fit in as many as possible when travelling, and 36 hours gave us the chance to see two. We did not want to take the chance on half-price ticket booths so had pre-purchased our tickets to *Jersey Boys* and *Les Miserables* before leaving Australia. The security checks were quite stringent and our bags were sealed with yellow tape before we could enter the theatre. Both shows were great, the lack of leg room our only problem. With my post marathon legs I suffered big time from the lack of space.

Our London tourist run
Tuesday 24 June

Sightseeing runs are one of our favourite forms of Partnerunning and have been a great source of enjoyment for us over the years. They can take many forms depending on our fitness and timing. We've sometimes used this form of Partnerunning to do serious long training runs 3 weeks before major marathons. At the other extreme, we've done slow sightseeing runs with significant walk breaks when ill or recovering from injury. We've also used sightseeing runs to spend quality time together after we arrive somewhere, explore new cities and revisit favourite destinations, and for business activities such as searching for investment properties.

The idea in London was for a slow recovery run allowing us to check out some key landmarks in as short a time as possible. Sightseeing runs are a very efficient way of seeing a city. You can cover far more territory than by walking, avoid the hassles of driving and parking, and you don't get the crowds of official tours. We often check out a city by running and then later return to places we want to investigate further.

With our London run, we were careful to monitor our legs after Mauritius. We decided to adopt an adventure-style approach which involved running from one landmark to the next, taking a photo and then running on to the next location. Our course was designed to take us past Green Park, through Hyde and St James Parks, into the Parliament district, along the River Thames, past Trafalgar Square and then back to our hotel in Piccadilly opposite the Green Park tube station.

The first landmark we came to was the original London Hard Rock Café, located opposite Green Park. It was advertising a big weekend of concerts; Eric Clapton was headlining on the following Saturday night and The Police on the Sunday. The posters prompted a 'running discussion' of just missed great concerts, including Dean Martin in Las Vegas, Warren Zevon in Melbourne, Bruce Springsteen in New York, Crosby Stills Nash in Melbourne and The Rolling Stones in New York.

We then paused at Hyde Park Corner to marvel at the traffic and watch the hordes of cyclists and runners dodging the vehicles, crossing the Hyde Park roundabout, before heading off into Green Park towards Buckingham Palace. We studied their route carefully as we planned to follow them after our run through Hyde Park, by now crowded with walkers, runners, cyclists and horse riders. The first three managed to share many of the same paths, and while we are used to seeing people cycle to work, we were struck by how many runners had backpacks and appeared to be on their way to work. After watching a large pack of horses on 'Rotten Row', which has a special surface for riding, we followed the road until we reached The Serpentine, a lake in the middle of Hyde Park, where we were astonished to find a section marked out for swimmers and about 50 people swimming laps. After taking some photos and feeding the ducks with food donated by a passerby, we headed off to the Princess Diana Memorial and then the Albert Memorial for some more photos.

I crossed the road from the Albert Memorial to photograph the Royal Albert Hall (a well known concert venue) and check out the gig guide, and returned holding a flyer about a forthcoming Brian Wilson concert at the Royal Albert Hall. I was disappointed we'd miss it. Several years ago we'd seen Wilson at the Royal Festival Hall in London and I have great memories of his performance.

We then ran back through the park, taking a few snaps of sculptures and memorials, before reaching the Reformers Tree outside the Hyde Park concert compound not far from Speakers Corner where workers were preparing for Mandela's 90th birthday concert. We took short walk break here and then ran past the concert venue, with me again expressing disappointment that we wouldn't be in London on the Friday night.

As we ran through the Hyde Park corner roundabout we took in the war memorials and then joined runners, walkers and cyclists as we dashed in front of the traffic, under Marble Arch and along the side of Green Park towards the front gates of Buckingham Palace. At this early hour tourist numbers were small and we shot some footage of Sue running past the Palace before heading off through St James Park towards the Parliamentary precinct.

As we went under Admiralty Arch I pointed out the section of the park where I'd run into Sting on a previous London run. Then we made a right turn past the horse guards and the Prime Minister's residence at No 10 Downing Street before zapping past Westminster Abbey, Parliament House and Big Ben. After turning to run along the River Thames, we passed the London Eye (a large Ferris wheel) and Victoria Embankment. By now we were looking forward to breakfast and a morning of strolling around.

Soon we turned away from the river and ran up to The Strand and back along to take in Trafalgar Square. As the time moved toward

9.30am, and crowds of tourists and workers filled the busy streets, we decided to start our cool down by walking back to our hotel. In just under 2 hours we'd covered approximately 14 kilometres – hardly a cracking pace, but by combining our run/walk approach we were able to see and take photos of many of the major London sights. And given it was only a few days since we'd completed a marathon distance run in Mauritius, we were thrilled to have covered as much ground as we had. The run had combined footpath, road and gravel trails, and for many people would comprise a 1 or 2 day walk. What a wonderful way we'd chosen to re-explore this city!

A dose of culture
Tuesday 24 June pm

We'd checked out of the hotel and stowed our luggage before heading off to our theatre matinee, planning to return about 5.30pm to pick up our bags and head straight to the airport for our 9.45pm departure to Rio. The thought of dragging our bags through peak hour London walking traffic to the nearest tube station was abhorrent, so we decided to taxi to Paddington Station and catch the Heathrow Express – a more expensive option but definitely better for our health and safety. It would have been terrible to be injured between marathons.

We both have mixed feelings about London. I dislike the smoke in particular. O'B loves the theatre, the bookshops and the wonderful parks to run in. When it's sunny, the city looks beautiful with its historic buildings, quaint pubs and shops with colourful flowerboxes. On the other hand you have the expense and in some cases rude customer service. At a Pret a Manger shop a couple of days earlier I'd asked the cashier for a receipt only to be told, no,

I couldn't have one. And while O'B found himself delighted to be back in London he also wanted to get away as soon as possible; he has something of a love/hate relationship with the city, for sure. Maybe I do too. We both felt a sense of relief as our plane left the ground, but also a sense of regret. When we would next return? Maybe for the London Marathon.

Partnerunning Tip

QUALITY TIME

Spending time together without distractions and doing something you enjoy provides a foundation for relationship success which flows through into all aspects of your relationship.

Quality Time is:	
Enhanced by	**Hindered by**
• Planning regular activities	• Failing to allocate time
• Being present during planned activities	• Allowing distractions (e.g. Blackberry and Iphones)
• Selecting enjoyable activities	• Selecting activities one or both partners do not enjoy

How do I get started? Spreading the word in London

On the plane from Heathrow I recalled an incident that had happened in a shop near our hotel. It was just before 10am and, being nearly at the end of our 'tourist run', we decided to buy breakfast from the Marks and Spencer express store adjacent to the Green Park tube station. It had a wide selection of fruits and other breakfast items and after making our selection we joined the checkout line. While Sue was purchasing the goods one of the managers approached us. 'Hey, have you two been running?'

The shoes, shorts, singlets and sweaty bodies must have given us away.

'Yes, on such a beautiful morning it's a great way to spend a couple of hours checking out the city.'

Then came the next question from the slightly chubby manager. 'I really want to get into running but I am not sure how to get started. What do you think I should do?'

Well, this is the question we always love to hear and we managed to delay the checkout line quite some time making a few suggestions which, in summary, were:

- Find a running /walking buddy
- Start with a combination of walk/run at the 30 second walk/30 second run ratio
- Increase the times to 1 minute/1 minute, then 2, 3 and so on until 10 minutes run/10 minutes walk
- Once at this level, increase the run by 1 minute and reducing the walk by the same amount until settling on 20 minutes run and 5 minutes walk

- Take it slowly, with no more than a 10% increase per week
- Purchase a pair of good, individually fitted running shoes
- Read *Runners World* magazine
- Check out our website www.Partnerunning.com
- Seek advice on any injuries
- Make sure you enjoy yourself.

At this point we were really holding up the queue. We wished her luck, pleased with the opportunity to help someone in starting to run – but wondering if she was serious or just good at engaging with customers.

REST AND RECOVERY

Status report

O'B was feeling in excellent shape with great recovery from the Comrades and Mauritius running. Sue was pleased with her muscle recovery and pre-existing heel injury. Unfortunately, a lump on top of her right foot that appeared after Comrades was still causing problems. We were hoping anti-inflammatories, ice and rest would solve the problem before the Rio run next Sunday.

Lesson for life

Face reality.
Be candid about today by acknowledging positives and negatives.

Running with a partner teaches you to be brutally honest. There is nowhere to hide and you can't pretend if you haven't 'done your homework' or don't 'have the work assignment under control'. Facing reality sooner rather than later helps solve problems before they get out of hand and is great for enhancing the experience itself as well as the results. Taking a walk break when Sue had severe foot pain in Mauritius was just one example of where facing reality rather than ignoring it allowed us to avoid potentially drastic consequences.

Going to Rio de Janeiro: Brazil

'Piglet sidled up to Pooh from behind. "Pooh!" he whispered. "Yes, Piglet?" "Nothing," said Piglet, taking Pooh's paw. "I just wanted to be sure of you."'

A.A. Milne

Cumulative flying distance:	**37,773 kilometres**
Cumulative flying time:	**51 hours and 10 minutes**
Cumulative total travel time:	**108 hours and 10 minutes**

We had imagined gliding down into the city, looking out the window and seeing Sugarloaf with that golden sweep of sand and sun glistening off the blue Atlantic Ocean. But we were met with grey skies full of low lying clouds and drizzling rain. This was *not* the Rio de Janeiro of the glorious postcards and TV travel shows.

We'd pre-arranged through the hotel for a driver to pick us up and were very glad to see Antonio standing with a sign for Dr O'Brien. He spoke some English too; like most drivers in Rio, he had learnt the fundamentals for the job, such as 'Is this your first visit to Rio/Brazil?' and 'How long are you staying for?' On our ride to the hotel, Antonio gave us a great description of some of the landmarks we passed, and we later found out he was running in the marathon or 'maratona' on Sunday as well.

The traffic was bumper to bumper, in multiple lanes, as we ground our way towards the popular beach area of Leblon, passing many 'favelas' en route. Many of Rio's 6 million people live in these slum-like dwellings that are like small brick boxes stacked on top of each other, some with sheet metal roofs, others with rooftop balconies. Many had lines of washing stretched across their balconies, others had broken windows or no windows at all, while some had silver insulation paper up or metal grilles instead of glass. Graffiti covered many of the walls and on the dirty mud pitch created between the structures we caught glimpses of kids playing soccer before school.

For decades, favelas have been largely built by their occupants and are still being built in the newer areas of the city, although today's structures are both safer and more comfortable than the older wooden creations. They can also be very dangerous areas, with their own laws, and no tourist would think of entering the majority of them, but they're a fascinating part of the Carioca (as natives of Rio are referred to) landscape.

As we drove the 27 kilometres to our hotel we craned our necks around to try to see Corcovado (Christ the Redeemer) on top of his mountain, but the huge statue was shrouded in low-lying misty cloud and would have to wait for another day. The city is surrounded by hills with many Cariocas living in condominiums on the hillsides. It reminded us of Hong Kong and Honolulu and this feeling was reinforced as we began to go through tunnels to reach the beaches. The Tunel Reboucas was in two sections, the first some 1,800 metres long, the second 2 kilometres. On an average day it services over 200,000 cars!

Emerging from the tunnels we were suddenly in a much better class of area, with high rise condos looking sparklingly fresh and white with glass balconies to capture the views of the hills and Jardim Botanico, a huge botanical garden and parkland area. This area – the Lagoa – is set around beautiful Lake Rodrigo de Freitas, and even though the weather was far from perfect there were boats on the lake and joggers and cyclists on the 7.5 kilometre track round the lake. Antonio told us there were many private clubs, pointing out one called Caiceras where wealthy cariocas go to socialise, sail, play tennis and use the gym facilities. Not sure how much it costs to join but we could only imagine it is beyond the reach of most of the population here. From this area, you could see to Corcovado on clear days. What a spectacular regular jogging circuit!

Our first view of the beach was at Leblon but it was almost deserted due to the poor weather. However, we saw the Watchtower 12 with the surf lifeguard inside. These 'postes' are numbered to let you know where you are along the Copacabana, Ipanema and Leblon beachfront. Each attracts its own clientele. Supposedly there's a watchtower for singles, one for families, one for gays and so on.

REST AND RECOVERY

Status report

After two long haul flights in as many days we were both feeling rather tired and O'B's back and adductor muscles were particularly tight. Sue was continuing to struggle with a swollen and sore right foot and was really upset and angry about it. After enduring 12 months of pain and cortisone injections in her left foot, now the other was giving her grief.

Some free time
Wednesday 25 June

We were very happy with our hotel's location, perched in the shadow of the Two Brothers Hills. Having decided to pay an extra

99R or AUD$75 to check in early, we found ourselves with several options for the next few hours. We could go for a walk and explore the Leblon beach, try to go for a run, or take advantage of the free shuttle bus service to Rio Sul, one of the big shopping malls.

Even though it was tempting to shake off the cobwebs after yet another long haul flight, we discounted the run option as Sue's foot was still sore. On previous overseas marathon trips we've often gone for a run soon after arriving somewhere and have found it a great way to get our land legs. Walking would have been our first choice in many of the cities of the world, except for maybe this one. Before we left we'd been inundated with warnings about personal safety in Rio. Some had told us stories of being mugged at knife point while out for a jog, having both their watch and runners stolen from them. Others had been bailed up so frequently that they had prepared a fake wallet to hand over and save time. We had even heard of taxis stopped at red lights and surrounded by thieves. Even former residents had warned Sue not to wear any jewellery, even cheap earrings. So understandably we were somewhat nervous to head off into the unknown, especially being a little fuzzy after the long flight from London.

The drive to Rio Sul gave us a good understanding of the layout of the southern side of Rio, as we crawled in the traffic before arriving at the large mall. There seems to be an almost generic quality to these places and really we could have been anywhere in the world – until we tried to buy some food for lunch. The Portuguese that the Brazilian people speak is like nothing we have heard before. Soon we began to understand why chain restaurants such as McDonalds and KFC are so popular with foreign tourists. But we couldn't find either the Colonel or the golden arches at Rio Sul and finally decided to just buy an ice-cream. Surely that would be foolproof. Well, after some confusion and much pointing at pictures we did get our food, although it wasn't quite what we wanted. But we gave the 'thumbs up' sign and a tentative 'obrigado' and hoped it meant thank you.

Then it was back to the hotel for a massage. We were treating massage as a vital part of our recovery and preparation for each of our runs, knowing the benefits it can provide for injury prevention. We'd each booked a sports massage which turned out to be a 75 minute mixture of stretching, vigorous rubbing and kneading. Our legs, arms and necks were pushed and then pushed again to increase the range of motion in the joints before the muscles themselves were worked. Again the language barrier provided a minor hiccup when my therapist Viviane mistook 'No more' for 'More ' and just about wrenched my arm out of its socket!

The hotel staff seemed quite impressed that we were running the full 'maratona', or 'championship' as they referred to it. There didn't seem to be any massive awareness of the race, but there were signs up about road closures and placards and posters promoting the event, so we were curious to see the size of the crowds cheering the runners on Sunday.

Maratona!
Thursday 26 June

We woke early to a glorious sunny morning, the waves crashing onto the rocks outside our hotel room. With clear blue skies the views across the ocean and to Ipanema beach were spectacular, a great background for a few hours' work in our hotel room. A language problem resulted in us enjoying what we thought was a complimentary breakfast at the cost of US$50 per person – the most expensive fruit, muesli, toast and coffee we have ever had. The travel guides had warned about being robbed in Rio, but this was not the way we expected it to happen.

After breakfast we booked a hotel car to the Centro underground railway station in downtown Rio to register for the marathon. We arranged for our driver to drop us at the entrance and pick us up one hour later. As we walked out of the hotel the car service manager told us to call him on the car radio if need be as the driver could not speak any English. Now you tell us, we thought as we drove away. Just 500 metres down the road we were startled by the perfect English coming from the front of the car: 'How are you today' followed by 'Is this your first time in Rio?' and 'How many days will you be staying?' There soon came some excellent descriptions of the key sights along the way. We were impressed. What had the car service manager been talking about?

We had told the driver we were in town for the marathon but as we approached downtown there was some confusion regarding where we were going and for how long. We handed the driver the internet print out of the registration location.

'Ah running, championchipa, maratona!' he said excitedly.

It finally dawned on us that while he was very good at delivering the lines he had been taught, he hadn't enough English to understand what we had been saying to him. In spite of all this, the drive to the downtown area was fantastic. We followed the last 15 kilometres of the marathon course through Leblon and along the world famous Ipanema and Copacabana Beaches before crossing the marathon finish at Flamengo Beach. Travelling slowly in the busy traffic, we were able to take many photos of the beaches and the people walking, running, sun baking, drinking coffee, playing soccer and working along the beachfront. Once we moved past Flamengo Beach our driver told us to hide our camera and to stop taking photos as this area was 'a little unsafe'. On a tour the next day the guide told us that at certain times of the day there is no way he would go into the area where we had to register.

Soon we reached our destination and agreed to meet our driver at the same place an hour later. Walking through a crowded market plaza looking for the station entry, we quickly became lost, but a security person pointed us in the direction. As soon as we found the expo we were asked if we were international. Being dark-haired and tanned, Sue blended in nicely with the Brazilian women but I was rather easy to pick as not being a local. We were escorted to a special area where English-speaking volunteers arranged our registration and provided us with an escort to go and pick up our race numbers and timing chips.

We then checked out the expo, including a small merchandise booth where we bought a running cap for me, two drink bottles, and a pair of marathon thongs for Sue. Our saleperson had been schooled in the same approach to being understood in a foreign language as I often reverted to. Basically, you say the same thing more and more loudly until you are yelling at each other. Thankfully an English speaking volunteer heard what was going on and came over to assist. We took a few pictures in front of marathon banners, then tried (unsuccessfully) to access an automatic teller machine before venturing back into the crowded mall. We found a bank, and there was our driver, spot on the agreed time. Mission accomplished, we spent the afternoon at our hotel enjoying the sun before it disappeared behind the hill at 3pm, leaving us in the shade. Never mind, we set out for a 40 minute run along Ipanema Beach, which was also well shaded by now.

After a short and somewhat nervous jog along the pathway that separated the beach from the road we were ready to return up the hill to our hotel. Our confidence boosted by running safely and our legs feeling okay, we decided to run past the hotel and explore what was around the corner and further up the hill, expecting to find another magnificent ocean view. No more than 200 metres past the hotel the landscape changed dramatically. As we reached a side street that disappeared into a favela the sun literally disappeared too and it was not just the scenery but the atmosphere that changed. I quickly realised we were in a place we probably should not be and instantly decided we were ready to head back. I promptly turned around, put my arm around a somewhat surprised Sue and directed her towards the hotel. We scurried down the road and into the safety of the hotel lobby where I explained to her my concerns for our safety and the sudden change of direction.

Sugarloaf
Friday 27 June

Two famous landmarks define Rio de Janeiro. One is Corcovado Mountain with its massive statue of Christ the Redeemer. The other is Sugarloaf Mountain with its cable cars taking tourists up to the peak for the spectacular views. Like countless tourists before us, we felt our visit to Rio would not be complete without visiting these famous sites. Magnificent, amazing, sensational – all these were appropriate adjectives as we looked down from Sugarloaf to the golden sunset over Ipanema and Copacabana. By the time we descended, night had fallen and the landscape was punctuated by millions of glittering, sparkling lights. It was a fabulous way to see the city, and one that we probably would not have considered, preferring a daylight view.

Corcovado
Saturday 28 June

A stunningly sunny morning heralded our excursion to Corcovado – a huge relief as we'd heard that tours up the mountain can be disappointing if it's swathed in low-lying cloud. No such problems for us!

Corcovado, meaning hunchback, stands some 710 metres above sea level. A road goes only part way to the top, the peak being reached by funicular train, which makes the engineering feat of erecting Christ the Redeemer seem even more amazing. The statue stands 30 metres high, has a span of 28 metres and a total weight of 1.145 tonnes. Construction took 5 years, with building materials being transported up the hill by the aforementioned railway.

After exiting our carriage, we walked up the final staircases to the base of the monument. When Christ the Redeemer came into view it was truly one of those goosebumps moments. Awesome! The 360 degrees views from the lookout were also amazing. Quite a few of the international marathoners were on the tour with us and many were taking the opportunity to try to follow the course from start to finish from this vantage point.

Unfortunately there was a rather long wait standing in the sun to return back down the mountain and we were very glad to be seated on the train and returning to the relative cool of the bus. Ever since the Paris Marathon eve in 2001, when our tourist excursion proved to be exhausting for our legs and caused fatigue early in the marathon, we've been wary of too much standing and walking the day before a race.

The night before the Rio Marathon

By 9.30pm the night before the Rio Marathon we were getting ready to sleep. Once again we'd made it through 2 days of pre-race eating and hydrating. We'd prepared our race gear, booked a 4am wake up call and arranged transport to the start. We were looking forward to running on a very beautiful course. The marathon started at 8am and temperatures of 29 Celsius were predicted. It would be a 'tough day in the office', but with almost the entire run along the coast we were hopeful the sea breeze would keep us cool.

Dinner had been at a restaurant in South America's largest shopping mall at Barra da Tijuca. Barra's on the ocean at the 15 kilometres mark of the marathon and 15 kilometres towards the start of the course from our hotel. So by now we'd seen 25 kilometres of the course and it was very scenic indeed – like a cross between the Gold Coast and Great Ocean Road Marathons in Australia, or Big Sur and Fort Lauderdale Marathons in the US. Often on the night before a marathon you see water stations being set up along the course for the runners the following day. But this was the first time we'd ever seen armed guards keeping a close eye on the drinks!

REST AND RECOVERY

Status report

Sue was in good shape other than the injury she sustained during Comrades. She'd seen some improvement this week and we were hoping her foot would be okay for the run in the morning. O'B had no notable injuries at this time.

Ready to rhumba
Sunday 29 June

Our 4am wake up call had us both jumping out of bed and into action. We'd slept well and it felt good to have a solid 6 hours' snooze time behind us before the big day. Breakfast was electrolyte drink and protein bars, and after showers and the lathering of any body part that might chafe or blister, we quickly dressed. I dealt with a couple of quick work emails, then we checked we had everything and left the peace and quiet of our room. In the lobby I asked the all night concierge to take a quick photo of us as we headed out the door ready to battle the Rio heat.

Our driver Jose was waiting and had the Renault in prime position at the front door ready for action. He seemed even more excited about the marathon than we were as we raced along Ipanema and Copacabana Beaches towards the finish line which was also the pick up point to take us the 42.2 kilometres to the start. We'd been impressed with the way Jose handled the busy Rio streets but on this occasion he ran every red light. As we approached each one he'd slow to make sure there were no cars coming and then accelerate. In a strange way we felt safer; it made it more difficult for people roaming the streets to approach our car. But we later discovered he was not breaking the law; at night drivers can run red lights in order to reduce opportunities for carjackers and thieves.

When we arrived at the bus boarding zone workers were busy loading trucks and directing runners. We'd noticed the lack of kilometre markers on the course along the way and now realised race officials had not been prepared to risk the signs being damaged or stolen by putting them out the day before. It also explained the police guarding the water for the drink stations.

It was just after 5am. We arranged a pick up point with Jose then scampered across the park and on to a bus to take us to the start. Half marathoners were also boarding buses and we were thankful for an English speaking volunteer who steered us on to the correct one. Sue struck up a conversation with two local lads who had worked in the US. Meanwhile I got chatting to an accounting lecturer from San Francisco who was on a mission to complete 100 marathons. Rio was to be his 84th (or thereabouts). A walk/jog exponent, my new friend was expecting a 5 hours 50 minutes finish and had a wealth of knowledge of marathons all round the world, especially those with a course cut-off time of six hours.

Marathon walking is not widely practised in Australia, with many courses closing to runners and reopening to traffic after 5 hours. According to this guy, there are few marathon walkers who travel under 6 hours and less than 5 hours 30 minutes is very rare. This restricts the number of possible races for marathon walkers although there are many races that cater for them in the US and other parts of the world.

The time passed quickly on the bus ride to the start and we were pleased that Sue's new friends from Rio interpreted for us as a volunteer made a number of announcements in Portuguese on the way to the start. Before we knew it the first signs of daylight were with us and we could see the beach area adjacent to the start.

Waiting to run

There were less than 100 runners and with nearly 2 hours until the start we were in for a long wait. As the sun rose over the mountains we stood on the shore watching the surfers and more runners arriving by bus.

Being in a country where you can't read or speak the language means you don't know as much about what is going on as the locals do. We were unaware of the participant numbers but noticed considerably more men than women. Even so, and unusually for marathons, there were adequate toilets for women but men had long waits. The first time we used the toilets, about 90 minutes before the start, Sue thought this was great. But a visit closer to race time revealed a unisex approach as the men took over the women's toilets and created massive waiting lines everywhere. The Brazilian portable toilets also seemed to be the worst we have encountered anywhere and the smell particularly off-putting. Once on the course we chose to go bush.

Many of the locals had brought breakfast to eat before the start – a clever idea and one we wished we'd adopted as by the time the run started it was more than 3 hours since we had eaten. Supplies for runners at the start were poor, with only water available, and we suspected that once again language differences had gotten the better of us.

As far as race starts go, the air was fresh but not cold and apart from Sue, who felt chilled, there were very few people wearing garbage bags or other tops to keep warm. As a general rule, comfortable conditions when standing around waiting to start a marathon are a bad sign; it usually means the race temperature will be too hot.

With 15 minutes to go, the starting chute was opened and we made our way to a position behind several hundred people. Our best guess is that there were 2,000 to 3,000 marathon runners, though we'd heard a rumour that when the marathon, half marathon and family run were added together there were 14,000 participants in total. Runners amused themselves by cheering at the sweeping camera that hovered above the starting chute, much to everyone's enjoyment.

As 8am approached a police helicopter dominated the sky above. The runners surged forward and all of a sudden took off. Unlike many other races there'd been no countdown or starting ceremony. As we crossed the line, however, we did notice a starting hooter that looked like it had seen better days. Not to worry, we were off and running.

The barefoot runner

About 30 minutes before the race start we'd noticed a local man dressed in a traditional costume warming up. With no running shoes and his timing chip tied around his ankle, he was carrying out a well-practised series of tai chi style warm ups and stretches. A number of people approached him to shake hands and wish him well so Sue strolled over and did likewise. Later in the day we noticed this fellow's photo in the early pages of the marathon program. Clearly this was not his first barefoot run, but unfortunately we could not find out any more of his story.

Over the years we have come across some weird and wonderful costumes being worn by marathoners and the Brazilian warrior reminded us of the Hawaiian runner we have seen many times. Another barefoot runner, he runs in a loin cloth with a circlet of leaves on his head.

Running 42 kilometres on hard roads barefoot? We just shook our heads. Although on a hot course it may well provide the extra incentive to run fast!

Running into the sun

By the time we finally started the sun had climbed quite high in the sky and we knew from previous experience at the Honolulu

Marathon it would be really important to get as far into the course as we could before the sun felt as if it was burning through our skins. The late starting time meant there was little chance of avoiding some very warm temperatures, even for those running in less than 3 hours. To make matters worse, with the exception of the initial stretch and a couple of small tunnel/underpass sections, the entire course was directly into the sun.

The first 1.5 kilometres ran away from the finish line before we turned around and headed back past the start towards the finish at Flamengo Beach. O'B usually takes about 75 minutes to 'warm up' and feel at his best. But he expected to be a little slower at the start today, as the muscle in his right calf felt slightly strained. We decided to monitor it but thought that within the first hour it would become another long forgotten momentary sore spot. What a misguided thought!

As we ran along the very straight, very flat and very exposed first 15 kilometre stretch the gap between drink stops seemed endless. We had taken good care prior to the race to work on hydration and bought six packs of electrolyte drink from the local shops, but the 3 to 4 kilometre interval between drink stations seemed massive. When we did see them we were taking two each of the sealed plastic cups, one for now and one to consume midway to the next. Before we started we had checked out these cups and looked at various opening options. The top did actually peel off but in the interests of efficiency we decided that the puncture method was the way to go.

By 9.00am the locals were out in force along the beachfront, not many shouting out support, but just enjoying the glorious Sunday morning. Two locals commented that conditions were warm even for them; they'd not realised that 'it would get hot so quickly and be a bitch weekend'. What did they mean? Then we realised they meant *beach* weekend!

Prior to the race we'd been on tour with a group of Canadians who had travelled down for the event as part of a charity fundraising organisation. We also saw Danish flags and a group of Germans in the red, black and yellow colours of their flag with 'Deutschland in Rio 2008' across their shirts. We chatted to a South African and saw a couple of Comrades 2008 singlets as well, but as to how many internationals were actually competing and their demographics we had no idea.

It soon became apparent that electrolyte stations were not going to be frequent. In fact there were only two on the entire course: one at the 15 kilometre mark and one at the 35 kilometre. Again we'd not been able to access that information, and being used to having electrolyte drink or a sponsor's drink at least every second station, that is about 5 kilometres apart, this was disconcerting, especially given the warm conditions. Moreover, my 'strained calf' from the first minutes of the race was still bothering me.

We were trying to take an energy gel at every second refreshment point and that was working well energy-wise for the first half, which was great after struggling to keep it down during Comrades 2 weeks earlier. The water was now being poured over heads, necks and wrists as well as consumed as we tried to keep our core temperature down. Luckily, as we got close to the 15 kilometre mark, there were large stretches of shade as apartment buildings and trees cast shadows across the road. This area was a comfortable middle class suburb and Sue got quite a few cheers from the local women. So few women running was such a contrast to races in the US. Our American friend on the bus, who had run many marathons in Europe, said that there too the numbers of female runners are significantly lower, with less than 20% of the total field being women. However, in a race such as the Chicago Marathon, there is now parity, or very close to it.

Leaving the Barra da Tijuca area we reached the half marathon start at Lagarda. It sure was a relief to get past that milestone! By now

I was worried I had pulled a calf muscle and was starting to feel the heat quite badly. The temperature already felt into the mid 20s and it was only 10.00am. Sue's right foot had begun to hurt too and she took the first of two anti-inflammatory tablets at the 2 hour mark. As we moved past the halfway, it was 2.02 hours on the watch. We agreed that with the heat and the stopping for videos and photos, we would not break 4 hours, and that 4 to 4.30 was going to be a more realistic time. But with the gorgeous scenery, we really couldn't complain. Indeed, in retrospect the extra walk breaks and slower time may even have helped our recovery for Calgary the following week.

Partnerunning Tip

SCENARIOS

Whether you are training, running or walking your local 5 kilometre course, or travelling to the other side of the world to run a marathon or ultra marathon, considering scenarios and developing strategies for each is vital for success as it prepares us to take action in the moment and helps us avoid making poor decisions on the run.

Scenarios are:

Enhanced by	Hindered by
• Identifying options and alternatives	• Failing to consider options
• Considering best and worst case scenarios	• Failing to develop strategies
• Developing clear strategies and actions for each scenario	• Thinking only of the 'best' scenarios

Overheating

We started off with a strategy of 30 minutes running and 1 minute walking, then shortened this to 20 minutes running and 1 minute walking. But the unpredictability of the drink stations and the increasing heat made a regimented ratio difficult and after the 28 kilometre mark we opted for 10 minutes running to 1 minutes walking and decided to keep to this until the end of the marathon. We have found this sort of strategy provides a focus and discipline, rather than waiting until one of us is exhausted and has to stop.

Moving away from the beachfront after the halfway mark, we headed onto the highway past the lush tropical vegetation of the Fioresta da Tijuca, through tunnels in the mountains and over long two-storey bridges before we headed towards the golden sands of Ipanema and Copacabana. Perched precariously above us, the houses here – not shanty-town favelas but solid, architect designed homes whose balconies would offer spectacular views – seemed as if they were about to tumble down the hillside.

The tunnels offered respite from the relentless sunshine and the breeze that seemed to have sprung up made things a little more comfortable. Finally we hit 'the Hill'. Our earlier reconnaissance of the course had revealed that there was really only one climb, just before our hotel. Driving out to Barra shopping the day before, we'd checked it out and decided it was not a particularly difficult gradient and the length was manageable, although we agreed that after the Comrades hills most inclines would not appear too steep or long. Strange how at the 30 kilometre mark, with temperatures nudging 29 degrees Celsius, your strategy for a climb can change! We found ourselves taking the Comrades bus approach and running for four light posts and walking two, which helped keep our momentum up.

O'B was cooking by now and throwing water on himself, but it was not really helping lower his core temperature. He was getting worried about the pain in his right calf that was slowing him down too. I could tell he was struggling not only because he was starting to limp but he was also trying to distract himself by taking lots of photos. Meanwhile, I had taken my second painkiller as the pain in my right foot had begun to move up my shin, making walking in particular very uncomfortable.

Passing the favela a few hundred metres before our hotel meant that we were just over 10 kilometres to the finish. This section of the course was notable for the large number of heavily armed police patrolling it and the major entry point in and out of the shanty towns. When we'd jogged out this way from the hotel on Thursday we'd experienced one of those 'I don't think this is the safest place to be' moments and turned around very quickly. Today the huge police presence meant we at least felt safe but we would not have wanted to take a wrong turn. As we ran past the police, who looked more like soldiers than traffic cops, we realised how lucky we had been to run through the same area a few days prior without the armed escort.

Looking to change the subject, we wondered if it was possible to pop in to our hotel room en route for a mid race quickie. It certainly would have been another first and the hotel was well located for such an interlude. But we decided we should plan for such some other day, one when we weren't struggling with injury and where English was the local language just in case we had to do some explaining. Still, it was another possible advantage of Partnerunning – and quite in keeping with the romantic atmosphere in Rio.

Barrelling down the other side of the hill brought us at last to Leblon and Ipanema Beaches which were absolutely packed. Some wore brief Brazilian bikinis, others the small man bathers known as sungas (a bit like the ones like Daniel Craig wore in James Bond, although I'm not overly impressed with them). Some women were out in high-heeled sandals and skimpy miniskirts, while the men wore casual shirts and dress shorts. Many were walking dogs or taking espresso at the kiosks along the waterfront. I still marvelled at the fact that O'B had run Comrades, Mauritius, the streets of London and now Rio carrying – and using – a video camera. But I noticed he seemed to be taking more crowd shots today than in our previous runs. Must have been all those women in their 'dental floss bikinis'!

The temperature had hit 29 by now, and despite some shade it was hot. It was such a tease to have the water so close and watch the swimmers and surfers cooling off. As we were staring longingly at the cool blue ocean, O'B became aware of someone running alongside him dressed in a polo shirt and casual shoes. How weird! 'The plane, the plane,' he kept saying.

And sure enough, it was the Englishman who had sat opposite us with his lady on the flight down from London. They'd decided to come down to watch the run on the slim chance they might actually see us go by. What were their odds of being in the right place at the right time? Whatever, this chance meeting gave us a real boost.

From the beaches it was merely 2 kilometres to the finish and, as is often the case, the last stretch seemed relatively pain free. We floated the few hundred metres to Flamengo Beach amid the roars of a very enthusiastic crowd. As was our custom, we held hands and soaked up the support as we ran the last 100 metres through the finishing chute where volunteers were waiting to remove our timing chips and present us with our hard earned medals.

Carnivale finish

We took a moment to watch others crossing the line, marvelling yet again at the power of an event like this to demonstrate people's ability to complete a major challenge. Whether they were family runners, first time half marathoners or veteran 6 hour pace marathon runners, people of all shapes, sizes and abilities were achieving great things and reminding themselves, 'Yes, I can do whatever I set my mind to.' And in many cases they will apply this approach to the rest of their lives.

As we left the finishing area we reflected that we had now completed a marathon or greater in each of the six continents – a thought that quickly was replaced with ones of recovery and the fact that five more marathons over the next 5 weeks still awaited us.

Our time of 4 hours 25 minutes and 32 seconds was our slowest ever and left us with mixed feelings. It was disappointing, but on the other hand we reminded ourselves of the recovery benefits of taking at least 30 minutes longer than we would have liked. We later discovered we took more than 100 pictures on the course and more than 10 minutes of video footage, which would have slowed us considerably. But we'd agreed the marathon was a unique opportunity to capture the sights of Rio so took every opportunity to do so.

Of course the heat was another major factor and we were worried from the halfway point that a major meltdown would have a severe impact on Calgary the following Sunday, so the slower time was important to offset the risk of injury and extreme fatigue. I was in a very bad way from the heat and my leg was also a cause for concern. From the beginning of the Rio run I had a constant pulling on my shin and calf which, despite stretching and getting warmed up, continued to get worse not better as the day went on.

We suspected the soft surfaces, early start time, cold Coca Cola and some leftover runners' high from Comrades may have made our Mauritius run easier than we deserved. Possibly we lacked that extra bit of energy in Rio when the heat became intense, but after all it was only 2 weeks since the gruelling 87 kilometres of the Comrades run.

On the bright side I was 1,008th of the 1,618 men and Sue was 107th of the 220 women who completed the Rio Marathon, so there were many people finishing after us and even more who never made it at all.

The post race activities quickly developed into a huge party, with a live band playing samba music on a big stage and families and friends gathering in the park. The Brazilians are renowned for their party spirit so I suppose we should not have been surprised. With no one to cheer for or meet we went in search of Jose and were extra pleased to see his smiling face and congratulatory handshake waiting for us where we had agreed to meet earlier in the day. I climbed into the back seat of the Renault but poor O'B had a little more difficulty squeezing in. But we were soon underway, driving at a sedate pace back through the streets of Rio. Even though we had finished running, O'B was still very overheated, flushed and sweating profusely, and his aching calf pain had not abated. Combined with my foot problems we were both getting concerned about our physical condition, and this was only marathon number 3!

With the beach area still closed Jose took us via an alternative route past a university and the botanical gardens before winding his way around the Leblon lagoon and back to the hotel. O'B had even more trouble getting out of the car so we headed straight to the pool where we spent the rest of the afternoon. I made a quick detour to grab a bikini from our room and we ordered food and drinks to down as we relaxed in the warm afternoon sun and cooled our aching legs in the pool.

By the pool we met Matt and Louise, an Australian couple from Melbourne who were travelling around South America and running in the marathon before flying back home We traded race stories, celebrated Louise's first half marathon and finished the afternoon with a cold beer as the sun disappeared behind the hill overlooking the hotel pool.

By now it was 4pm. Next on our agenda was showering before heading out to a churrascaria (Brazilian barbeque restaurant) and samba show for our last night in Brazil. It was the perfect way to celebrate.

Some post race reflections
Monday 30 June

We were feeling very tired by 11.45pm when the show finished, and the hard seats had proven particularly uncomfortable for our post marathon legs and backs, so we were glad to head back to the hotel. Usually when you stand up at these sorts of shows it is to join in the dancing, but in this instance it was the pain in O'B's muscles and joints and not the rhythm in his feet that saw him standing for most of the performance.

We awoke feeling good although still somewhat disappointed with our marathon time of the day before. We could not help but compare Rio with the events and training runs of the past 6 months. In all of these, O'B had been the one to run well with plenty of strength and energy, especially in the second half. So the way the Rio heat knocked him about was a massive contrast. On the other hand, I'd been struggling with injury and had drawn on his strength on many occasions during this trip as well as in the half year of lead up. Yet in Rio it was me with the strength and energy to help us across the line.

O'B's leg was extremely painful but he wasn't sure if it was a specific problem or the result of running three marathons in 3 weeks. We were worried that as the weeks passed our recovery would become more difficult, and it would be harder and harder to tell the difference between muscle soreness and injury. I thought ice, massage and rest would be extra important this week to make sure O'B was in good shape for Calgary, where at least it would not be so hot.

One really pleasing aspect of the Rio Marathon, however, was we could truly see the benefits of Partnerunning. The course was magnificent and it was wonderful to share the experience together and see the city in such a unique way. As is often the case, on marathon day you can visit places that are closed or unsafe every other day of the year and this was very much the case with Rio. More importantly, the Rio Marathon highlighted the way in which Partnerunning can allow each runner to benefit from the other and to balance strengths and weaknesses, good days and bad, and assist each other over the line.

The day after

At 3pm our original driver Antonio was waiting to take us to the airport and proudly showed us his medal from the family run the day before. During the trip to the airport we traded stories and Antonio showed us a picture from 5 years back when he was on the podium receiving a medal for 3rd place in his age group in a big race. Crossing to the airport side of town involved driving through tunnels under the mountains. As we left the cloudy beach side for the last time we were amazed when we emerged on the city side to beautiful clear sky and sunshine. What a shame the clouds had not followed us the day before, rather than this one when all we wanted was some nice poolside weather.

As we reached the airport I remarked to Sue that Rio is truly a spectacular city. If not for running marathons, I can't imagine I would ever have seen it. Running has provided us with so many wonderful unexpected experiences – all of which are topped off for me by being with Sue.

Our next stop was Miami Beach where we were hoping for some warm beach weather and recovery time. After a short flight to Sao Paulo we changed planes for our 9.50pm American Airlines flight to Miami, Florida. As the plane took off we ordered champagne.

REST AND RECOVERY

Status report

O'B's strained calf and shin soreness had reduced and he seemed to have the least amount of post marathon soreness he had ever experienced. There were no lingering ill effects from the heat during the marathon and we were hoping the slow run time would augur well for a good recovery. Sue was in good shape in terms of leg recovery, but her right foot, ankle and shin were swollen and sore.

Miami
Tuesday 1 July

Cumulative flying distance:	**44,682 kilometres**
Cumulative flying time:	**60 hours and 40 minutes**
Cumulative total travel time:	**126 hours and 40 minutes**

What a relief to be able to check in when we arrived at our hotel at 7.00am. The flight had given us just enough time for a late dinner followed by about 4 hours' sleep – not quite long enough.

Rain was glistening on the bitumen as we drove through the dark streets. After being in South Africa, Mauritius and Brazil, areas that we had never visited before, arriving in the US was like coming home. We were excited about getting a few days' rest, maybe sitting by the pool, hanging out in Barnes & Noble and Borders bookstores, and eating food we were familiar with.

After a quick unpack we decided a stretch of the legs was in order and set off for what turned out to be a 2 hour walk – perfect for clearing our fuzzy heads after our overnight flight from Brazil. But our intention of doing the same walk the next day backfired when my lower back and adductors became very sore. Some unexpected calf and shin pain as a residue from Rio popped up as well. Sue's foot also found the long walk more than enough weight bearing exercise for the day so after breakfast we spent a few hours at the beach lying on our hired sun lounges, trying to catch a few Zs in between some cooling ocean plunges as the heat picked up to 90 degrees Fahrenheit (mid 30s Celsius).

Relaxing
Wednesday 2 July

We woke to a gorgeous sunny day and decided to head out for another long walk, this time with camera in hand. I was keen to check out the atmosphere at funky South Beach, with its Art Deco hotels and 'beautiful people', and not even think about running for a short while.

REST AND RECOVERY

Status report

O'B's lower back and hips were sore and concerning him quite a bit. He also complained that his right shin and calf were a bit tight. Sue's right foot was still a bit swollen after the flight but the pain seemed less than 24 hours ago. Neither of us had experienced that sort of trauma before and it was scary! All we could do was apply ice and hope for the best.

Some beach time
Thursday 3 July

We had a really restful day, enjoying the beach and catching up on emails and blog writing. Receiving a backlog of emails gave us a real boost, and some were especially fun. We really enjoyed the comment from one person following our blog:

> I love reading the blogs, although I've had to change when I read them, as after Comrades, all the race info came through one night, so I sat in front of the computer and read greedily, savouring every word, looking at the photos, and feeling the pain. But then when I went to bed, I couldn't sleep and drifted in and out of a dream like state, where I was running behind you two and you were yelling at me to hurry up, and I just wanted to go to bed, but you wouldn't let me. I finally fell asleep exhausted two hours before the alarm went off! So now I only read them during the day. I am completely addicted and can't wait for each entry.

We also became aware a number of families and schools were following our journey on maps and teaching children about the locations we were visiting.

On our way to Calgary
Friday 4 July

We were up at 4am on American Independence Day. We had an early flight to Calgary via Dallas. Some 40 million Americans – double the population of Australia – would also be travelling this weekend. We were worried about congestion and hoped to beat the traffic to the airport and avoid any flight delays, especially on the first leg, as we didn't want to get stranded in Dallas. There were huge celebrations planned and we'd been amazed by the number of places selling fireworks, especially the tents on street corners and in carparks.

We'd have liked to have stayed longer in Miami Beach. We'd both been feeling very tired, which we put down partly to the relief of returning to more familiar territory. At the same time we hoped it was not marathon related tiredness, as we were looking forward to the Calgary Marathon and were particularly interested to see how we'd recovered from Rio.

REST AND RECOVERY

Status report

O'B's right shin was very sore and rest and massage seemed the only option. The pain was manageable walking around, but he couldn't jog without suffering and he started anti-inflammatories to try to get some quick improvement. Without realising it, he must have sustained an injury during either the London tourist run or in Rio. Sue's foot and shin continued to improve. Whereas 48 hours before she was concerned about a stress fracture, now she was fairly optimistic that the worst was behind her and that she'd be in good shape for Calgary. How ironic that we had found ourselves in a role reversal! Would we ever both be injury free and comfortable at the same time?

Lesson for life

Help others.
Despite differences we can work together.

It's hard to explain but for some reason when we do something to assist others, sooner or later someone does the same for us. In a race where we could not speak to other runners as English was not widely spoken we were still able to help and encourage each other to the finish. It made us focus on the value of working with people who are different to us as well as those who are similar.

The Calgary Stampede: Canada

'The best way to cheer yourself up is to try to cheer somebody else up.'

Mark Twain

Cumulative flying distance:	**48,933 kilometres**
Cumulative flying time:	**66 hours and 40 minutes**
Cumulative total travel time:	**139 hours and 40 minutes**

Check in at Miami was a worry, with only three counter staff for a huge line of people. With all our luggage, we were worried about the $15 charge for checked bags and hoped our long ago purchased Round the World airfares would exempt us. But luckily any extra fees were not mentioned and we went on our way. As our luggage had grown with each race, I hate to think what the extras would have come to.

Our flights from Miami to Calgary via Dallas were hassle free, although on both legs American Airlines ran out of food (more cost cutting). With minimal time to change planes we were lucky we'd brought some pretzels along; at least we had something to nibble on. We snoozed on the flights, caught up with some reading, and tossed and turned as our legs and backs grew tired of the cramped seating.

There was a short delay at passport control after needing to explain why we wanted to run 8 marathons in 8 countries in 8 weeks. The reaction from Canadian customs was similar to in the US. We got the impression they thought we were crazy but believable; no-one could possibly make up such a story.

As we emerged from the customs hall we could hear country and western music. A couple of cowboys were on a small stage, giving departing and arriving passengers a rousing version of 'Momma Don't Let Your Babies Grow up to Be Cowboys'. Our arrival in town had coincided with the world's largest rodeo!

The Calgary Stampede is the busiest and most exciting time of the year in this town, when rodeo enthusiasts from all over the world arrive. Hotels are booked out and restaurants are full. Luckily we had pre-booked our car. We soon discovered our hotel was also in cowboy mode! The lobby was full of decorations, parties underway and crowds of people everywhere. Checking in among the hay bales and wagon wheels at the front desk, we felt somewhat underdressed, being the only people not wearing cowboy hats and boots. I was just waiting for O'B to let out a 'Yeehah'!

Something is not right

We had left hot weather and afternoon thunderstorms in Miami, and Calgary was offering the same weather menu. The rain began as we got out of the car and we made a quick dash to the Old Armoury building where the expo was being held.

Our first attempt to run since Rio proved a disaster as my sore right leg was lame and refused to join in with the rest of my body. After a few more attempts it became clear that the painful right shin was more than just post race soreness but a mild form of shin splint or some other injury. As we headed inside we discussed our concerns and agreed that it would be hard if not impossible to run a marathon today but hopefully by Sunday my leg would come good.

We registered, and received our race numbers, timing chips and goodie bag, including a very nice long sleeved Brooks running shirt. After a couple of small purchases we were directed through to the Running Room stand. Running Room is a Canadian based retailer and promoter of running and other fitness activities and we checked out their merchandise and gathered information on a 3 kilometre Friendship Run they were sponsoring the next morning. The run started opposite our hotel which solved any transport challenges. Looking for an opportunity to test my bad leg, we decided to sign up.

We then spent the next hour trying free samples of electrolyte drink, power bars and other products while collecting information on a range of marathons and other fitness products. After a short demonstration we purchased a new product called the 'travelroller' which is like a foam tube and is designed to assist with massage and stretching. Over the years I have collected a few of these devices and enjoy visiting expos as there is usually a range of new products and ideas to discover and I can add to our collection of sticks, bricks, balls, rollers, lotions, massagers and other wonderful toys.

The Friendship Run
Saturday 5 July

The Running Room and the affiliated Walking Room are the creation of a Canadian, John Stanton. In addition to selling all manner of running products they promote their running/walking programs which can be accessed online or in person at the various store locations. As well as his business success, John has enjoyed great personal and physical success by giving up smoking, losing his extra body weight and experiencing great general overall health. He is also the author of many books on running and fitness walking and we were lucky to meet the man himself as he turned up to welcome runners. He was intrigued by our 8–8–8 adventure and said he'd like to feature us in an edition of his store's magazine.

Before the run began we were treated to a fashion parade, with running gear modelled by local runners of all shapes and ages. It was a hoot! They certainly seemed to be enjoying their moment on the catwalk. As we sipped the complimentary coffee and snacked on cookies, fruit and dips we were also introduced to the 'pace bunnies' and the race director, Helen Kolodziejzyk who explained that from next year the race would be changing its course, expo location and date. We were very lucky that we had selected 2008 for our runs as the date in May 2009 would not have suited our Round the World schedule.

Formalities completed, we set off on a very leisurely 3 kilometre jog to the expo. Over the bridge and around the riverbank we ran, before going back past the Children's Museum. We chatted to Keith, the 3.45 hour 'pace bunny', who coincidentally had just returned from an extended stay in Australia where he had run the Great Ocean Road Marathon and the Puffing Billy fun run. It was interesting to compare notes. He said he believed the Great Ocean Road was one of the most beautiful courses he'd ever run and the changeability of the weather held interest, rather than being a nuisance factor – a very Canadian attitude, we figured. He'd enjoyed a few quiet beers in the Apollo Bay Hotel and who knows, we may have been there at the same time doing the same thing.

After our soreness in Miami we were both a little apprehensive, and the Friendship Run gave us a good chance to check the state of our legs. I was relieved that, while still sore, I felt minimal discomfort in my right shin and thought maybe the rest had cured whatever problem had existed. Sue also felt good, not feeling any pain in her foot at all. So we were two very happy runners as we moved through the expo one more time to pick up a few free samples and drinks to supplement our breakfast snack at the Running Room.

The weather was much hotter and more humid than we remembered on our last visit to Calgary in July 2002, and it was a great relief that this morning's gentle jog had been relatively pain free. Little did I realise what was around the corner

Time to muster
Sunday 6 July

At this time of year Calgary has very long days and when our wake up call came at 5am it was already broad daylight. When we arrived at the hotel we discovered the staff were unaware of the marathon and so hadn't made any special breakfast arrangements for runners. Almost by auto-pilot we ate a breakfast of protein bars and electrolyte drink and went about our pre-race ritual – anti-chafe balm, run gear, energy gels, camera pouches – as we contemplated the day ahead. A few years back we learnt the hard way that once the novelty of preparing for a race wears off it is easy to overlook the basics. On occasion one or both of us has forgotten to apply anti-chafe balm to all our chafing parts, left the timing chip in our hotel room, forgotten sunglasses, or arrived at the start without the required garbage bag or warm clothing. We have developed a pre-race checklist and before leaving for any run we ask each other a series of questions.

It was a 2 kilometre walk to the start so we decided to leave at 6am to ensure we had plenty of time for checking in our bag of post-race clothes and visiting the portable toilets. The morning air was fresh without being cold and while Sue wore a jacket I was comfortable in a singlet. The first half of the walk was quiet, the downtown streets deserted. Closer to the start we noticed another runner, then a couple more. By the time we were 500 metres from the start a steady stream of marathoners was joined by cars and taxis containing more runners, volunteers and supporters.

After a few photos under the start sign it was off to join the line at the portable toilets and drop our post race bag. The Old Armoury building had been reconfigured and the expo booths replaced with a massage centre and baggage holding area. I hate it when pre race portable toilet lines are extensive but these were at least fast moving and I was impressed by the tables set up with anti-bacterial hand wash adjacent to the toilet area.

A series of speakers were in place around the race start and Tom Petty and the Heartbreakers enhanced the atmosphere as runners in the marathon and half marathon stood around, met friends, stretched, and in a few cases ran up and down the street warming up. More than one person could be heard suggesting they were saving every bit of energy they could for the race ahead. Ready for action, we went in search of the 'pace bunnies'.

Pace bunnies

Pace groups, where an experienced runner leads a group of runners to finish the race in a targeted time, are common in many marathons. In South Africa the pace group leaders were called 'bus drivers'. We'd met a few of the pace bunnies as they're known in Calgary the previous day and decided to start the marathon with Keith, the 3.45 hour pace bunny, although realistically this would be too fast for us.

The pace bunnies were all wearing red Running Room race shirts and caps with pink bunny ears, hence the name! Each bunny had their target time written in their ears and was carrying a sign as well.

Partnerunning Tip

Planning your race/event not only helps match your running with your training, it enables you to perform better and over time to review, learn and improve as you are able to compare expected with actual performance.

Event Strategy is:	
Enhanced by	**Hindered by**
• Considering options and linking to broad goals	• Having no race strategy
• A clear race plan based on fitness	• Changing strategy 'on the run'
• Encompassing all aspects of the event	• Adopting someone else's strategy without training for it
• Implementing ground rules	• Setting unrealistic goals
• Focusing on the desired outcome	• Getting carried away
	• Going too fast too early
	• Not considering other possible scenarios

The Stampede begins

As we huddled in the starting corral, the race announcer informed us that 52% of the 896 marathoners were men and 59% of the 2,300 half marathoners were women – so many more women participants here in Canada, compared with South Africa and Brazil.

With fewer than 3,500 runners in the marathon and half-marathon the race start was busy but not crazy. We still could not find pace bunny Keith so we lined up near the 1.55 half marathon bunny, still well in front of the 4.30 one. The starting crowd seemed rather relaxed and we enjoyed the fact that the usual pushing, shoving and jockeying for position was missing. Runners seemed to be giving each other plenty of personal space and with everyone crossing the starting line soon after the gun, and confident of the chip timing system, we experienced one of the most civilised race starts ever.

Prior to the countdown we wished each other luck and expressed our hope that our bodies would hold together. Hopefully it wouldn't be too hot and we'd spend less time on the course that we did the previous Sunday in Rio. Sue was feeling good and her injuries were continuing to improve, while I was looking forward to the experience but still worrying about the heat, humidity and the emerging injury in my right shin.

Saddledome and beyond

When the hooter sounded the crowd was off with a yeehah! We charged down Eighth Avenue in that excited way, too fast to sustain and full of enthusiasm. Somehow most runners find themselves caught up in this kind of excitement and when they check their time for the first kilometre are a bit shaken that they have gone out way too fast. When a half marathon and a full marathon start together the chance of this happening to the marathon runners seems to increase dramatically.

With so many females on the course, I was intrigued to note how popular the running skirt had become. I'd not really seen them that often at home, but here huge numbers were wearing the skirts with their inbuilt bike shorts underneath. I don't think I'll be adopting them any time soon. I've tried them on and don't find them either comfortable or particularly flattering for my petite stature. Nor do I think O'B will go for the knee length shorts that many of the younger men seem to be donning; he finds them too hot, too restrictive and thinks they'd cause too much chafing.

After leaving the shopping precinct we headed towards the Stampede Grounds with its distinctive Saddledome, an indoor arena for rodeo, shaped as its name suggests like a huge saddle. Even though it was only 7.15am, the crowds were quite large, waiting to get in. Surely not to cheer us? No, definitely not. There was dead silence and bemused expressions on most of the spectators' faces. O'B tried to rouse the crowd by turning his video camera towards them and calling out, 'Come on, what about some cheering?'

It transpired that our early morning crowd were lining up for free pancakes which were available on Family Day at the Stampede!

Our course had kilometre markers instead of the mile ones used in the US and the UK, and we were both pleased they showed distance completed rather than distance still to run. For some reason we prefer to be told we have run 5 kilometres rather than have 37 kilometres to go, and towards the end if feels better to see we have run 37 kilometres rather than have 5 kilometres to go. Sue prefers the kilometre markers to miles too, as they appear quicker and grow faster in magnitude. I have no definite preference – both seem to go on forever.

Either way, we both find it incredibly frustrating when drinks are scattered through the course at irregular intervals. It makes it very difficult to plan both taking on fuel and short walk breaks. Such was the case in two sections of the Calgary Marathon – one in the early part of the first half, and then again for a section at the start of the second. Overall though it was a very well organised race with great volunteers. The aid stations were well manned and provided both water and electrolyte drink (this was in various flavours from one station to the next, which was very thoughtful of the organisers). Along the course there were also three energy gel points and Sue ended up with more gels in her bum bag (or fanny pack as they are known in the US and Canada) at the end of the marathon than she started with.

Our course now led us out to and through the Calgary Zoo. It was great fun seeing the camels and flamingos and taking photos as we cruised past. The pace had steadied by now and we chatted to a few local runners as we moved along, including one who told us that her father was a judge at the Stampede Chuck Wagon races, which was of great interest as our Sunday night plan included tickets for this event. We're not sure how many international runners there were; not counting US citizens, we only came across one couple from the Netherlands. It seemed most were local Calgarians or from other provinces in Canada.

Horse man

Some marathons are renowned for participants in fancy dress. At the Rock'n'Roll Marathon, for instance, you'll inevitably see at least one runner – or ten – dressed in Elvis suits. Or as monkeys or various other sorts of animals! And some local runners dress in their country's native costumes, as did the Brazilian man.

Being the Stampede Marathon we expected to see at least one cowboy, which we did – but he came complete with his cardboard 'horse'. About the 16 kilometre mark we came upon Sean with his stallion, galloping along Parkside Drive. Sue asked him if he was running or riding, to which he replied the latter. As I captured him on film he said he'd really wanted to get into the spirit of the event and thought the horse box option would still enable him to run quite freely, although it meant he'd had to leave the camera at home. Good on him! It couldn't have been the easiest way to run a half marathon, but Sean had a huge smile on his face and was clearly lapping up the attention. The crowd certainly got into the spirit of things and calls of 'giddy up' and 'horsome' kept everyone entertained.

As we headed out of town and over some picturesque bridges that flanked the extremely fast flowing Bow River, we got a spectacular view of the city and the snowcapped Canadian Rocky Mountains. After following the river for a few kilometres we came upon the 10 kilometre run markers, and knew that we weren't far away from the point where the field would split and the half marathoners would head back towards the finish. In addition to the full marathon and half, there were three other races: the 10 kilometre, the 4 X 10 kilometre corporate challenge and a kids' marathon. The kids' event was a cumulative marathon over the month prior, which left them with just over 2 kilometres to run or walk on race day. Several years ago Sue's daughter Shelley and a girlfriend of hers had completed just such an event as part of the Canberra Marathon. It's a great way to get children involved in a fitness event and give them a real sense of achievement as well as a regular exercise program.

By now the crowd was getting excited as the majority of runners were about to turn and cover the last few kilometres to the finish. I was suffering badly with my right shin; in fact, it had been feeling uncomfortable almost from the start, and I was now in considerable pain. It was very tempting to turn with the half runners and get some relief from the relentless agony in my lower leg. This type of injury had been one of our chief concerns during the planning of our world tour. How would we cope if one of us developed an injury that not only hampered our progress but meant we did not get a chance to recover between marathons? Sue had struggled with her right shin and ankle and now, just as she was feeling good, I had succumbed to a similar problem. Neither of us could pinpoint how or when we had hurt ourselves, and neither of us had realised the seriousness of the soreness in our legs at the onset and gotten onto icing and treating the problems when they occurred.

The soreness in my right/good foot had well and truly returned but luckily for me the painkillers had effectively taken the edge off, making running more comfortable, even though walking was not so pleasant. Unluckily for O'B, these medications had little or no effect and running was becoming more and more difficult for him although he was finding walking relatively pain free. What a pair we were! We hypothesised that lack of massage and a tightening around his hips and adductors had caused the absence of smoothness in his running gait, and this in turn had led to injury in the lower limb. It was a lesson to us in the importance of proper recovery and care post race, and we were determined to try to hunt out some proper therapy in Arizona before next week's run in Missoula and hopefully get an informed diagnosis of his injury as well.

The Robin Hood Marathon in the UK had one of the most attractive first halves of a marathon that we'd completed, but then petered out to one of the most boring second halves that we have run. This Calgary run wasn't quite as bad, but there was a distinct change in interest factor as we launched into the second half. It was with some trepidation that we moved beyond the 20 kilometre mark. Would O'B's shin go the distance running or would we need to walk? The temperature was climbing into the mid 20s Celsius by now and the humidity was increasing too. Our energy levels were good and we were coping okay with the altitude although O'B had noticed an increase in breathing rate. The field had thinned considerably and it was now just the marathoners on the road. There was little crowd support out there but a few very enthusiastic volunteers were yelling encouragement and reading our names from our bibs as we passed, giving us just the boost we needed.

Determination

Well into the second half unbelievably we were dealing with road issues. Not only were parts of the course not closed to traffic but the road surface itself was abysmal. We had to dodge potholes and, even more distressing, eruptions on the bitumen had created almost wavelike undulations. It was very difficult to navigate on tired legs and in O'B's case with an injury. My problematic foot was struggling to balance as well. The gravel and unmade roads on the course had been much easier to negotiate than this tricky surface, and even though the neighbourhood was quite pleasant with tree lined streets and nice houses it made for very uncomfortable running for about 8 kilometres all up, as we covered the same stretch on the return journey.

By the 25 kilometre mark O'B's injury had caused us to modify our original 10:1 run/walk ratio. The pain had become intense and we were taking 30 second breaks when needed, but apart from that our actual running pace was quite fast. Energy-wise we were feeling good, taking on gels every 40 minutes or so and electrolyte drink at every aid station. There was only one section where we mismanaged our regular drinks. One station was supposed to cater to the needs of runners on both the out and back sides of the road. However, it was not signed as such and was on one side of the road rather than in the middle – hence the confusion, causing us to stretch our fluid intake to an interval of over 4 kilometres. Not good by any means in warm conditions at the 30 kilometre mark.

It felt really good reaching the furthest point of the course at scenic Bowness Park. On the river, it was a very attractive spot with picnic tables and playgrounds. Without complete road closure, supporters of some runners were driving alongside for a chat, handing over personal refreshments, then driving ahead and parking and getting out of their cars to run beside the marathoner they were supporting for short periods. We were down to the business end of the run now and the going was getting tough.

The out and back nature of the course gave us a chance to see the lead runners, which is always a buzz. Were they leading the field comfortably or was there another runner who looked stronger and was closing fast? Calgary is not one of the foremost marathons in the nation and there were no 'name' runners in the event, but the elite always look fast and smooth when you see them on the course.

Bowness Park and the Olympic Park were the two highlights of an otherwise unremarkable second half that wound its way through suburban neighbourhoods, some not particularly attractive. The Winter Olympics were held in Calgary in 1988 and the purpose built facilities are now a recreation park used in winter for seasonal pursuits and in summer as a tourist attraction and mountain bike course. The massive ski jumps were spectacular, perched so high above us. It was awesome just contemplating the nerve required to throw yourself down any of the three mountainside runs.

As we finally retraced our steps along Bowness Road and Parkdale Boulevard back towards the city, the sun was climbing higher. We were in the top 40% of the field and we certainly saw many stragglers. We yelled encouragement, but it must have been sobering for these back markers to realise they were at least 7 kilometres behind us, and while we were heading towards the finish line they were still running in the opposite direction!

As the roads became busier and less suburban we ticked off the kilometres. Other regular Sunday exercisers were out and about along the riverbanks but again crowds were quite thin. I was feeling strong and so relieved that my foot injury had not flared up. This had been my strongest marathon so far in our 8-8-8 journey and I felt really fresh in the legs. O'B was bravely pushing on, trying to manage the pain and looking forward to the end of the running. For him, today's effort was an achievement in determination. He was trying to deal with adversity and battling through. Over the last few runs we'd really needed to help each other through some tough times, and it was a huge relief when the skyscrapers came into view around the river bend.

As we passed the 40 kilometre mark we noted that we had 10 minutes to reach the finish line in order to break 4 hours. Most times we would have taken up the challenge and bolted for the last 2 kilometres, but as we approached the end of our 4th marathon in as many weeks we were mindful of protecting ourselves as much as we could. Besides, with the level of pain O'B was experiencing it was doubtful he could increase speed. One of our ground rules is that we stay together and while others may have separated at this point, for us it was not an option.

We soon crossed the river and the final bridge, then an overpass, around the corner and down to the finish line near the Armoury. We held hands as we cruised the last 100 metres of the finishing chute to end very close to where we had started some 4 hours 2 minutes and 17 seconds earlier. Yeehah!!!!

The finish

Relieved more than anything else, we crossed the finish line. The course announcer called our names and encouraged the crowd to cheer the couple from Black Rock, Australia. The cheers grew louder as we stopped for an extended kiss a few feet over the line before being told to move on. Hay bales provided seating for volunteers as they removed our timing chips. Some runners looked as fresh as they had at the start, others looked like they could not walk another step. Most of us, while a bit wobbly on our feet, were doing our best to move through the finishing area as quickly as we could.

Another group of volunteers hung belt buckle medals around our necks and we asked one of them to take a photo of us together before we moved to the finishing area where a giant party and refreshments awaited us. The adjacent carpark was the scene of much celebration as exhausted runners met up with family, friends and each other, removed shoes, feasted on fruit and drinks, and sat on the grass to enjoy the country and western band. After a quick wander through the festivities and chatting to some of the runners we had seen out on the course, we headed for the baggage claim and a post race massage.

Our preference after a marathon is to refuel as quickly as we can and then to keep moving for at least half an hour, with a 2 or 3 kilometre walk being our ideal cool down. But the queue for the massage did not allow for this. The waiting area comprised a row of chairs. The longer we sat, the cooler our muscles became and the more challenging it was to stand. As the person at the front of the line was called, we all moved up one place, watching each other struggle just to move a single chair to the left. In a strange way we enjoyed each other's suffering, but it was a painful way of playing musical chairs and a huge relief to finally reach the massage table.

Sue's massage was quick and relatively pain free. O'B endured the usual advice that he was very tight in the calves, shins, back and everywhere else followed by tips on the latest stretching techniques, a recommendation to go back to the hotel and have a hot bath, and the seemingly well intentioned question, 'Did you do any training before deciding to run all these marathons?'

After taking a deep breath, O'B provided a week-by-week description of our training, starting in September 2007, which seemed to satisfy the trainee masseur. Once off the tables and back into our shoes we set off to walk the 2 kilometres back to the hotel, hoping a cold drink and the massage would assist our recovery for the following week.

Pardner Running

Pain and suffering aside, we had a great time in Calgary and can't speak highly enough of the Canadian people we met, particularly the race organisers and Calgary running community. The Calgary Stampede is very special and it's well worth visiting the city at that time, even for non-cowboy types. The atmosphere and hospitality was so awesome we had to use all our restraint not to grab some boots, jeans and a hat and spend our time on the party circuit.

Running together, we often dream of what we'd like as a post marathon treat, but more often than not when the time arrives our stomachs don't agree with our minds and that beer or giant cheeseburger or ice cold frappucino with cream becomes the last thing on earth we feel like. This was very much the case after the Calgary run although the cold drink and fruit we settled on really hit the spot.

As we looked back on another marathon in another city we reminded ourselves that in Partnerunning – or pardner running, as we'd started to call it in Calgary – the benefits of encouragement are immense. Positive feedback is so often missing in our workplaces and private lives but encouraging others is so easy to do and can have such an impact on the actions and achievements of others. Throughout this challenging run, O'B and I tried to focus on the enjoyable, fun aspects. As partners we always try to encourage, reassure and help each other – and this was definitely needed this day. We strongly believe that together we can achieve so much more than we can alone.

Our Calgary Marathon experience highlighted some of the benefits to the giver of encouragement too – it really helps in focusing on the task at hand and overcoming pain. Calgary also allowed us to see the futility of negative feedback. We could never imagine telling each other – or other runners – they were too slow or to give up. Such comments can be so destructive, in any areas of our lives.

The Calgary Stampede Grandstand Show

It was with some excitement that we headed out to Stampede Park for our post marathon celebration. Luckily a shuttle trolley had been booked for a private group and the organiser asked if we'd like a lift.

We don't think he knew we'd just run a marathon when he asked us, but he would have been in little doubt after seeing us hoisting our rapidly stiffening leg muscles up and down the steep stairs to get on and off the shuttle bus! The crowd, all in their western gear, ranged from wizened older stockmen to young women in short denim cut-offs.

After checking out the showground attractions and Wild West events, we took our seats for the main event. One of the highlights of the 'Greatest Outdoor Show on Earth' is the chuckwagon races. Each team has a covered wagon or rig, one driver, a team of four thoroughbred horses and four outriders. The outriders load the wagon with a metal stove and jump aboard their mounts. The rig driver then proceeds to steer his team between two barrels, turning 180 degrees in the process before racing around one lap of the track. A huge screen shows spectators the action at the back of the track before the teams again come into view, thundering down the finishing straight. At any one time in each race there are four wagons and 32 horses on the track, and the crowding and tightness of the manoeuvres makes it a dangerous event. As the wagons and horses surge past the winning post, the sound really is like rumbling thunder.

We were just settling in for the evening when a real thunderstorm hit. While we found the heavy rain refreshing, our tired bodies had had enough. It was time to make our way back to the hotel.

The day after
Monday 7 July

We tried in vain to find a work area and accessible power point at the airport so we could spend some of our 2 hour wait working.

Unable to use our laptops for long (we didn't want to deplete our battery power before our 6 hour flight) we decided to check out the airport shops. Just 2 minutes later, after we'd looked at all there was, we found the best location we could and sat back, taking it in turns to walk up and down the terminal while the other guarded our hand luggage and endured the noise and discomfort of the waiting area.

We were relieved when our plane finally arrived and we had only 45 more minutes to wait. But as our revised departure time grew closer, the sky rapidly darkened. We figured we had about 15 minutes up our sleeves to make our connection in Dallas. Any delay was liable to create a major problem for us.

By the time we finally began boarding the sky was pitch black. Meanwhile, there was a lot of shuffling around among passengers in our section. The airline staff were doing their best to hurry people along without being seen to be rushing them. By this time the first drops of rain had begun to fall and we were convinced making our Dallas connection was an impossibility.

We focused on counting the time between the thunder and lightning to calculate the flash to band ratio, and therefore the distance between our location and the electrical storm. A flight attendant noticed what we were doing and said he thought the storm was between 6 and 7 miles away. We'd learnt about the flash to bang ratio when running the Disney Marathon in a storm and had discovered on our way to the Honolulu Marathon that in Sydney, if lightning is within 6 miles of the airport, planes can't leave or arrive because ground staff are not allowed to work outside in such conditions.

We crossed our fingers and hoped Calgary had a lower minimum requirement than Sydney. Finally we heard the door close and the plane started to taxi. We were in with a chance.

Scottsdale
Tuesday 8 July

Cumulative flying distance:	**52,821 kilometres**
Cumulative flying time:	**72 hours and 10 minutes**
Cumulative total travel time:	**154 hours and 10 minutes**

Our Dallas transfer went smoothly and soon after 9pm we arrived in Phoenix and drove to our hotel in Scottsdale, our recovery location for the week. It was 34 degrees Celsius at 10.30pm and temperatures of 110 Fahrenheit/ 43 Celsius on Tuesday and Wednesday were predicted before a cool change and 103 Fahrenheit/40 Celsius on Thursday. Overnight lows of 83 Fahrenheit/28 Celsius were expected each night. Hot!

With daily temperatures like this, July is a quiet time in Scottsdale. Many locals leave town on vacation, university students return home, fewer people come to play on the numerous golf courses and not many tourists visit. The result is significantly cheaper hotel rooms and we were able to save a few dollars as well as stay at a very nice hotel in the Kierland Commons area. An added bonus was that with few people in the hotel the facilities were not very crowded – and nor were the roads, restaurants and everywhere else we went.

As we entered the pool area we were puzzled by a huge rack of sandals and thongs on display, along with a vast array of sun protection lotions. After a quick spell on the deluxe padded lounges we decided to take a dip in the pool. The ground was incredibly hot, impossible to walk on. Now we understood why all the footwear was for sale.

We tried to make the 5 metre journey from lounge to water in bare feet a few times but realised it was impossible. In fact on a 20 metre dash to the restroom I was concerned that I'd burnt the skin off my feet – the last thing we needed with another marathon looming.

We spent most of our time at the pool, floating around in giant inflatable tubes. Our legs, particularly the quads, were still too sore from Calgary for a massage but we wanted to book appointments for Wednesday or Thursday. The cost of a 45 minute session at the hotel was a ridiculous price, so we asked around.

When we had enough sun we headed off to check out the local running store. The staff were most helpful and we left with a couple of leads for finding a well priced massage and the suggestion that we return on Thursday evening for a run with the store's run group. Deep down both of us knew this would be unwise, if not downright stupid. But I refused to give up on the idea at that stage, even knowing that in the extreme heat and with our sore legs a 10 kilometre run would not be good a couple or so days out from the Missoula Marathon. In the end commonsense and the pain in my leg prevailed, but we vowed to run with the local run group next time we were in Arizona.

I was very worried about O'B and wondered if he had a stress fracture. He was determined he did not so we headed off to look at some local real estate and have dinner at a PF Chang's restaurant, one of our favourite US eating places. Normally walk-ins need to wait 15 to 30 minutes for a table but we were seated straightaway and enjoyed our first big meal since Calgary. We decided to go with three courses. After all, we'd pencilled in a stop at PF Chang's as a halfway treat and had been looking forward to it for several weeks.

REST AND RECOVERY

Status report

Sue had been recovering well after her 'comfortable' run in Calgary. Although he was determined he did not, it was looking more and more likely that O'B did indeed have a stress fracture in his right leg. In addition to the running and travel, the constant blogging was taking a toll on our rest and recovery. However we were determined to keep going, especially after an email arrived saying, '4 down, well done. Following the blog and enjoying it guys, first time I have ever followed a blog.' Well, it was the first time we had written one!

Camelback
Wednesday 9 July

Depending on the condition of our legs, we'd contemplated an early morning hike up Camelback Mountain before the day became too hot. Located in the middle of the Phoenix, Scottsdale and Tempe area, the mountain is a real feature of the landscape. Multi-million dollar houses have been built into the side, along with luxurious golf resorts. And from the top are spectacular 360 degree views of Sun Valley.

Unfortunately I was still in severe pain. Camelback would have to wait for another day. We contacted a local sports therapist who turned out to be a great choice for a massage. Stephanie was a marathon runner herself with considerable experience working on runners and triathletes. She worked our legs and other sore bits, gave us some feedback on the status of our various injuries, and made some helpful suggestions as to the areas we should work on as well as those we should leave alone. I left the massage confident my bad leg was just muscle tightness. Since there was no 'hot' spot, it could not possibly be a stress fracture.

REST AND RECOVERY

Status report

Sue was in pretty good shape and confident the massage would further assist her recovery from the Comrades foot/shin soreness. O'B was feeling slightly better and although he was used to being told that his muscles were very tight and he needed to stretch more, this time he found it rather confidence sapping.

Rush Limbaugh and 3AW Melbourne radio interview

Driving back to the hotel we were listening to a nationally syndicated show on US talkback radio. *Family Guy* fans and those with an active interest in US politics will be familiar with conservative mouthpiece Rush Limbaugh. Like many US talkback hosts, Limbaugh is passionate and excitable in his delivery, and regardless of the politics is great entertainment when dealing with heavy traffic on US freeways.

As we listened in Limbaugh launched a tirade on one of his favourite topics – global warming and the alarmist position of left wing politicians. The prompt for his outburst was an article printed the previous day in our hometown paper, the *Herald Sun*. Written by Andrew Bolt, it told of a young boy who was scared to drink water in case he increased global warming and contributed to the death of others. Bolt was a regular guest on Melbourne's number one 3AW breakfast show hosted by Ross Stevenson and John Burns. I'm a regular listener to Ross and John; in fact, Sue is sure some of the topics I suggest we discuss to pass the time on a long run are borrowed from them.

It was no surprise to us that Limbaugh was pretty happy about Bolt's article and he kept talking about someone called 'Rude'. It was not until he called him Australian Prime Minister Rude that we realised he was talking about Kevin Rudd. Back at the hotel, I sent an email to Jay Mueller, the producer of the 3AW breakfast show. With the time difference, the Limbaugh outburst was well timed for Melbourne radio. I emailed Jay at 5.27am Melbourne time, Jay responded at 5.44am and at roughly 6.15am Ross was introducing me on the radio. He and John interviewed me about the Limbaugh comments as well as about our 8 marathons.

That evening Sue and I headed south to find some dinner. Jay from 3AW had given us a recommendation and we figured the least we could do was check it out. Joe's Real BBQ turned out to be fantastic, like nothing we had come across before, and a real meat eaters' delight. Caféteria style, and with a John Deere tractor parked in the dining room, it might not have looked five star but it was!

Pinnacle Peak
Thursday 10 July

Our Thursday morning options were a 5.45am spin class for US$20 each at the local gym or a hike to Pinnacle Peak just north of Scottsdale. We chose the latter for a short 3 mile walk from the car park to the peak and back. Pinnacle Peak is a very popular trail, providing views of the valley, some great houses and beautiful golf courses. Like Camelback, the vistas are stunning and you can see back towards Scottsdale and Phoenix as well as to the north of Sun Valley. Wanting to keep active between marathons, walking was a great option without the impact on our joints and muscles of trying to run.

It was in the low 90s and very sunny when we headed out about 7.30am. The trail was busy with walkers and a few runners and we took it easy, trying to protect our legs. I found it comfortable going but the return down the hill reminded O'B his legs were still recovering from Calgary. Although he didn't say so, his right calf was still worrying him. I was aware of him wincing as he picked his way down the rocky trail.

It was time to turn our attention to the Sunday marathon in Missoula, Montana. We returned to the hotel early, packed and prepared for a 3am wake up call. Next stop was Seattle for a 24 hour stopover.

Seattle
Friday 11 July

Cumulative flying distance:	**56,943 kilometres**
Cumulative flying time:	**77 hours and 40 minutes**
Cumulative total travel time:	**166 hours and 40 minutes**

Amazingly for Arizona there had been thunderstorms in the night. We had heard via the television that some of the freeways were under 3 feet of water and had been closed for a few hours for safety reasons. Maybe it was lucky we had such an early start. We would never have dreamed that arid Phoenix would cause us this sort of concern, but the trip to the airport proved uneventful and the forecast thunderstorms did not delay our departure.

Our flight with American Airlines meant it was back again to Dallas, the 'hub' port for many flights. From there it was on to Seattle. Flying in, the sky was as clear and blue as you could wish for, making for perfect visibility over the Rocky Mountain Range. We had uninterrupted views of Mt Rainier, snowcapped even in the middle of summer, and we were flying in so low it seemed we could have reached out and touched the peak. Surrounded by pine-covered lower slopes, with trails snaking around and small lakes sheltered in the foothills, it was easy to see why this is such a popular recreation area.

Other mountains, such as Mt St Helens and Mt Hood, were also visible in the distance, although at first we thought they might have been merely white clouds. As the plane came into land the overwhelming impression was of evergreen trees and grassland. No wonder Seattle is sometimes referred to as the emerald city!

We'd decided to spend a night here because it was a city that I'd not been to before. Having seen *Sleepless in Seattle*, I was keen to check the place out on our way to Missoula. As soon as we could we headed out into the afternoon sunshine to stroll down Pike Street to the famous Farmer's Market, located in an old historical building and full of handcraft shops as well as fruit, flower and vegetable stalls and the famous Pike Place Fish Market. Here a crowd of tourists had gathered, cameras in hand. What were they waiting for? The fishmongers behind the counter were singing, as was the one outside the stall, standing among the crowd. Suddenly one guy behind the counter hurled a massive fish to the one standing among us. The air filled with delighted squeals as people ducked for cover. We tried to photograph the fish flying in the air, at the same time avoiding being hit. One spectator was not so lucky and walked away with a big fishy splodge on his shoulder.

The next morning we both woke before our alarm. What was happening with our body clocks? Again it was a lovely sunny morning with crisp, clean air and bright light. I really thought everything was fresher here and the colours more brilliant. The short drive to the airport showcased the snowcapped mountains and with the sunlight glistening on the water of Elliott Bay, it really did look like a postcard.

REST AND RECOVERY

Status report

Sue was feeling good but O'B was still very sore in the right leg, only improving slowly if at all. As he hobbled along Sue was certain there was something seriously wrong but kept her conjecture to herself. O'B was still convinced it was just a muscle strain. Had the questions he asked of the medical staff and the answers he gave them to theirs been designed to convince himself this was the case?

Lesson for life

Stay positive.
Encourage others and maintain a can do attitude.

What started out as strategy to take the focus away from the pain associated with O'B's leg became a real energy boost. It reminded us of how effective it is both at work and at home to stay positive and encourage others. People tend to live up or down according to your expectations of them, and once again we discovered that the better you treat others the better they treat you.

Partnerunning
Reader bonus number 2

Bonus Download Offer from www.partnerunning.com

A complimentary ebook introducing Partnerunning is available for download from www.partnerunning.com

Please feel free to send the ebook on to your friends and family. While you are there you can subscribe to our free **Couple On the Run** Podcast.

The Community Run: Missoula, Montana, USA

'You don't understand anything until you learn it more than one way.'

Marvin Minsky

Cumulative flying distance: **57,579 kilometres**
Cumulative flying time: **79 hours and 10 minutes**
Cumulative total travel time: **172 hours and 10 minutes**

We were very worried about the size of the Dash 8 that would take us to Missoula and wondered if our ever-growing baggage would be accepted. Our fears proved to be groundless and we relaxed – or at least tried to – in the cramped conditions. We flew over more snow covered mountains and then lower slopes of very rugged, pine covered terrain before dropping to a long, wide valley between the Clark Fork and Bitterroot Rivers.

Missoula is a pretty small town, which explained why none of the hire car agencies had satellite navigation. Home to the University of Montana, the town was in the middle of the college summer break and a lot of the population was away, so the whole place had a very laid back feel. As we drove down Main Street to our hotel overlooking the Clark Fork River, we were immediately taken by the charm of the city centre – lots of homely shopfronts and wide streets with stop signs rather than too many traffic lights.

Once checked in, we walked the 100 metres or so to the expo which had been set up in a large open space known as Caras Park which had a massive permanent shade cloth suspended above it, somewhat like an open sided tent. The first trestle table we came to was for marathon merchandise: t-shirts and singlet tops, hats and visors, bags, water bottles and 'fanny packs'.

The second table was for registration. Jeri was hearty in her welcome – we suspected we were the only international entrants – and said she had seen us on the marathon website and was keen to find out more about our previous exploits and Partnerunning. She told us that for this race we were required to wear ankle timing bracelets, quite similar to the ones Sue used to wear in triathlons.

The next trestle was for the photography group covering the race. The local run shop also had a display, as did the race physio group Alpine Physiotherapy. One of the therapists, Sam, was able to give me a greater understanding of my shin soreness and suggested various treatments and stretches. He was convinced the problem was muscle related and definitely not a fracture. Acupuncture was also available and we decided to come back later and give it a try.

Also on displayed at the expo were 26 plaster cast legs and feet which had been painted and decorated by local artists. At first we thought they were simply art for art's sake but were told they were mile markers for the race and would be available for purchase after the race as a charity fundraiser.

We had arranged to meet a local sports reporter Varun Sriram from the ABC network in the afternoon and did a lengthy interview with him beside the river for a feature appearing on the network the following week. We seized the chance to say more than we usually get to about Partnerunning, and about our fundraising for Oxfam. Varun promised to post us a copy of the interview and said he'd be following us the next morning in the red ABC van.

After seeing him off, we headed back to the expo to test out the acupuncture. Brian inserted two needles into my left hand to release the nerve pathways that affect the shin area on my right calf. Sue had a needle in the area between her knuckles in both hands, aiming to release calf tension. Assistants Tina and Lindsay also offered advice and support as we hoped to get relief in our legs. After walking and stretching for about 20 minutes the needles were removed and we felt optimistic that the treatment would have a positive impact.

So there'd be no unpleasant surprises the next morning, we drove over the course. Not being able to face pancakes again, we decided to have dinner at the McKenzie River Pizza Company – a magnificent feed! All would be revealed the next day as to whether pizza was a wise decision or not. It was marathon eve again. The forecast was for a sunny warm day with a cool start. Excellent! Anti-inflammatories were back on the menu for the next 24 hours, but fingers crossed all would go well.

Yellow school buses

Our alarms were set for between 4am and 4.05am. With one mobile phone alarm, one watch alarm and one hotel wake up call, we were not taking any chances! Imagine having to tell our friends, 'Today we slept in and missed the marathon.' It was a scenario we were keen to avoid.

I had been awake since 3am so the first alarm was a welcome relief. Our routine breakfast of protein bars and electrolyte drink was followed by the usual thorough application of anti-chafe balm. We systematically worked through our checklist to make sure we were wearing all the right clothes and were equipped with race numbers, timing chips, energy gels, money, painkillers, cameras and garbage bags. As each week passes, the chance of us becoming blasé and forgetting something vital increases.

This time we were staying at the official marathon hotel, conveniently located near the expo, the finish and the loading area for the buses. Buses were scheduled to depart for the start at Frenchtown between 4.30am and 5.30am and we planned to get the 5am bus. As we left the hotel and joined other runners Sue was wearing a warm jacket while I was just in a race singlet. The temperature was approximately 59 Fahrenheit/15 Celsius and we both felt comfortable.

By the time we arrived at the loading area, buses for the marathon and half marathon were leaving. We waited in the dark until the next one arrived. Having just missed a bus, we were at the front of the line and so got to sit in the front row of the next bus that turned up. The organisers had provided yellow school buses – pretty standard fare for the locals but quite a novelty for us.

As we hit the freeway to make the 20 mile journey to Frenchtown, we noticed the speed limit was 75 miles (120 kilometres) per hour. We were cruising along with little scope to go faster as the speedo peaked at 85 miles (136 kilometres) per hour. No big deal as far as Missoula residents were concerned, but interesting to us being used to maximum speeds of generally 100 kilometres per hour.

We arrived in Frenchtown with a little over 30 minutes to race time. Daylight was just breaking. Once off the bus we quickly joined the queues for the portable toilets, chuckling when we saw they were provided by Sweet Pea. Since seeing the Australian movie *Kenny* a few years back we've paid more attention to the names – and appearances – of portable toilets at the various races we participate in. Some of them are winners!

Drinks and a bag drop were located near the starting line and we had plenty of time to prepare for the start. Sue put on a garbage bag to ward off the cold and we passed the time talking to race organisers, journalists and fellow runners. The next thing we knew it was time to take our place at the starting line.

Meeting Elvis

Not long before the start we'd noticed a runner with a guitar in hand. His costume and glasses were stunning and could only belong to one man. When Elvis was only 20 metres away we knew we'd found our costumed runner of the week. Dressed immaculately, he looked ready to take to the stage in Las Vegas or to bring *Blue Hawaii* to life. Only a pair of white running shoes gave the hint that he was in Missoula to run. He was quickly nabbed by a journalist from the *Missoulian*, and when the time was right Sue asked if he would mind posing with her. The King kindly obliged but then whipped out his camera and asked a passerby to take a photo of him with the two Aussie runners he had heard all about!

Over the years I have seen many Elvises out and about on marathon courses. In my first marathon in LA in 1999 there were both individual Elvises and groups of Elvises, some with guitars, some with pre-recorded music, others just out for the run. There was something disconcerting for a first time marathoner to be continually passed by the King. As I battled my way through the 26 miles for the first time, I did my best to pass Elvis more times than I was passed by him! To this day we use this as our guiding approach to running in any marathon that has attracted an Elvis.

We did not see the Missoula Elvis on the course but sometime after we had finished we spotted him crossing the finishing line in Higgins Street and talking with the media and fellow marathoners. It seems Ron is a very experienced marathoner who occasionally leaves Elvis at home and steps out to run as himself. No doubt he thrilled many of the runners, spectators and volunteers out on the course that day, but the idea of running a marathon in full stage outfit, complete with guitar, sounds like hard work to me. We are always grateful to these dedicated runners who have the courage – and stamina – to run in costume. They make it so much more fun for the rest of us.

Cheered by horses

We have had starters' guns, hand held hooters and electronic signals, but never had we heard a Civil War cannon start a race before! That crisp Sunday morning, some started wearing long sleeves and gloves; others, like us, decided they'd warm up quickly, although I did start in the glamorous gar-bag coat that I'd brought with me for just such conditions. Feeling the cold as I do, it was a highly effective and very cheap windbreak.

Despite the pain in O'B's right shin, we ran well at the start. We were being shadowed along the first half of the course by Varun Sriram and his crew, and had made arrangements for a post marathon interview with him at the finish line.

The first few miles went at quite a brisk pace. With a field of under 500 runners, there was little crowding on the bitumen as we headed out along Mullan Road, a wide two-way road that catered to local traffic. There was not total road closure on any part of the course probably because there were neither sufficient participants nor enough traffic to warrant it. But today there was a steady stream of participants' support vehicles cruising up and down.

Our first two aid stations were very spread out, over 2 miles apart, and we made sure we took both electrolyte drink and water to keep up hydration. It was obvious from the clear blue sky that it was going to be a hot day once the sun climbed higher.

What a beautiful start to the course! Mullan Road is surrounded by small farms, some with small herds of cattle, but most with beautiful thoroughbred horses in their pastures. As we passed, the animals pranced excitedly and neighed – an equine cheer squad! Most of the farm owners were sitting on deckchairs at the end of their driveways, eskies containing their breakfast beside them, mugs of coffee in hand. This was so wonderful. Many not only cheered for all they were worth but had turned the music in their farmhouses up to maximum volume to pump up the atmosphere.

Just before the second aid station we came to a huge pulp mill with white smoke puffing from its chimneys. Shift workers were coming and going, and calling out 'Looking good!'

After the fourth aid station, where we'd paused for a vox pop with ABC news, O'B became extremely uncomfortable in the stomach. He had been battling flatulence and indigestion since the start of the race and these now developed into stomach cramps which required an urgent stop at the next Sweat Pea portable toilet. We then joined up with the 4 hour pace group and had been running very comfortably, listening to people's stories and backgrounds, when O'B's gut pain again became intense. We said farewell as he joined the line for the single toilet at the next aid station. What a disaster! He'd need to make three more porta-potty stops over the next few kilometres, which would ultimately cost us about 20 minutes' running time. We weren't to know that yet, of course, but still it was frustrating. All I could do was to try to encourage him and hope his pain would soon pass.

We had been concerned about his shin and the pain that was building in his leg, but this stomach problem was completely unexpected. Was it the second part of a virus that he'd had in Scottsdale earlier in the week? Or a reaction to the anti-inflammatory tablets he had been taking for his shin soreness? Perhaps last night's dinner was to blame? Was the type of the food the culprit, or the quantity? Or was it something completely different? For the next 8 miles he was in various degrees of misery. We stopped at the next aid station at 11.4 miles, and then again in the second half at the aid station at mile 15.6. The pain in his shin faded as his stomach issues increased and O'B jokingly referred to the old adage: if someone has a sore leg, punch them in the face and it will surely take their mind off their sore leg! He was putting on a brave face but I could tell that he was in great distress, and nothing in my running medicine kit could be of assistance.

Thankfully, we had the distraction of the beautiful scenery. Leaving Mullan Road, we'd turned down Kona Ranch Road at 9.4 miles and headed directly towards the pine covered hills, crossing over an old iron bridge that spanned the fast flowing Clark Fork River. Again the enthusiasm of the local community and the volunteers manning aid stations and directing traffic was remarkable. Everyone was so vocal and hearty in their wishes of good luck and calls of 'Looking strong'.

Turning again, we moved onto The Big Flat Road (yes, that is really what it's called). Further along, we decided it must have been named by someone with a bleak sense of humour, but at this stage we were just rolling along parallel to the river. Again, the vivid greens of the trees and pastures and intense blue of the sky were postcard perfect. As we approached the halfway mark the gradient changed and we began to climb. We had driven over the course before and knew of the incline ahead, but to the uninitiated this was a steep winding climb that demanded respect. Around us most if not all of the runners had slowed to a walk. At this point O'B had not needed a toilet break for quite a while and I hoped his troubled stomach had settled. I was still wondering about his shin and calf pain however. Dare I ask? I was reluctant to in case he snapped, 'Don't remind me!'

We decided there was nothing to be gained by pushing the pace and chatted to a few other runners as we walked. Chuck was a 60-something man, a veteran marathoner, with a nut-brown tan and a long white ponytail hanging halfway down his back. He was running bare-chested (maybe to work on the tan?) and had entrusted his precious 50 state shirt to a race official to take to the end for him. The 50 state status is particularly coveted among American runners. It is a club that many aspire to join, planning their races to cover different states rather than do a run in a state already visited.

We'd overheard a discussion on the bus between two runners, one of whom had run 25 marathons.

'Wow, you're halfway!' his friend said.

'No,' came the disappointed reply. 'Four of them were in California.'

Finally reaching the top of the hill, we picked up the pace again as we headed down to the halfway mark, complete with timing wire across the road to pick up the signal from the chips on our ankle bracelets. Reassuringly we heard the 'chirp' record our times as we passed the 13.1 miles in 2 hours and 7 minutes, much of which had been Sweat Pea time.

Holding it together

I was hanging in there, going through some very tough times. Our partnership in running was important to me – to both of us – and at this point staying focused on the big picture of 8 marathons in 8 countries 8 weeks was crucial. So often we have found that when one of us is feeling very ordinary, the other will be feeling strong enough to help by distracting with humour or a witty observation, or even by suggesting a walk break or different pacing strategy. All these tactics are ways of breaking up the bad and sad patches that many runners go through. This is the hidden strength of Partnerunning: you are not alone to deal with your demons.

If I'd been attempting this race on my own, it would have been easy to become depressed. But this marathon was only one piece of a bigger picture, of our shared journey. And if it wasn't a perfect fit, so what? We knew that we would get there in the end. Next week there would be Pattaya. Our 8–8–8 vision was still intact; we just had to readjust the parameters slightly.

Continuing our downhill run, we reached the 15.8 miles aid station at River Pines Road. As its name suggests, the road was lined with pine trees – again a deliciously fresh scent filled the air – and we ran directly parallel to the river as we headed back into town and finally reached the part of the course that the half marathoners had run.

Despite the long day, the volunteers and crowd lining the road remained as enthusiastic as ever. Some were dressed as elks with full sets of antlers; others were decked out in matching, brightly coloured sponsors' t-shirts. It was here at the River Pines Road that I took my last toilet break before the finish. Luckily I was still able to retain the electrolyte drink and the energy gels needed to get through the day. The pain in my leg wasn't overwhelming but in hindsight I suspect that was due to the focus on other problems; I was too busy 'holding my cheeks together' and actually ran with a roll of toilet paper tucked in my shorts in case an unscheduled and sudden stop was required.

Turning into Clements Road and then 7th St West we found ourselves on the outskirts of town. Full credit goes to the local sheriff's office; the local police officers on duty were polite to traffic and supportive to the runners as we passed, often giving hearty verbal encouragement. As always, we tried to thank as many officers, volunteers and spectators as we could.

At about the 20 mile mark, there is always a sense of relief that you are on the home stretch. We'd passed two aid stations, at the 17.7 and 19.3 mile marks, that were full of supporters. Anticipating the runners, they held painted posters and had hung up banners along fences urging us along. I'm not sure if those coolers they had held alcoholic beverages or not, but there was definitely a jovial, picnic-like feeling in the air.

As we'd driven over the course on the Saturday afternoon, I'd commented to Sue that all the turns through the suburbs would be good as a lot of distance would be covered without us realising it. But there sure were a lot of turns! Sue, who has a poor sense of direction at the best of times, was convinced we were doubling back on ourselves. Even the marshals were telling runners 'not too many more turns to go'.

The day had warmed up, but it was insignificant after the heat of Rio. Around 20 miles, the streets were lined with big oak trees and beautiful, brightly painted two storey weatherboard houses, complete with verandahs and spacious front lawns. Now mid morning, there was even more crowd support. One group at about the 24 mile mark got right into the spirit of my videoing, chanting along to my instructions and playing to the camera.

Aid stations had been coming every mile, which psychologically was great as they acted as targets to reach. Despite our toilet stops and injury concerns, we'd actually been running very strongly and our speed was good. Comments from bystanders and supporters on the side of the road let us know how good we looked, how fresh, how strong. Boy, can appearances be deceiving! Apart from my stomach troubles, my right shin and calf were getting extremely sore by now, and Sue's calves were tightening up and becoming very painful. We were both very glad – indeed always are – to hear the loudspeakers at the finishing line.

Against a background of snowcapped mountains, it was time for those final few turns and the short climb to the Higgins Street Bridge. The run to the finish was lined with cheering spectators and a triumphant arch of brightly coloured balloons awaited us. Whether it's been an easy day in the park or a tough day in the office, the thrill of the finish and the surge of adrenalin remains the same, overpowering pain and exhaustion. We were smiling broadly as we ran that final 50 metres, holding hands and waving to the crowd. The clock showed 4 hours 17 minutes and 35 seconds, but was not a true indication of our run time, given the 20 minutes I'd spent in the portable toilets. Our race positions put us 222 and 223 out of 406. We agreed it had been a very tough day at the office, but one we'd not have traded. We enjoyed every minute of it – well, almost every minute. How important our strict training regime had been, not just to stand us in good stead for the physical challenges we faced in this particular marathon but also the mental ones.

Partnerunning Tip

TRAINING

Training is the hub of Partnerunning. It provides the quality time together which generates relationship and fitness benefits. Whether you are a 'training only person', enter an event once a year or race more often, training a few times a week sets you up to be more successful in everything you do.

Training is:	
Enhanced by	**Hindered by**
• A training plan	• Lack of a plan
• A slow build up	• Doing too much too quickly
• Clear goals	• Having no goals
• Regular times	• Irregular times
• Quality equipment	• Poor equipment, especially shoes
• Rest and recovery	• Ignoring injuries

Lights, cameras, action

Once over the line, we noticed that some of the spectators we had seen along the course, in some cases on multiple occasions, were in the finishing area waiting for other runners. This was a great feature of the Missoula Marathon. Like Calgary, it was big enough to have a terrific atmosphere yet small enough to be able to connect with spectators and officials before, during and after the race.

The local TV stations filmed our traditional hand-holding cross of the line, and newspaper and online media were waiting for to do post run interviews with us. After a few photos we proudly ducked our heads as our medals were hung around our necks and tried to compose ourselves to talk sensibly to the journalists. As middle of the field participants, we rarely have the opportunity to speak to the media after a marathon and had spent some time in the last few miles trying to come up with a handful of words by which we could do justice to the efforts of the volunteers, the organisers, the race officials and the Missoula community, all of whom had done a wonderful job and given us a memorable experience. At the same time we wanted to recognise the spirit and camaraderie of the other runners. We decided on a couple of themes and hoped we'd have the opportunity to thank everyone and get our message across.

In each marathon we'd run I carried a video camera and every 10 kilometres or so we recorded our thoughts and tried to capture some useful footage. Most of it is shaky as I can't seem to hold a steady hand, but I have captured some great atmosphere shots and it has been a worthwhile means of gathering our impressions. A key theme for us this week was partnerships, having experienced how Partnerunning had enabled us to finish the marathon and, despite the hardships, have a fantastic experience, and seen the way the Missoula community had banded together to overcome many challenges and provide so many people with an unforgettable marathon.

Another emerging theme since we'd been running the 8–8–8 challenge was the 'tough times' – the times when it hurts and you just want it to be over or you are worried you will embarrass yourself in front of others. During these patches we always seem to say to each other that although we're feeling bad we know that if we keep going, sooner or later the pain will pass and the satisfaction of achievement will be well worth any sacrifice along the way.

Having mulled over what to say, Sue found it quite bizarre to suddenly be surrounded by TV crews and microphones and wished she'd had a mirror with her for a quick check! As we did our best to answer media questions and thank people, I became aware of a new marathon related challenge, one we had not had to deal with before: post race lost voice. Throughout each race we try to thank as many volunteers and spectators en route as we can. When we add this to our own chatter we tend to finish with not much speaking voice left. When we quietly slip away to our hotel this is not a problem, but when the task at hand is to record television interviews then maintaining some voice becomes rather important.

If only I'd realised this ahead of time. Once it was clear we were not going to make 4 hours but were well under 4.30, we spent some extra time cheering the crowd and taking photos of some families and younger volunteers handing out drinks. About 2 miles from the finish I turned on the video and charged onto the sidewalk to film a large group who were cheering the runners rather loudly. With the camera in one hand, I led the group in a mighty cheer.

'What city are we in?'

'Missoula!'

'What state are we in?'

'Montana!' came the enthusiastic response.

'What country is this?'

'The USA,' yelled the group in unison.

They seemed to be enjoying themselves, then one of them said, 'I thought we were meant to cheer the runners, not the other way round.'

Making my way back onto the road but with camera still filming I led the group in a passionate version of 'Aussie, Aussie, Aussie' and left what was remaining of my voice on the course.

With interviews underway and my voice already starting to squeak, Sue disappeared, quickly returning with two bottles of water which provided just enough lubricant to keep the voice box going and enable us to finish answering questions.

Just as we were about to leave the finishing area we realised we hadn't taken our own photos. We quickly snapped off a few before asking one of the volunteers to take a picture of us together before we went in search of some sustenance and our gear bag. The post race food included icy poles and watermelon, which was excellent, however just as we reached the tables my stomach took over again. Off I went in search of another Sweet Pea.

Back with Sue but still crippled with stomach pain, I registered for a massage and returned to the hotel room for further relief and a much needed shower. Clean but scared to eat I returned with Sue to the post race awards and massage area where we cheered the winners before getting our massages. Missoula used a system of $1 per minute for a 10 or 20 minute massage, an increasing trend which seems to work well. My masseur Gary did a great job on my legs and Sue was very pleased with the treatment she received from one of the other therapists. We were hopeful the massage would help with our recovery and the difficult conditions facing us in Thailand in six days' time (we were to lose a day crossing the date line from the USA to Thailand).

With material to gather for the local media and a radio interview scheduled with Ross and John on 3AW in Melbourne, I was quite happy spending the afternoon in the hotel room with private facilities at close range. A wise move, as it turned out. After icing our legs, we snoozed for 30 minutes around 5pm before deciding to stay in and eat at the hotel restaurant. Another wise move; while Sue enjoyed her meal immensely I struggled to keep mine down.

Why Missoula? Why not Missoula?

Sometimes when you go to a new place you notice things which the locals don't. It happens with companies, schools, universities, hospitals, all types of organisations as well as families and towns. Many people we met in Missoula told us they had read about our trip and thought it was great we'd come to their town. Then they'd ask the inevitable question: 'Why Missoula?'

Before we went there the answer to that question would have been pretty straightforward. We wanted a US marathon that fitted with our schedule and ideally was somewhere we had never been before. But after spending time in Missoula and running the marathon our answer changed. 'Why not Missoula?' we'd ask.

At the risk of encouraging swarms of people to flock to the town and its surrounding area, Missoula is truly a hidden treasure. It's one of those places not many people go to, but the people and the countryside are magnificent and we can't wait to return.

Departing Missoula
Monday 15 July

When we planned our itinerary I remember noticing a few early flights but at this stage it seemed as if pre-dawn rising was becoming habitual. We had another early start with our flight out of Missoula scheduled for 7.00 am. At least flights were one way of catching up on some sleep!

Missoula airport is memorable for its stuffed animals, and I don't mean the teddy bear kind! High on the walls above the baggage claim are full sized mountain goats and elk, and standing pride of place in the middle of the terminal is a glass cabinet containing an absolutely enormous grizzly bear. Standing about 9 or 10 feet high, he is up on his hind legs, with paws outstretched and teeth bared ready for attack. Quite terrifying! But the small size of the airport did mean a minimum of hassle with check in, and thankfully our bags passed their weight test with ounces to spare.

It was a very cramped fit in the small plane, particularly for O'B's sore leg. Quite a few runners returning home to other states after the weekend were also gingerly lowering themselves into their seats. We'd just settled in when the lady across the aisle from us, a local Missoulian, asked if we were that Australian couple on the front page of the paper. Wow! We felt like celebrities.

Arrival back in Seattle during our transit meant negotiating steep stairs to both disembark the plane and climb to the arrival deck. Poor O'B's leg muscles had stiffened up terribly and he had to hoist his wheelie bag up three steps, then lever himself up one step at a time, gripping on to the bag. When the ground crew asked if he needed a lift to get to the arrival deck he refused. But when passengers from the flight after ours arrived and were chasing him up the stairs, even offering to help with his bag, the elevator didn't seem like such a bad idea. I am ashamed to say that while I was terribly concerned for him, I couldn't help the urge to giggle!

San Francisco

Cumulative flying distance:	59,307 kilometres
Cumulative flying time:	82 hours and 40 minutes
Cumulative total travel time:	184 hours and 40 minutes

Due to bad weather in the Bay area, our flight to San Francisco was delayed by 90 minutes. The low lying cloud and fog meant there was not much to see as we finally made our descent into San Francisco, although we caught glimpses of a huge pall of smoke that was covering northern California. For several weeks, we'd seen on the news and read reports in the papers that wildfires had devastated large areas and were continuing to blaze out of control. Even Big Sur National Park, the scene of one of our previous marathons had not escaped unscathed.

As we arrived at the rental car pick up O'B had a call from a producer from 4BC in Brisbane requesting an interview on breakfast radio. Just 15 minutes later he was chatting with Kim and Sophie about Partnerunning and our world tour. We'd no sooner arrived at the hotel when we received a request from Perth radio station 6PR for an interview, and it was great being able to continue spreading the word and talk about our efforts to raise funds for Oxfam.

Driving to our hotel at Fisherman's Wharf we were again reminded of what an attractive city this is. With its distinctive landmarks – such as the Golden Gate Bridge, the Transamerica Building, Coit Tower, Lombard Street (the crooked street), cablecars and Alcatraz in the middle of San Francisco Bay – it's little wonder it is so crowded with tourists pretty much year round. We headed along the Embarcadero, around the Harbor, past the Piers which are numbered from 1 through to 43. It was lunchtime and the pavement near the restored docks was crowded with walkers, joggers, tourists and office workers. Ferries were also bustling around the Harbor, and there was lots of traffic on the roads too. This city always seems to be busy.

Wading in the Bay

It had been suggested to us on the plane that the frigid waters of San Francisco Bay would be the perfect location for soaking our sore muscles. So after checking in, we wandered a few hundred metres to the nearest 'beach' to test this theory. Now, I should explain that the weather had cleared for a few hours, and even though the air temperature was in the mid 60s Fahrenheit and there was a cold breeze, some local families had headed to the water for the kids to swim and play. There were also a few hardy adult swimmers heading into the bay, although one was in full wetsuit with gloves and booties on his feet!

Unfortunately, when we started our wade, the clouds closed in again and with grey sky, grey water and even grey sand the water felt freezing. We got used to the cold after a while though. Or was it just that we got numb and lost feeling? Somehow I managed to wade hip deep into the icy water, while Sue took the soft option and only got wet to her knees. Still, it was a very scenic backdrop for our restorative bathing. Behind us we could see both the Golden Gate Bridge (the lower part anyway) and Alcatraz (the former prison that it was claimed no-one ever successfully escaped from.)

A reward

After we'd completed the Oxfam Trailwalker 100 kilometre run back in early April, I decided that once we'd run the first 5 marathons I'd have earned a feed of fish and chips. Sue had been looking forward to some spicy Cajun Bay shrimp. It was time for this long awaited reward and where better than at Bubba Gump's on Pier 39 with a window seat overlooking the Bay? We enjoyed our meal and after passing the Forrest Gump trivia quiz it was time to check out some of the sayings posted on the restaurant walls. We enjoyed 'Run Forrest Run' but were a little unsettled by 'I'm tired, I think I'll go home now'. As we left we walked under a sign saying, 'At least I didn't lead no humdrum life'. It certainly resonated with us after the past few weeks.

It must have been round 1.00am before we finally got to sleep. We had another fairly early start planned as we'd decided to hire bikes and ride over the Golden Gate Bridge to Sausalito in the morning. This was the third night in a row with very little sleep and we needed to address this very soon before one of us got sick. It probably wasn't helping our recovery from the previous marathon, let alone our preparation for the next.

REST AND RECOVERY

Status report

O'B had really been suffering with his right shin and tight calf on the same leg although the muscles in his other leg were in good shape. It had been agony for him to walk, with his leg giving way on a few occasions. However, particularly after the Bay immersion, the soreness eased up dramatically and walking became much freer. Maybe as a sign of getting rundown he also developed mouth ulcers (or canker sores as they call them in the US).

Sue was very happy with her recovery. During the Missoula race she'd had extremely tight soleus muscles low in the calves, but a night in the compression tights and stretching helped a great deal. The only peculiarity was that her left ankle had swollen into what we describe as a cankle (a combination calf and ankle) and she could not work out why. As the day progressed, the swelling decreased, but it was quite unnerving and decidedly unattractive for a while.

Hiring bikes
Tuesday 15 July

The distance of our bike ride was approximately 13.5 miles and we felt we could easily accomplish this and return by 12.30 to the hotel. Over the years, we'd enjoyed some memorable runs in San Francisco, it being one of our favourite cities to run in. But unfortunately this was not an option this time. So it was off to Blazing Saddles bike hire, wearing three layers of clothing and me in gloves as well to ward off the cold, hoping that the name 'Blazing Saddles' did not refer to how uncomfortable we were going to be after a morning on these bikes!

Riding to the Golden Gate Bridge

It was easy riding as we pedalled along the recreational trail at Crissy Field. This whole area used to be an army landing field but is now a large park with bike and walking/running trails. Whether it is the weekend or mid-week, afternoon or morning, there are always lots of people out jogging, walking (lots with dogs) or bike riding. With an uninterrupted view across San Francisco Bay and out to the Golden Gate Bridge, it would be a lovely area to have as your regular run course and we regretted that we couldn't make use of it. Even the surface was soft, quite a change from pounding on the concrete.

I was finding the riding easy but I could see O'B was struggling. He was in mild discomfort with seated pedalling, but his leg was actually buckling underneath him if he attempted to climb standing up. The calf tightness and shin pain from Rio was continuing to haunt him, and neither of us dared to say the words 'stress fracture' as this could mean an end to our marathon dream.

On the Golden Gate Bridge we stopped to chat to an American couple who were showing the sights to a German exchange student. Decker was sporting a UCSB hat and we discussed what a wonderful campus it was, O'B having visited it some years back. As with many people we met, they were amazed at our trip and wanted to find out more. We gave them the details of our website and they wished us good luck for the challenges ahead.

What an amazing thing it was to ride a bike over the Golden Gate! I'd driven over it a few times in a car but had not been able to fully appreciate the view. It was a real buzz to leisurely ride, stop and take pictures at our leisure. Exhibiting great balance skills on the bike, O'B videoed our path across, steering his way among other cyclists and pedestrians coming from both directions on the narrow shared laneway, then pausing to switch to still photography at the various lookout points along the way.

Our ride ended at Sausalito, one of the area's most beautiful and tourist-friendly bay front cities. Its main street is full of shops, boutiques, galleries and restaurants, and has a fantastic view back across the Bay to San Francisco. The distinctively top end homes here look like they're about to tumble down the hillside. The whole place had the air of an exclusive weekend getaway location. Sadly, we had little time to linger and enjoy the atmosphere and were soon on the 11.55 ferry heading back to Pier 41.

Talking to Millsy and Tony Mac in Perth

Back at the Pier we returned the bikes and walked the short distance to our hotel to get the car and drive to the beach at Crissy Field for another quick soak before our 3.30pm interview with Perth radio station 6PR. Even though it was sunny, again the water was absolutely freezing, and unlike the day before O'B had the water to himself. I completely wimped out, citing the improvement in my legs, although the reality was I couldn't face even dipping the end of a toe in those icy waters.

REST AND RECOVERY

Status report

O'B's right shin and calf continued to be of concern. He was experiencing ongoing pain and still had some swelling in the ankle and lower leg. His other leg muscles appeared okay however, and he was walking freely. On the next flight, he would try to ice this area a few times and keep it elevated when possible. Sue's leg muscles were good, a little tight in the quads when she tried to stretch, and she was also experiencing pain in the soleus in her left calf when it was stretched or touched.

Lesson for life

Learn by doing.
Experience enhances learning and makes it personal.

You can only learn so much through conversation, reading and formal lessons. When you actually undertake an activity, what may have previously been unclear or sounded like a cliché makes sense to you in ways you can learn from and make future use of. As we looked back on Missoula we realised O'B s approach to carbo loading was better described as overloading and he is now more careful about how much he eats before a marathon (most of the time).

Stormy Weather:
Pattaya, Thailand

*'There are only two mistakes one can make
along the road to truth; not going all the way,
and not starting.'*

Buddha

Cumulative flying distance:	72,126 kilometres
Cumulative flying time:	99 hours and 40 minutes
Cumulative total travel time:	212 hours and 40 minutes

We decided to eat a late supper on the plane and then sleep. Hopefully this would help us adjust to the major time change we were going to experience on our next travel leg. We both managed about 7 hours' sleep, which is fantastic on a plane. Mind you, we had built up a sizeable sleep debt over the past few days.

Flying into and out of Hong Kong en route to Thailand was wonderful. At the old airport the plane seemingly landed between buildings, just as my father had often described during his stories of an end of season footy trip with Essendon in the 1960s. The new airport out at Lantau Island also makes for an amazing arrival; the plane swoops around the Bay affording brilliant views of the dozens of small islands that comprise this former British trade outpost, now officially part of China since 1997. We caught a glimpse of the giant Buddha that perches benevolently on the hillside and the new cable car system that takes tourists and worshippers up to the adjacent monastery.

Our stop was brief but we were reminded of what a dynamic city Hong Kong is. The massive airport is highly organised, with rail and ferry links to the city and a hub for every airline imaginable. We worked at the state of the art computer terminals, looking out gigantic windows to the tarmac and hills of Lantau beyond.

The next stage of our journey passed very quickly as we tucked into our third breakfast of the day and re-adjusted our watches again. By this stage we really had no idea what time our body clocks were running to, but it was 10.30am when we arrived in Bangkok so we just rolled with that.

Bangkok's recently opened Suvarnabhumi Airport is a massive structure of glass and concrete. Pronounced 'su-wan-na-poom', it is vastly spread out which means a lot of walking. Airport guides, immaculately dressed in purple suits, assist and the signage is good so at least we were heading in the right direction.

Unsure of the best way to transfer to Pattaya, we'd asked our hotel to organise a driver. Again, this worked out very well. Our man was waiting for us as we left the arrival hall and steered us past the gaggle of taxi and limo drivers screeching at us and signs promising a cheap and reliable deal. We were definitely in Asia!

We couldn't remember how long the journey to Pattaya was. Maybe 60, 90 or even 120 minutes? We hunted for signs along the way but didn't see any. Eventually, just as the traffic ground to a halt in a huge jam, we spied one saying 20 kilometres to go. Our driver informed us that it was the start of a four day weekend; hence the huge number of vehicles on the road.

Continuing along Sukhumvit Road we were very excited when we spotted some signs welcoming runners to the marathon. They were about 20 metres apart and promoted the major sponsors – Blackmore's vitamins and Singha Beer. What a contrast! There were also huge banners across the road, welcoming runners and announcing the marathon start at Soi 4. Exactly what this was we were not sure.

Pattaya is busy, dusty and noisy. Brash too, with loud advertising and people spilling onto the road as they wander along crowded shopping streets. Shops, bars, restaurants and massage salons are jammed close together on the narrow lanes and sois (secondary roads) and along the main drag, Pattaya Beach Road. Everywhere there was noise, from the tinny piped music pouring out of shops to the incessant engine drone and honking horns of motor bikes and taxi trucks.

Our hotel was on Buddha Hill, which divides the beach areas of Pattaya and Jomtien. This is one long steep hill and we were horrified to realise it was part of our marathon course and we were going to be forced to climb it at the 35 kilometre mark. Straightaway our dread increased even more. Heat and hills are not an appealing combination!

After the clamour of downtown Pattaya the hotel was like a sanctuary. Designed in the traditional Thai style and set among lush tropical foliage with fountains and open balconies, it truly was beautiful. But as we were shown to our room we had a sinking feeling. There were a hell of a lot of steps! Lifts? Well, maybe to Level 1, but the tiered design meant that there were five flights of steps to the pool and three to the breakfast restaurant. How on earth were we going to manage on Sunday after the race? Let alone Monday, and then Tuesday?

We walked down to the beach but it was closed to swimmers due to jellyfish. So after a short swim in one of the hotel pools, we decided to go into Pattaya and check out Soi 4 which, we discovered, was a road. We'd been told it would take about 15 minutes to walk to the shopping streets, but after only 3 minutes we already had sweat trickling down our backs! Down the hill, past dozens of boats in dry dock at the Port and onto the notorious Walking Street we went. During the day this is not a pedestrian zone, as we soon found out, dodging motorbikes and cars and trucks. At night though it is closed to traffic. The neon lights flash and the place comes alive. This area used to be strictly adults only, but these days all age groups wander down there in the evenings, although there is still the profusion of 'go-go' bars and all manner of men, ladies of the night and 'lady-boys' out and about, trying to find a 'date' with one of the many middle aged Caucasian male tourists.

Time for our first massage and we were spoiled for choice. Opting for a 60 minute oil massage for the princely sum of 300 baht (about AU$10), we were surprised that we were expected to shower and then take off all our clothes. Had we picked the wrong sort of place? But after this and subsequent massages – and why wouldn't you for that price? – keeping underwear on only elicited giggles from the masseuses.

I am not built for the combination of extreme heat and humidity. Rio had been tough going but nothing like marathons I've run in Singapore and Lake Placid where the humidity and heat were extreme. Pattaya was shaping up to be the hottest and most humid yet and it was unnerving.

REST AND RECOVERY

Status report

O'B was still concerned about his lower calf and shin pain. His right leg was very sore and not up to running yet. Hopefully further massage and anti-inflammatories would help. Sue had some pain in her left soleus, one of the deeper calf muscles which she was unaware of until the massage found a sore spot. She was not sure whether this would be a problem running, but the area had caused concern during the latter stages in Missoula. At least it was not the dreaded plantar fascia pain under the foot and it seemed like the cortisone injection was still working.

Friday in Pattaya
Friday 18 July

One of the challenges of our trip was adjusting to the climate changes and different weather conditions every few days. After the cool of San Francisco, Pattaya was going to take some time to adapt to. Taking the hotel taxi, we were again nervous at how long and steep the hill was. O'B joked that it was the Polly Shortts of the Pattaya Marathon. It sure would be a strong runner who managed to actually run up this hill at the 35 kilometre mark!

Jomtien, the next beach along, is a fraction quieter than Pattaya but still not walkable, with a huge number of deckchairs and umbrellas set up. Being Friday afternoon and a public holiday, the beach was crowded with locals, sitting and chatting happily on the breezy waterfront. Along the road were shops, bars and restaurants, with a few hotels in between.

We were just about to select our massage bar for the day when my phone rang. It was a Sydney radio station checking if they could phone back in about 40 minutes to chat about Running for Relationships. Graham Gilbert from Talk Tonight on 2SM and other affiliated stations, including one on the Gold Coast, was very interested that Gold Coast mayor Ron Clarke was my uncle. He also wanted to talk about what fuel we take with us and the logistics. Trying to find a quiet place was difficult. We tried hotel lobbies and air-conditioned shops with doors that closed, but everywhere we went we encountered the same problem – piped music. Eventually we decided on the carpark in front of the Jomtien Park Hotel, much to the bemusement and concern of the security staff. But even there buses and motorbikes were revving their engines.

Interview out of the way, we embarked upon a two-massage day. We started off with a full body oil massage, followed by a foot massage which incorporated reflexology techniques designed to create equilibrium within the body. At this stage we figured we needed all the help we could get!

We had booked an 8.00pm buffet dinner at the hotel but were rather late arriving back and couldn't get a table in the air-conditioned section of the restaurant so sat outside on the dimly lit balcony. At least it was comfortable temperature-wise. Unfortunately the food was not that suitable for a pair of marathoners trying to carbo load. There were no pasta dishes and only one spicy rice option so we tried to eat as much bread as we could. We had planned to eat at the hotel the next night too and we hoped there'd be more suitable food then. Otherwise we'd have to run on a low-carbohydrate preparation, or risk a restaurant in Pattaya. Something of a dilemma as after O'B's stomach upset in Missoula we wanted to be extra careful.

We turned in early, looking forward to a full night's sleep in a bed for the first time in several days and wondering how our arrangements for this marathon would pan out. Earlier that day, we'd gone to reception to find out what time the shuttle bus was taking marathon runners to the start, only to be met with a blank look from the guest relations manager. We explained that the official marathon website said that the hotel was running a shuttle for guests but this seemed to be the first time the hotel had heard of this. We left it in her capable hands. Luckily we had asked with a few days' warning! As events unfolded we would discover how vital transport to the start would become.

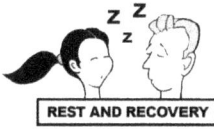

REST AND RECOVERY

Status report

There was not a huge amount of improvement in O'B's shin soreness and calf tightness and his leg had felt painful as he tried to run across a road in Jomtien; clearly running was still not an option. He started on anti-inflammatory tablets, hoping the inflammation would go down. Meanwhile Sue's heel spur pain had returned, and on the same leg she had some soleus tightness. Maybe the foot massage had stirred things up a bit? She started on anti-inflammatories too, a real worry as the pain in her heel and foot had been crippling before she'd had the cortisone injection in May. With three marathons yet to run and both of us carrying injuries we were becoming very concerned!

Hot and bothered
Saturday 19 July

We were awake by 6.00am and thought an early breakfast, then work was a good plan as we needed to make an extremely early start the next day. An early morning swim first was delightful. It had rained heavily overnight and the air seemed a little fresher. This would not be quite so bad to run in, we thought.

After as much breakfast as we could hold comfortably, we headed back to the room for a few hours' work before it was time to register for the marathon. We were not sure what awaited us in Pattaya city but we came upon a series of tents and temporary stages set up along the beachfront. The official marathon tents were manned by many volunteers whose bright green shirts proclaimed 'Stop Global Warming Pattaya Marathon 2008'. There was also a huge Blackmore's stand with girls (we think) dressed in aqua mini-dresses and stilettos trying to attract customers. For some reason quite a few photographers were hovering around them. There were lots of lesser displays too, many from discount sports stores with table after table of sports shirts and shorts and cheap runners all with Adidas and Nike labels. Were they real? At 150 baht (about AU$5) for the shorts and 750 baht (AU$25) for the shoes, probably not!

As in Brazil, dental health seemed to be big business, so it was little wonder that there was a dental tent too. Another tent was promoting safe sex and Sue was handed a box of condoms as she strolled past. This was definitely a first at a marathon expo!

We had registered online but when we tried to pay credit cards weren't accepted. The preferred method of payment – money order – would have cost three times the entry fee, so we decided to pay when we registered. The English of the volunteer in charge of online entries was adequate at best. Some European entrants in front of us had been there for ages and even when they left we weren't sure if they had succeeded in registering. After much shuffling through a multi-ringed folder, the volunteer finally found our faxed entries and after a cash transaction we were on our way to pick up our race packets. The whole process had been much smoother than we anticipated and we counted ourselves lucky.

With receipts in hand we proceeded to the bib and race packet collection area and received our numbers and ankle bracelets with timing chips attached. Age groups were in 10 year brackets, but strangely the men were grouped 35 to 44 and so forth, and the women 40 to 49. With only the first number showing on the bib, however, I was happy to wear M35 and Sue was very pleased with her F40!

Instructor and student. We met in a fitness class. Sue was the instructor and O'B was attempting to regain his fitness. One day Sue suggested a movie. The rest is history.

Family football. Sue and brother Ian playing with their father Jack Clarke at the famous Windy Hill Football Ground in Essendon, Australia.

Wedding day. We had our wedding photographs taken at the Black Rock Beach. Years later it has become a popular spot for doing television and newspaper, video and photo shoots about our running adventures.

Our first finish line together. The instinctive hand holding the first time we crossed the finish line has become a tradition which has continued for more than 50 marathons together. Photo courtesy www.marathonfoto.com

Our first family fitness event. Completing the 1998 Olympic Dream 10km in Melbourne with Anthony and Shelley.

Keynote speakers. Here we are ready to speak to a corporate conference audience. Photo by Passion8 Photography, www.passion8photo.com.au

Streets of Chicago. The moment of truth in our first marathon in Chicago is captured here as a signature story from one of our speeches on the power of partnership and going further together.

Graduation day. Andrew's parents, Estelle and Arnold along with Anthony and Shelley enjoyed the day O'B became Dr O'B. Partnerunning and Desired Futures are the result of commercialising O'B's doctoral research.

A family celebration. For the Goofy Challenge at Disneyworld in January 2008 we ran the half marathon with Shelley on Saturday and the marathon on Sunday. Anthony had the tough job taking pictures both days.

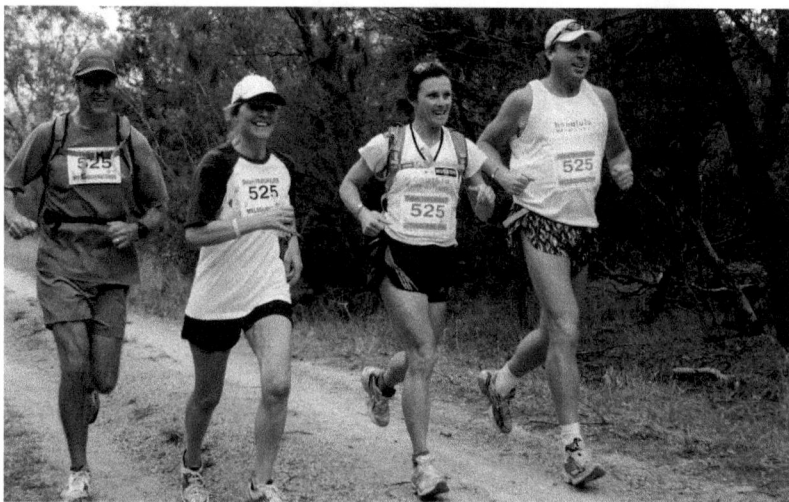

Boosting confidence at Oxfam 2008. With friends Chris and Leanne in March. Running 100km in the Oxfam Trailwalker in less than 16 hours convinced us we were a chance to complete the Comrades 87km.
Photo courtesy www.sports-pix.com

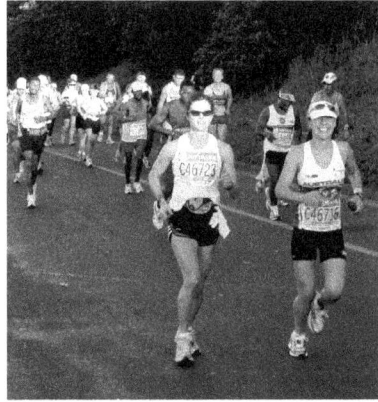

Comrades: Only 42 km to go. With 45km behind us we joked about making the finish as we figured 'We can run a marathon'. (Even if the warm up was longer than usual)

Sue and Mari-Mar during Comrades. We ran the early stages with Travelling Fit Founder and Director Mari-Mar Walton. Here Mari-Mar and Sue run up Fields Hill while O'B does the camera work.

Ten hours and seventeen seconds later. We were elated to cross the line. The drama and excitement of the 12 hour finish cut off is amazing and like nothing else we have experienced. Photo courtesy www.actionphoto.net

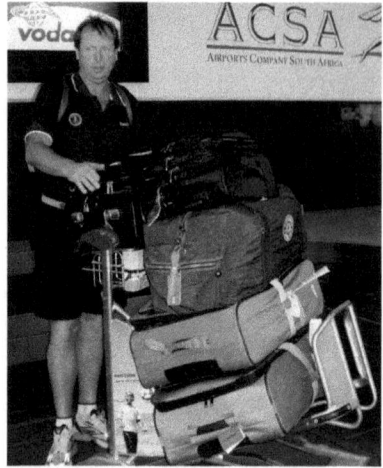

Ultra unwell post race. We were both 'a bit off colour' when we cooled down after running for 10 hours. Sue paused for this photo before spending the next hour in the medical tent.

At the airport on the way to Mauritius. Eight weeks luggage was a challenge and it seemed to grow with each marathon expo.

Post run breakfast. It felt good to be back at the hotel in time to enjoy the full buffet breakfast and Mauritian entertainment – a bonus for making an early start.

Heading for home in Mauritius. Beautiful scenery, tough conditions and a tricky course made Mauritius one of our most difficult runs.

Corcovado. Also known as Christ the Redeemer this famous site is one of the many places we may never have seen if not for running together.

Cool at the start. It may seem unusual to non-runners to wear a garbage bag but for those getting ready to run in cold morning conditions it is a common sight as modelled here by Sue.

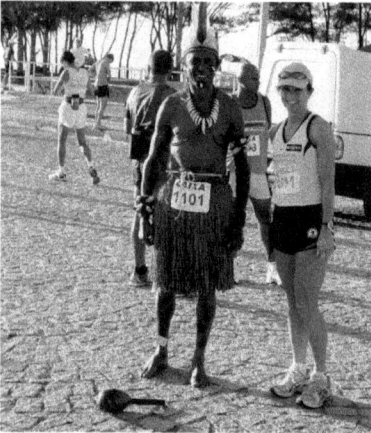

Meeting Barefoot. Running 100 metres with bare feet is hard, let alone a marathon. We have met many amazing people as a result of our Partnerunning.

Partnerunning in action. The Partnerunning approach includes different types of runners and relationships. It encourages planned conversation to improve productivity and motivation.

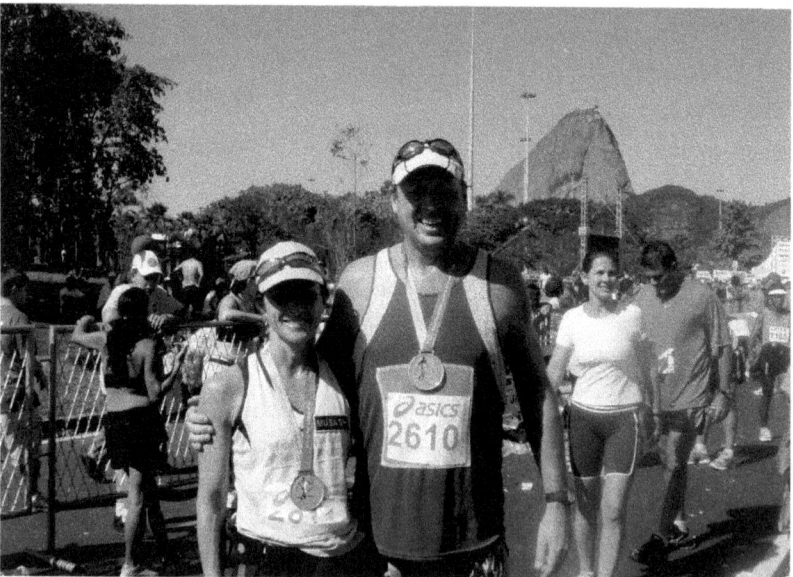

The Rio finish at Sugarloaf. Surely one of the best backdrops to finish a foot race anywhere in the world.

Calgary cowboy welcome. After a sleepy flight we were wide awake as the country and western music welcomed us to the Calgary Stampede.

Paris and turning 40. We often pass the time talking about past and future races. We ran the Paris marathon to celebrate Sue turning 40.

Running Room Founder John Stanton. Meeting best selling author and leading Canadian business person John Stanton at the pre-marathon breakfast was a real thrill.

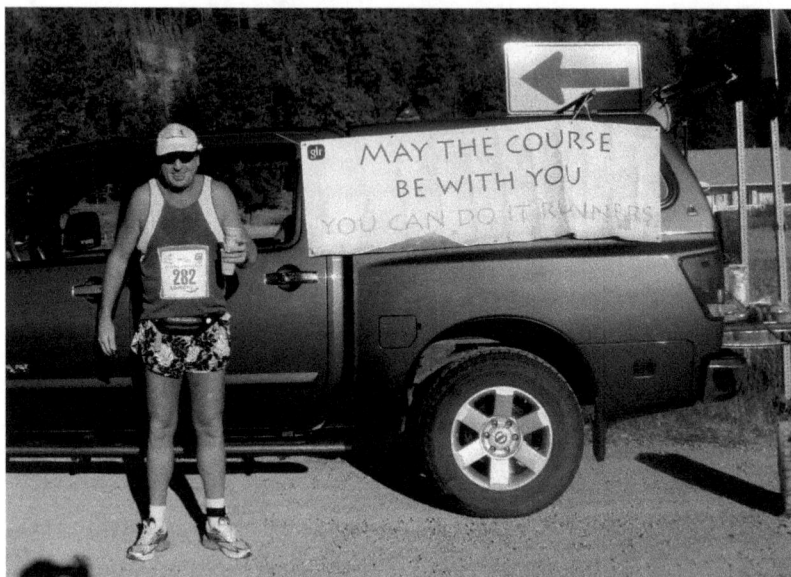

Great course encouragement. Marathon day almost always brings amusing signs of encouragement. We especially liked this one in Missoula.

Carbo overloading. Enough of the pasta and pancakes! O'B was lured into overeating by this delicious pizza, always one to make new mistakes.

Scottsdale recovery walk. Arizona is one of our favourite places in the world. We love the desert scenery and climate.

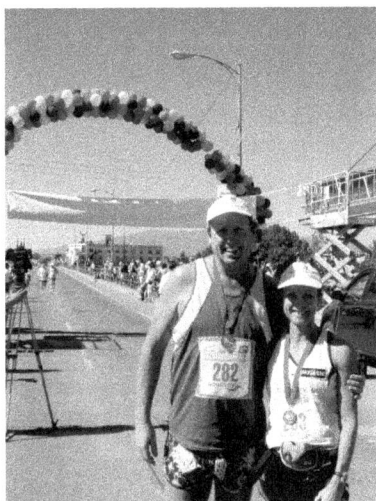

The Missoula Finish. After a very tough race and a few interviews we captured the moment.

Spreading the word on our cycle tour. Any chance to talk about Oxfam and healthy relationships. Sue chats to a family from California on the Golden Gate Bridge.

A walk in San Francisco Bay. Sue took the camera while OB took to the very cold water. We think it helped and the views of the Golden Gate Bridge and Alcatraz were fantastic.

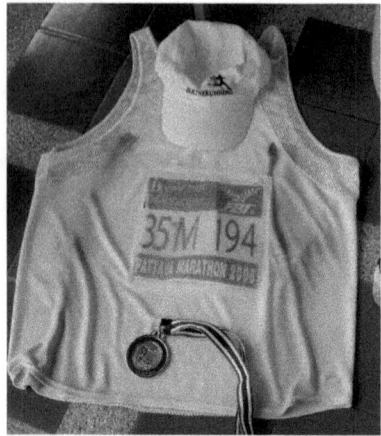

Pattaya entertainment at the start. The tropical storm made for chaos but this guy did his best to entertain people.

Blood on the tracks. Maintaining clean clothes is a real travel challenge and removing the blood from O'B's singlet after Pattaya was more challenging than normal.

We love Thailand. The rain, humidity and language difficulties made for tough going in Pattaya. Very pleased to finish, we enjoyed every moment.

Not what we expected in the Swiss Alps. Single file up the mountain trail was not what we envisaged for a marathon.

Stunning scenery. We look forward to returning to the Swiss Alps and taking on the 78km event that goes over the Jakobshorn Mountain.

Picture perfect (the alps not us). What better way to experience the beauty of the Swiss Alps? The hills were alive with the sound of runners and O'B moaning in pain.

Great to see family and friends. It was a wonderful weekend with Jane, Sue, Gary, Shelley, Anthony and O'B (from left).

Unexpected recognition. We were honoured when the Townsville Road Runners presented us with a trophy after our 8th and final marathon run.

What leg? Another signature story cartoon by Jock which we use when speaking about the power of focussing on your desired future.
Photo by Passion8 Photography

Sue. Speaker, trainer and coach.
Photo by Passion8 Photography

Andrew. Speaker, facilitator and
mentor. Photo by Passion8 Photography

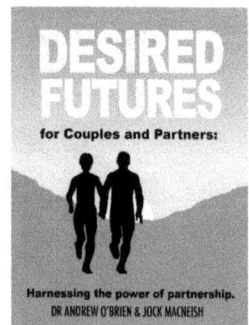

DESIRED FUTURES
for Organisations:
Why shared vision and what it means.
DR ANDREW O'BRIEN & JOCK MACNEISH

DESIRED FUTURES
for Individuals:
Creating the future you truly want.
DR ANDREW O'BRIEN & JOCK MACNEISH

DESIRED FUTURES
for Couples and Partners:
Harnessing the power of partnership.
DR ANDREW O'BRIEN & JOCK MACNEISH

Creating Desired Futures. Corporate, partner and individual success
practices are at the heart of Partnerunning and Andrew's Desired Futures
approach. Collaboration with Jock Macneish uses pictures to connect with
diverse audiences. Book covers courtesy of www.andrewob.com

Our race pack contained an emerald green shirt like the volunteers had been wearing, a lime green baseball cap, and a lime green and white mesh sports bag; both the hat and the bag had the Global Warming motto printed on them. Unfortunately there was no race info in the kits; indeed there was no information booth to answer our questions about drinks, aid stations and portable toilets, and we began to fear the worst.

We escaped the heat for a while by wandering through Mike's Shopping Mall. What a shock when I went to use the restroom: you had to purchase toilet paper from a machine in front of the toilets that I thought was for sanitary products. Even more of a shock was that the paper was not flushed away but put in a bucket beside the bowl. After this, I felt even more concerned about the marathon's arrangements. I'm one of those people who likes to line up as close to the race start as possible and wasn't sure what I'd do if there were no toilet facilities at the start. Other women will relate to this, I'm sure.

It would have been very easy to snooze beside the pool in the sun after a swim, but we didn't want to take any chances with our hydration, so we stayed inside and worked and dozed before heading to dinner at the hotel's pizza restaurant. One of the traps with vacation marathons – along with too much sun and overdoing the walking – is poor food choices. The wrong sort of fuel can undermine your performance.

By now there were at least three things we could put O'B's gut problems in Missoula down to. First, a stomach virus he had in Scottsdale had not completely left his system; second, the anti-inflammatory tablets he had taken for his shin; and third, the pizza he had eaten the night before was both too big and too rich for his digestive system to handle (even if it was the best pizza ever, anywhere). Or was it a combination of the above? Whatever, here we were, the night before the Pattaya Marathon, having pizza and O'B was back on the ant-inflammatory tablets. Understandably he was somewhat nervous about how his stomach would react, but we didn't want to get too paranoid. O'B took the view that a one-off event did not warrant an overreaction. Unless the stomach problem occurred again, we should follow our normal routine. The only change he made was to reduce the amount of food he ate and make sure it was very plain.

Following a delicious meal it was back to the room for some more hydration from the electrolyte drinks we had bought from one of the convenience stores that abounded in town. Luckily everywhere except Mauritius we'd been able to buy electrolyte drinks but we'd brought a container of Endura powder with us in case of emergencies.

Apart from when each of us ran our very first race, contemplating the Pattaya Marathon was the first time we'd been scared about what was likely to happen on the course. Apart from being concerned about sore legs, and particularly O'B's right leg, the challenge of running in the heat and the unknown cause of O'B's stomach problems the week before had us worried. Language difficulties meant we were unsure about the number and location of drink stops, food supplies and portable toilets on the course. We figured there'd be enough convenience stores along the course for us to stop and purchase drinks. But the locations of toilets – or lack thereof – really had us nervous. McDonalds might be the solution but what if they were not open at 4.30am or soon after when we needed them? And what if the anti-inflammatories and/or painkillers were the culprit and O'B's stomach problems flared up again?

Then there was the heat and humidity. We had been drinking extra fluids for the past two days but still hadn't achieved the clear urine recommended. Outside O'B was sweating like crazy and indoors the air-conditioning dried us out further. I felt okay about running in the heat but for O'B heat and humidity are just about his biggest fear.

We were being picked up at 3am for a 4.30am start and were worried about waiting around for a long time in the dark streets of Pattaya. This would be a good one to have behind us, we agreed. Then we could focus on my fear – the potential extreme cold running at altitude in the Swiss Alps.

Early morning chaos
Sunday 20 July

One reason for choosing our hotel was the promise of a shuttle to the marathon start. This meant we didn't have to worry about finding a taxi or walking through the nightclub district in the early hours of the morning. We thought 3am was a little early, but with no experience of the traffic and knowing that we had to pass through the nightclub district to reach the start area, we were grateful that a car would be coming to pick us up.

We opened our balcony door to heavy tropical rain and an electrical storm. A quick calculation of the flash to bang ratio told us the lightning was a long way from Pattaya Beach. We went about our usual routine – protein bar and electrolyte drink breakfast, showers and anti-chafe balm – before our now weekly check of everything we needed for the marathon. We discussed the positives and negatives of the rain. Maybe it would be cooler, but what would happen if the race was cancelled or delayed due to lightning? Would heavy rain make it a tougher run? Would the rain damage our feet or give O'B a nasty case of bleeding nipples? We'd once run in cold, heavy rain in the Canberra Marathon and found it very hard going.

At 2.50am we were just about to leave for the hotel lobby when our phone rang. Our pick up time would now be later and we should wait in our room for another call. Being all dressed up with no place to go made it difficult to wait without going back to sleep but we did our best to keep busy and at 3.30am went to the lobby to wait for our driver. By 3.45am no car had arrived. The night manager got busy on the phone and we were assured the car was on the way. More visits to the hotel's ballroom restroom and at 4am our driver finally arrived.

The trip of 4 kilometres took 20 minutes as we battled heavy rain and nightclub patrons, many on motor scooters. The soaked party goers, lady boys and women of the night kept us entertained as we slowly made our way in torrential downpours. Closer to the marathon start groups of runners were sheltering under shop balconies and some were stranded on the side of the flooded roads. Finally we reached the drop off point with 10 minutes to spare. As we hunched under a shop entrance to put on our garbage bags we were 'entertained' by a very overweight, very white, very drunk man falling out of a bar and attempting to swim through the street before falling back into the arms of some bar girls in the 'open' bar next door. All the while he wore his pants around his knees. Perhaps this was what they call a 'Full Moon Party' in Thailand, I suggested to Sue.

The 300 metre walk to the start was an exercise in dodging puddles. Marathoners and half marathoners took refuge in hotel lobbies, bars, shops, anywhere they could. It was chaos.

The stage full of officials looked on, waiting for the race start. PA speakers fell to the ground as the ground they were standing on turned to mud and slush. The starting area was flooded. We huddled in our garbage bags on the one part of the road that was above the water. We knew our shoes would soon be soaked but figured every minute we could stay dry was worth something.

Various announcements in Thai added to our confusion until after one Sue confidently said the race start had been postponed. It was 4.25am and with just 5 minutes to go we were not sure what to do. Then came a follow up announcement in English saying we could not wear two race numbers. What the …? Lucky for us we were still in the starting corral when a lengthy Thai announcement followed by another English one told us there was 2 minutes until race start. Sue has a very good command of French, Italian and German and with a great mind for numbers and languages is usually spot on in picking up on local languages. But she was way off the mark this time and I couldn't help but start sledging her. Then, 30 seconds after the '2 minutes to go' announcement, the start sounded and we were off and running.

Pleased to be out of the chaos of the starting area and no longer standing around in the rain, we giggled at the discrepancy. We reasoned the official Thai announcement was made with 2 minutes to go and by the time the other announcer repeated it there was only 30 seconds until start time. I'm not complaining about the organisation in Pattaya, mind you. Just trying to highlight some of the language challenges we faced in running in countries where English was not the official – or even second – language. Each time, we remind ourselves what it would be like for a Thai or a Brazilian running in Melbourne where there is even less recognition of other languages than we'd experienced in Rio and Pattaya.

Stormy weather

We were charging down Pattaya Beach Road! The road surface was uneven and the rain had collected in deep puddles. We found ourselves trying to leap over them, or changing course to avoid getting our feet too wet. In some sections the water was flowing like a river into the deep drains along the kerbside. By the time the next few kilometres had passed this would have become irrelevant as the heavy rain had soaked our feet anyway!

We had discarded our garbage bags at the start but were amazed to see local runners keeping their plastic rain bonnets on for the entire race. Neither of us had ever seen this before. Some had plastic, shower cap style bonnets on under peaked caps; others wore them on their own, both men and women. But the rain was so drenching for the next 4 hours we seriously doubted anyone could stay dry beneath those flimsy bonnets.

The wide road and the smallish field meant there was little jostling at the start. The first half of the run would be completed in darkness and, combined with the heavy rain and lightning, the whole experience was somewhat surreal. Along the way some bars and nightclubs were still open for business; indeed we'd see some patrons still sitting in bars at 8.30am as we made our return run!

We still had no idea how far apart drink stops were, or if they provided sports drinks, food or just water. We were relieved when the first one appeared out of the darkness at the 2 kilometre mark, but imagine our horror when we saw the volunteers doling the water into the cups from giant open buckets. This was definitely not the safe water from sealed containers of marathons in Singapore, Brazil, South Africa or Melbourne. Despite the rain, we were still concerned about hydration so just took a mouthful, swirled it around and spat most of it out. Not only did it taste strange but it was freezing cold; each cup had ice cubes floating in it. Throughout the rest of the run we'd notice a variation in the taste of the water, which was not very reassuring! On the more positive side, each station was equipped with sponges and lots of ice. We just crossed our fingers, hoping that neither of us would succumb to a stomach upset.

Partnerunning Tip

Learning this sound management technique and applying it to your running, exercise and travel is a great way to increase your enjoyment and overcome the obstacles you encounter along the way.

Risk Management is:

Enhanced by	Hindered by
• Using a simple risk management approach	• Ignoring risk
• Identifying risks	• Thinking only the best will happen
• Evaluating risks	• Adopting a risk approach not suited to your individual risk 'profile'
• Avoiding, reducing, transferring and accepting risk	
• Understanding and following your individual risk profile	• Lack of research

Leaving Pattaya Beach Road, we headed away from the waterfront and onto the major divided roadway, Sukhumvit Road which was closed to traffic on one side. Straightaway we noticed lots of police manning intersections and preventing traffic from interrupting the runners. In their orange jackets they stood out clearly against the overwhelming greyness, but most didn't look too happy. And who could blame them, standing out in heavy rain for hours on end early on a Sunday morning? Over half of the marathon would be going up and then back past Pattaya and onto Jomtien Beach and at this point we began wondering how much longer we had on this *#@* road! Vacant lots, petrol stations, closed car dealerships, the scenery was not very simulating, apart from the giant chicken sitting on a concrete fence. Apparently behind it was a chicken farm with ornately decorated buildings, but at first we had wondered if it was some strange chicken god with a bizarre temple.

The drink stops came with regularity about every 2 kilometres, with one offering watermelon and pineapple segments. We were fairly confident to take the melon which went down a treat, but unsure about the acidity of the pineapple. On the table were also cups of red liquid, which looked like a raspberry sports drink. O'B was hesitant but I cautiously tried it. Indeed, it did taste like raspberry, but more like a sickly cordial than an electrolyte drink, certainly far too sweet for me to be able to drink the whole cup.

We focused hard on implementing our race plan and tried not to waste energy worrying about what we could not control, like the weather, water and toilets. Thankfully, O'B's stomach had been settled so far, despite the uncertainty of the water, and this was a great relief as we hadn't spotted any public toilets or portable toilets en route. The illness of Missoula would have been a disaster here! Once we moved away from the waterfront, men were using the local foliage and vacant lots, but for the few women … well, standing up is a female marathon runner's skill and takes much practice! Once again the language problems added to our challenge. We couldn't ask if, with police lining the course every 100 metres, our impromptu toilet stops in the bushes meant we were risking arrest if we were caught with our pants down.

The terrain had been flat and the road surface much more even along Sukhumvit Road, even if the scenery had been uninspiring. Before we turned at the 14 kilometre mark to retrace our steps and go onto Jomtien, we passed the wheelchair leaders heading in the other direction. Next we saw the marathon race leaders coming back towards us. They looked so beautiful, running with their flowing graceful style, but as is so often the case with elite endurance athletes, with their gaunt faces and wraith-like bodies, they just did not look healthy. After the leaders passed we began to see ever-larger numbers of runners coming back towards us. And I do mean directly! While it was essentially 'keep left', we were sharing a laneway and aid stations on one side of the road were trying to help runners on both sides. Luckily the light was improving by now and the street light strong, otherwise crashing into an oncoming runner could have been a possibility. Finally reaching the turnabout point, we were handed blue hair elastic to put on our wrist to denote we had indeed made it all the way out and not cut the course short by a few kilometres. A new approach, which while low tech, proved highly effective.

We reached the half marathon in just over 2 hours and 6 minutes. Considering the conditions, O'B's leg and it being marathon number 6, we were pleased. Our average kilometre time had been pretty much spot on 30 minutes per 5 kilometres and we had been taking a 1 minute walk break every 10 minutes of running. Pattaya was never going to be the fastest course for us but we felt that if we could maintain this form we would finish in a respectable time about the 4 hour mark. It would have been nice if the rain had stopped, but throughout this first half it was relentless. Luckily our caps acted as gutters and diverted the rain from our eyes, but our clothes were saturated. Our waterlogged shoes were feeling heavy and we knew our feet would be wrinkled and discoloured, but thanks to our Injinji socks neither of us could feel any discomfort or blisters forming and feet-wise were generally oblivious to the rain.

At this stage O'B was happy with the state of his stomach, and we were becoming more confident of attributing last week's problems to a virus. He was concerned about his shin though and had taken pain relief tablets Tylenol Extra in addition to anti-inflammatories although unfortunately the loose capsules in my run bag had disintegrated during the heavy rain, and emerged as a runny mess. As for me, I was feeling strong and my legs, calf muscle and heel were all very comfortable – a great relief.

Persistance

Unlike in previous races we'd run, hardly any runners were using the measured walk break approach; most seemed to be running until they could run no more. We were trying to stick to our Jeff Galloway inspired 10 minutes running/1 minute walking regime, unless we saw a drink station in the distance. As a result, we seemed to pass, then be passed, by the same runners until eventually their pace slowed to the point that we lost track of them. We were trying to achieve consistency, a steady and safe pace that would minimise damage to our muscles and help with readiness for Davos next Saturday. That this time we only a 6 day break between races was uppermost in our minds!

I had gone for the Tylenol after the halfway mark. As Sue tried to scrounge more smooshy tablets from her bag we decided to buy a Coca Cola from one of the many shops along the side of the road. I don't know what the shopkeeper made of a marathon runner bolting into the shop but she took her time to serve Sue – and offered a plastic bag too! We later noticed another Western runner make exactly the same drink purchase, so clearly we weren't alone in wanting more refreshments than what were being offered on the course. It's hard to say whether the local runners used energy gels or the like; we didn't see them consuming any and the very few empty containers that we did see may have been internationals'. Sue used four gels for the race and I consumed six, and we both had a few sport jelly beans. Being able to consume gels without gagging was a great relief as in recent weeks I'd been finding them hard to take.

The Coca Cola also gave me a big lift in energy, as it had in Comrades, and from the 27 kilometre mark we again ran quite strongly. Past the outlet shopping malls, past Underwater World, past a life sized Bob the Builder outside a large hardware store (although Bob didn't look too sure about what was happening when I stopped to shake hands and have a photo taken with him). Finally we made it to Chaiya Phruek Road, our turn down towards Jomtien beach. At last we felt we were on the way home! This road was under construction in parts, the surface muddy and uneven, and again we were navigating potholes. On either side of us locals stared bemusedly before continuing with their daily routines. Some were cooking on small gas burners or acrid-smelling fires; others were sweeping concrete verandahs or sitting and chatting as they sheltered from the rain. Whatever, they were definitely not waiting to cheer marathon runners on! Such a marked contrast to Missoula the week before. Here in Pattaya, even the volunteers at drink and aid stations went about their work in silence. Language barriers aside, we did have some interaction with our fellow runners, even if it was a nod of the head or the universally understood thumbs up signal.

We hit Jomtien Beach Road at about the 32 kilometre mark and it felt great to have less than 10 kilometres to go. It was still raining and the many beach chairs and umbrellas were empty, although there were a lot of people about and a general sense of busy-ness as the day began and shops opened. Past our massage bars of Friday and the Jomtien hotels we ran, the palm-tree lined boulevard offering some shelter from the still persistent rain. How lucky we had decided not to bring the video camera! We'd had our doubts about its ability to cope with the extreme humidity but the rain that greeted us this morning had been the final straw. Just as well Sue's digital camera was waterproof, because a lot of water was getting on the lens whenever we paused for photographs.

Thappraya Road took us away from the beach, over the hill and down to Pattaya. As we turned on it we braced ourselves for the ordeal ahead. Originally my research had indicated a flat course so we'd been very surprised when we arrived to read local literature describing the race as 'holding the honour as one of the toughest marathon courses in the country' and having 'various hills and steep inclines'. However, the course seemed to take us beside Buddha Hill, not over it as we had originally expected.

For a few kilometres we still feared the worst, that we would suddenly turn and find ourselves climbing steeply. But it just didn't happen! The most gruelling part of the course had turned out to be the long straight Sukhumvit Road and the greatest ordeal of the day coping with the deluge. There was a slope, and some runners around us were reduced to a walk, but I'd by no means describe it as challenging. After all we were Comrades runners; we knew what real hills were all about! It would have been handy though to have a course map showing profiles, kilometre markers and drink stops.

Feeling as if we had been handed a gift, we rolled downhill into Pattaya City and around the Port before reaching Walking Street and the countdown of the sois to get to the finish at number 4. The rain had eased off and a huge number of pleasure craft were out on the water. There were also a myriad of parasailers in the air; it was a wonder they didn't fly into each other!

Walking Street

The entrance to Walking Street was marked with a small sandwich board sign denoting 3 kilometres to go. We felt a surge of adrenalin. At 4.00am this area had been busy, with patrons spilling out onto the street from bars, nightclubs and 'go go clubs'. Now as we passed, all was quiet; the shops and bars were closed. With the road closed to traffic as well for the marathon, there was an eerie stillness but the weird and wonderful names kept us amused as we contemplated buying a suit at Playboy Fashion Tailor, chomping on a T-bone at the Cowboy Steakhouse or finding out what was going on at Angel Witch Rock Dancers.

As we passed under the archway leaving Walking Street we were greeted by runners who had walked back from the finish and were encouraging other marathoners as they neared the end. A few were holding large trophies and cheering us on, some with calls of 'almost there'. At least that is what we think they were saying! By now the rain had stopped which made conditions much more pleasant. There were even a few non-running spectators and calls of encouragement from some of the bar girls hanging about waiting for the day's trade to begin.

The finish – at last

Once through Walking Street we could hear the music coming from the loudspeakers. We were within the final kilometre. As in Rio, miraculously our legs felt great and we picked up the speed and lifted our feet higher as the green archway came into view. Holding hands, we triumphantly passed beneath and heard that reassuring chirp of the chip as we stepped on the timing mat. Smiling and trying not to look too bedraggled for the cameras, we moved through the finishing chute. With the torrential rain, the day had been tough, but would it have been even tougher if it had been dry and we'd been faced with higher temperatures, sweltering humidity and a burning sun overhead? Almost definitely yes!

As the clock showed just over 4 hours and 17 minutes, we were elated to think that we were six down and only two to go.

Half marathoners were finishing at the same time as us, even though their race had started only 30 minutes after ours. These were runners at the back of the field, including one dressed as a white rabbit, complete with overalls and bow tie, running on behalf of the leukemia foundation. When he took off his 'head', we were surprised to discover he was an elderly Caucasian. I can only imagine the stuffiness and heat inside that suit in any weather conditions, but it must have weighed a couple of kilos after all the rain.

Our bibs were marked and we received our medals and had our ankle timing straps removed as we progressed deeper into the recovery area. Under a tent were plastic chairs with footstools where runners were treated to complimentary foot and leg massages. We don't know what was in the liniment, but it made my eyes water and created a burning hot/cold effect on the skin. This was one very welcome massage. Our therapists were excellent; they really found our sore spots and applied just the right amount of pressure. The Thai runner sitting next to me gestured at O'B's blotchy chest and suggested that he should go to the medical tent immediately for assistance. Indeed as we walked past, the staff came running out to drag him in!

Nipples

Many years ago I lost the tops of my nipples from chafing. Since then, attempts to avoid this problem with Vaseline, bandaids, nipple guards and surgical tape have all failed, although I've found a certain brand of anti-chafe balm effective in almost all conditions. The exception, as I discovered in Pattaya, was torrential rain or extreme humidity where my race singlet gets extremely wet. I was concerned this may be a problem and made sure I applied extra. We considered carrying a tube of balm with us, but with our pouches full of energy gels, painkillers, energy beans and emergency toilet paper we had no space.

By the time we'd run the first kilometre we were soaked and it was just a matter of time before the nipple chafing began. I checked at 10 kilometres and was surprised that there were no signs of damage, so continued oblivious to the emerging stains on my white singlet. As we passed the 20 kilometre mark Sue suggested I have another look since it was now daylight. Two bright red stains where my nipples had bled openly!

On the rare occasion when this occurs I dash into the next medical station and apply some Vaseline petroleum jelly. As we approached an ambulance offering assistance to runners I sauntered over and asked for some Vaseline. Just in the nick of time I jumped out of the way. The ambulance officer was within a few centimetres of applying the local equivalent of Deep Heat or Tiger Balm used to warm runners' tired muscles. A similar liniment had been massaged onto our calves and burned as it stimulated the muscles. My mind boggled as to what it would have done to my nipples.

Post race, a few things became clear. What we'd thought was growing crowd support toward the end was actually loud eeeeooow sounds as people noticed the two bright red spots on my singlet and the bloodstains running down each side of my race number. I assured Sue it looked much worse than it felt but even so was not looking forward to the first shower after the race; it would be far more painful than the rest of the race put together.

I was offered medical treatment in the finishing area treatment but, mindful of the near miss on the course, decided to treat the damage myself back at the hotel. The crowd's screams would soon be replaced with a loud %@%#@^% as I showered and then applied antiseptic cream. My new challenge was to avoid infection and hope my nipples healed quickly.

Food, glorious food

The post race food and drink were amazing! I'm usually prepared to try most new things, and this time there was a brand of sports drink that we'd never heard of, multi-coloured and set out in pre mixed cups. I took one look and decided to give it a miss, heading instead to the food tables. First up was rice soup. The process line worked with a ladle of rice, fish and prawn broth into a bowl, then a mushroom and finally chopped coriander on top. I was feeling quite chilled after the massage so this salty, tasty dish was just the thing. O'B was feeling somewhat less adventurous however and stuck with the watermelon pieces.

The next table along had massive woks. Noodles, chicken and vegetables were tossed together and placed into a polystyrene container with a lid and a pair of chopsticks. Many runners were walking home with these, and I'd have liked to try this dish as well, but the soup had been very filling and I simply couldn't fit anymore in.

The walk back

Even after some food, both of us were still feeling a bit cold and our clothes were drenched. At the end of the recovery area we noticed a section for gear check and many runners were picking up dry outfits to put on. Again, with no information booklet and unable to find English speaking officials to ask questions, we didn't know of this facility. We decided to walk back to the hotel for a late breakfast. This was the first time we'd done this after an official marathon – one advantage of the super early start.

With our medals hanging around our necks we received cheers and claps from the same group of bargirls we'd seen earlier that morning. Then it was time to offer our support to the runners coming along Pattaya Beach Road. Clapping and thumbs up signs were again our main forms of encouragement, along with a 'wai' or prayer like clasping of hands for the Thai runners. Often we called out 'almost there' or 'not far to go' but we really weren't sure if we were understood. Occasionally a Western runner would go by and we'd cheer them on enthusiastically, but really they could have been any nationality under the sun and have had absolutely no idea what we were saying!

It was about 5 kilometres back to the hotel so we'd warmed up and then some by the time we climbed Buddha Hill. Hopefully the walk is stretching out our leg muscles, we thought. We'd bought a drink and chocolate bar to have as we wandered back and enjoyed the stroll far more than jumping in a taxi truck and having a breeze blowing through our wet clothing, bringing the risk of hypothermia.

We were pretty sure we were the only full marathoners staying at the hotel, although there was one German guest running the half. But the hotel had a team of runners in the quarter marathon, so upon our return there was some interest. Or was it just my bloody chest?

After our 2.00am start we were exhausted. We spent the early part of the afternoon icing our legs and dozing. Unbelievably we both fell asleep with ice packs strapped to our legs! Amazingly, by the time we woke, the storms had given way to a sunny afternoon. Walking up and down in the pool, lying on banana lounges and more icing took care of the rest of the afternoon.

Following an early dinner, we spent a couple of hours writing our blogs and sending emails. We worked as long as we could but by 10pm were too tired. We packed away the ice, slipped into compression tights to assist with muscle recovery and called it a night. Six down, two to go.

Not feeling the best
Monday 21 July

We awoke to an email from Varun Sriram from ABC Sports Montana telling us he had posted his ABC television report on Partnerunning to YouTube. We were thrilled with the way Varun captured the spirit and purpose of Partnerunning and highlighted our efforts to raise funds for Oxfam, but a little shocked to see the deterioration in my running form. The footage had been taken on the day my right leg was at its worst and I was suffering severe stomach pains.

The day after the marathon the heat was overwhelming, and we concluded that the rain and cooler temperatures had been in our favour during the run. Apart from my chafed nipples there were no serious problems – but it would have been much, much harder if the sun, heat and humidity had been as intense for the race as it was today.

Farewell Pattaya
Tuesday 22 July

Even though we really hadn't bought anything, our Pattaya Marathon kit, some magazines and a few books had all taken their toll. We felt we needed to lighten our luggage by a few kilos at least and decided to post a package home. It is amazing how our luggage had just seemed to grow! One of our great concerns had been that different airlines have different baggage weight restrictions and we wanted to avoid incurring expensive charges for exceeding the limits. One of our mistakes had been to travel with the largest cases we could buy. Certainly we could fit a massive amount in them, but the meagre weight allowances meant they were at capacity when only half full!

There are many challenges when travelling. For instance, it is very unfortunate when hotel check out is at 1.00pm and your flight is not until 12.30am at night. But soon enough it was farewell to Pattaya, although we'd be coming back through Bangkok airport in less than a week after conquering the Swiss Alps of Davos. If O'B had been nervous about the heat of Pattaya, I was nervous about Davos, having had three immediate family members experience heart issues at altitude: my mother had heart palpitations walking in the Swiss Alps; my father's heart became erratic in Muskoka, in the Canadian Rockies during a triathlon world championship (later requiring a pacemaker); and my uncle damaged a mitral valve in his heart during the Mexico Olympics. One thing was certain, Switzerland would be very different from Thailand.

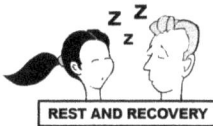

REST AND RECOVERY

Status report

With the exception of O'B's leg, we were both feeling well. We thought, optimistically as it happens, we had sorted out what the problem was, but were not sure of the best way to treat it and contemplated emailing our physiotherapist in Melbourne for some advice. At this stage we were thinking it was a muscle or ligament problem but Sue still wondered if it was a dreaded stress fracture – which really has no treatment other than rest for 6 to 8 weeks.

O'B was concerned that his hip had rotated more than usual which was putting undue pressure on the rest of the leg and impacting on the calf and shin pain. All of this was combining to make him a very concerned in the lead up to the Swiss Alpine Marathon, now only a few days away. All we could do was ice, rest, massage and hope for further improvement, but this time we only had 6 days between marathons.

Lesson for life

To do and not to do.
Behaviour counts so establish and use ground rules.

We discovered a long time ago that our behaviour determines our results. What we do and what we don't do are both important. Throughout our 8 marathon journey we focused on doing what mattered while avoiding anything that undermined our relationship or our performance. This approach was really helpful. We could see the benefit of it every day.

Partnerunning Community
Reader bonus number 3

Bonus online training program or Partnerunning course from www.partnerunningcommunity.com

Enjoy a complimentary membership and enrol in an online training and/or Partnerunning course. You can also check out our 'Great Running Destination' video series.

Ups and downs in the Swiss Alps

'Coming together is a beginning;

Keeping together is progress;

Working together is success.'
Henry Ford

Cumulative flying distance: **81,156 kilometres**
Cumulative flying time: **111 hours and 40 minutes**
Cumulative total travel time: **236 hours and 40 minutes**

No-one is happy when they are near a baby on a flight, particularly a night flight. The passengers immediately look concerned, the mother knows she is the brunt of stares and worried glances, and the airline staff brace themselves for a barrage of complaints. Our baby put in a solid 7 hours of screaming and yelling, and across the aisle from her was not the best place to be! Feeling very wiped out, having also had uncomfortable seats (there'd been an emergency plane switch and we weren't on the usual sort of plane for this route), we arrived at Zurich airport. Signs were frequent and often tri-lingual – English and French as well as German for some – and we had no trouble finding the train to take us to baggage claim.

Unbelievably, in the arrival hall there was a cow mooing! Yes, we were really in Switzerland, a country famous for its cheese, its chocolate and its efficiency. Everything was remarkably orderly, with trolleys all perfectly lined up and a carousel that delivered suitcases standing upright after announcements on a screen as to exactly how many minutes it would be until all luggage was out.

Baggage on a trolley, we thought about the train option into the city but realised that we'd need to get a taxi at the other end so it wasn't worth the hassle of trying to drag six pieces of luggage. At that point we received some shocking news via a phone call from travel agent Stuart; our Qantas plane home from Bangkok on 31 July had been cancelled due to operational problems. We were told there was a possibility we could fly with British Airways a day before we were scheduled and arrive a day early in Cairns, in plenty of time for the Townsville Marathon. But we were devastated; we'd really wanted to come back from our world challenge with our Australian carrier and the thought of boarding one of its planes at the end of 8 weeks' travel was one of those little things that we talked about to keep our spirits up when the going was tough. Still, we reflected, Qantas was known for safety and we respected that – and reminded ourselves that British Airways was not too shabby either.

Shaken up by this news, we were happy that we'd taken a taxi. The driver didn't speak English but Sue's German came to the rescue. We didn't really expect our hotel room to be ready when we arrived at 8.00am, but we were told it would be in only 30 minutes. We took a walk down to the lake, as the helpful concierge suggested. The sun was shining and held the promise of a warm day, but the morning was still very chilly, with a cool breeze blowing off the water. How beautiful it was down at the lake though, with the sun glistening on the water, and a brilliant blue sky with white clouds on the horizon. On the steep hillsides were beautiful villas with turrets and balconies with geranium filled window boxes. We could see church spires and the copper roofs of official buildings built in the French Empire style popular in the late 1800s. On the lake itself many small yachts were moored, and large ferries cruised about taking passengers on day trips. Lots of locals were out and about, some walking and jogging for pleasure, but most walking or riding bikes to work on the marked trails.

The air was crystal clear and we gazed in awe at the snow covered Alps in the distance. We shivered with the anticipation of our rail journey up to Davos the following morning. There were not many cars around but electric trams and bikes seemed to be the most popular means of transport. Staying as we were in the financial district, however, we did see quite a number of Mercedes, Audi, Porsche, Maserati and Lamborghini vehicles cruising around.

When we stopped for a coffee we were taken aback at the price. AU$5 for a small cappuccino! We'd been expecting things to be expensive in Switzerland but they were mind bogglingly so in contrast to Thailand. After paying $4.50 for a small bottle of soft drink, compared with 50 cents in Pattaya, we decided to be philosophical. It all evens out in the end and there is no point in depriving yourself of what you would really like to do or have when you have travelled so far to get to wherever you are.

REST AND RECOVERY

Status report

We were both very tired but overall our legs felt good with the exception of O'B's right leg which was still making walking difficult for him, especially on uneven surfaces. The 6 day break between marathons for the second week in a row will be a real test.

Trolley tour
Wednesday 23 July

If we hadn't been nursing our legs, or concerned about O'B's injury it would have been very tempting to set off on one of the nearby trails with a day pack. But that was not to be, and after taking a trolley tour of Zurich we boarded a train for a 30 minute ride to the top of one of the mountains overlooking the city. Our brief walk up to the 'Top of Zurich' was more than enough exercise for our weary legs and the view was well worth the trip.

Bahnofstrasse, the main street in the city, is pedestrian-only in some parts, and with the lack of cars the trams are the only serious hazard. There are some very expensive shops all along here – Cartier, Chanel and the like. Just around the corner we found Casa Mia, purported to have the best pizza in Zurich. It had not been easy to find but we were well satisfied with our choice. I was exhausted and I think O'B was too. Our body clocks were 5 hours ahead of Zurich time and again it seemed we were playing catch up with sleep.

A lazy day
Thursday 24 July

Our second day in Zurich saw us head down to the Pier (the Schifflande Burkliplatz) for a boat cruise on Lake Zurich. When we got back, the sight of so many locals lounging around and enjoying the sunny weather encouraged us to go to the park near our hotel and do likewise. After an hour or so, during which time I was bitten on my hand by a bee, we wandered to the railway station to check the details of our train trip to Davos. We got some great advice about catching an earlier train to give ourselves a few more minutes to transfer with the huge amount of luggage we had. The ever-efficient Swiss staff were very helpful and, print out in hand and having scouted the platforms to check the lay of the land, we felt prepared for the next day.

The train to Davos
Friday 25 July

After a 5am wake up call a taxi took us to the railway station where Sue bought breakfast while I stood guard with the luggage. After finding seats and storing our bags in a secure place so we could keep an eye on them, we sat down to eat and wait for the train to depart.

A change of trains at Landquart proved a fair challenge – we had just 5 minutes to get our bags off the train, change platforms and board a different train. With Sue taking our hand luggage and me pulling two suitcases (each with a 25 kilogram bag balanced on top) we figured we'd done a fair workout by the time we pulled away from the station. We marvelled at how the driver waited for the departure time, careful not to depart a second early or a second late.

After leaving Landquart we began our climb into the Alps. Klosters would be our next main stop. The town is a ski resort in its own right and we wondered how effective the quickly flowing streams and rivers we passed might be for cooling sore post-marathon legs.

As the train climbed from 1,000 to 1,500 metres we waited for our first glimpse of the Swiss Alpine Marathon area. Approaching Davos, we had a spectacular view of the town and its lake, nestled in the valley. We kept a lookout for our hotel, which we'd been told was located on a lake, but we couldn't spot it.

Soon we reached Davos Dorf (the village) and once again went to work removing our luggage from the train before it continued on its journey to Davos Platz (central), which we would soon discover was only 1.5 kilometres further down the line. Sue went in search of directions to our hotel while I once again kept a close eye on our luggage. When Sue returned she said the hotel was sending a car. We were only 200 metres away but at that point, with our heavy bags and my suspect leg, that may as well have been 200 kilometres, so I was very happy when the van arrived.

You must be kidding, was our first reaction. The lake adjacent to the hotel was no more than 30 metres by 30 metres, a pond at best, yet our hotel was named the Arabella Seehof (Lake Palace). Our amusement was quickly replaced by alarm. The hotel had no trace of our booking. They suggested it had been cancelled, but before things turned messy we provided the desk staff with our confirmation and panic was averted as we were given a room.

We quickly unpacked and made a note of our new room number. Even Sue with her special talent for remembering numbers was becoming a little confused with the constant changes in accommodation.

Expo and registration

After all the hype about world leaders coming to Davos to meet and the importance of the Congress Centre we were unimpressed. The Centre was unremarkable, nothing more than a town hall or middle of the road university union type of building, so we focused our attention on the marathon expo. With almost zero signs in English and no-one to provide assistance we did our best with Sue using her German speaking abilities to find the registration area for our event. Two envelopes were provided: one with race number and timing chip, the other with a few sample products, a bag tag and a range of brochures all in German. We soon found someone who could speak English and discovered our race shirt was a finisher's shirt and would be provided at the end.

The expo was spread over two levels with about 20 exhibitors. We tried a couple of drink and energy samples then checked out the official race merchandise. Nothing bigger than a large size saved me from purchasing any souvenirs and thereby further increasing the weight of our bags, but Sue was able to find one shirt in her size. Our explorations over, we picked up a few brochures about marathons and went in search of lunch.

Schatzalp and Jakobshorn

At 1,530 metres above sea level, Davos sits between two mountain ranges, each towering more than 1,000 metres above the town. There are many funicular railways and cable cars to access the ski runs and we decided to investigate a couple of them. After leaving the Congress Centre we came across the Schatzalp's departure point. A small train/elevator would take us up the mountainside which we thought would be a good place to get an overall view of the area.

After a quick ride to the top we looked at the restaurant and hotel (apparently well known from a Swiss novel) before discovering that to fully appreciate the views a 10 minute hike was required. Disappointed, we decided to return to Davos, not willing to risk precious leg energy or put O'B's suspect right shin under any unnecessary stress before the marathon the next morning. The temperature in the town was around the 20 degrees Celsius mark and in the sun was very warm, but despite the beautiful blue sky, on top of the mountains it was in the 12 to 14 degrees range, rather cool but much more pleasant than we thought it might be.

We grabbed some ham and cheese rolls and walked further down the main street and caught the cable car to Jakobshorn, some 2,590 metres above sea level. Lots of passengers were taking the cable cars to the top to the walking trails, while tourists and marathoners made up the rest. Many got off at the restaurant and tourist centre at the halfway mark but we continued on to the top where another bar/restaurant was doing a busy trade. Looking down into the surrounding valleys, we could hear the jingle of cowbells from the slopes far below. We walked up the trail towards the summit but found the height and the trail tricky going so after a few photos returned to the terminal.

By now the restaurant seemed full of marathon runners (their t-shirts from previous events gave them away!), many enjoying pasta and large steins of beer which they claimed was good carbo loading.

A check of the map told us that the route for the K78 Swiss Alpine Marathon would go from the valley below to the top of this mountain then back down to the finish line. It mightn't sound much but a 1,000 metres climb was seriously high and we were pleased our race was to go through the valley and along the side of the mountain rather than up and over it. The change in temperature as well as the climb and descent would present the sort of challenge we certainly hadn't trained for.

For some reason the ride up was easier than the ride down and, although we felt safe, the height was rather disconcerting and we were both pleased to be back in the village. We opted for an afternoon snooze and stopped off to pick up some electrolyte drink supplies on the way. With all the changes in time zones and early starts we felt totally zonked. A power nap was the only solution.

Pasta party

Many marathons provide a pasta party a night or two before the race but we rarely go, preferring to eat our own food at the time that suits us best. Two nights before a race is our big pasta night, which rules us out of most pasta parties as they are generally held the night before the race. But this time we decided to take up the offer. The cost was included in our race entry so we figured we had nothing to lose, and we also wanted to soak up the atmosphere. Besides, the 5pm timing meant if we didn't like the food we could try somewhere else later.

We were very pleased we went. The Davos Sportcentre, only a short bus ride from our hotel, was the start of the marathon so we got a chance to check it out at the same time. We shouldn't have been surprised, but there were no giant queues or standing around, as is often the case at pasta parties. Large army coolers of pasta and sauce were set up on pallets and used to restock a number of servicing points. An efficient system for checking tickets meant we were served very quickly and the food was plain and simple yet tasty – pasta, a tomato sauce, cheese if you wanted it and brown bread. Our full plates were more than either of us could eat.

Walking through the park nearby after the meal we shared our fears for the next day. Sue was worried about the altitude; I was dreading the now weekly stabbing pain in my leg. Once again we put into practice one of the key elements of Partnerunning: share problems and concerns. Soon our fears were in perspective and we focused on how lucky we were to be able to do this trip, how much we were enjoying being together and how much we were learning. We also talked of the great opportunities that lay ahead of us to promote Partnerunning and encourage more and more people to exercise together and improve their lives by working on their relationships. Our fears and doubts back in the context of our longer term hopes and aspirations, we took the bus back to the hotel with many of our fellow marathoners and, after checking our gear for the morning, turned in early.

The morning of the race
Saturday July 26th

The race commenced at 8am on the Saturday, 4pm in Melbourne, so we were up early for a quick Skype with the kids before heading off to the start. After the early start at Pattaya, this was extremely civilised and it was nice to shower, breakfast and walk to the race at a leisurely pace.

There were several events, including a 78 kilometre race and two marathons, the K42 and the C42. In general terms, the two marathons form the two halves of the K78 course. The K78 starts at 1,538 metres and drops to 1,032 metres before climbing to 2,500 metres and returning to 1,538 metres. We were running the C42 which included some climbing but overall drops nearly 600 metres. Our hearts would have liked to be running the K42 with its huge climbs, but several months back commonsense had prevailed and we selected the downhill run which we understood was mostly on roads and bitumen, whereas the other runs included large sections of mountain trails. At the time we entered, O'B had been keen to run the K42 but I was adamant we should take the 'flat' option. We were so glad we did! With O'B's leg injury we doubt we could have completed the trail climbing for the K42, although I must say the idea of returning one day with fresh legs to run the K78 is very attractive.

Our course would follow a beautiful valley through the Alps.

Injured leg and altitude aside, we were looking forward to our last run before returning to Australia. Our weekly routine out of the way, we worked through our checklist before heading downstairs. With this race being the seventh in a row, we could easily have become blasé and forgotten something.

The air was fresh but not icy and we guessed the temperature was around 12 degrees Celsius. Almost as soon as we hit the footpath a bus arrived and we joined the other runners on the short but welcome ride to the starting area. Some runners had put on many layers of clothing; we suspected they were K78 competitors on account of the hydration backpacks and other types of running packs they were carrying. It would be a long day for them, possibly 10 hours, and with a huge range of temperatures, even snow at the highest point of the run.

We arrived at the starting area with 30 minutes to spare and decided to drop our clothing bag and go in search of toilets. At this stage the starting area was empty but runners were spread out all over the large sports stadium, some resting but many performing elaborate warm-up rituals. Maybe it was the athletics track, maybe it was just the thing to do in Switzerland, but we'd never seen so many people running and stretching with such intensity before a marathon. If you didn't know better you'd have thought they were preparing themselves for sprint events.

We joined in by walking a lap, then it was time to line up. I listened intently to the announcements, hoping my schoolgirl German would shed some light on what was happening while O'B did his best to take photos. Before long, it was time to go. We braced ourselves for marathon number 7.

I thought you read the fine print

The air still had a crispness to it and many runners had chosen to begin the day with arm warmers and gloves. I had a long top under a singlet and a pair of woollen gloves, but O'B was dressed as usual in just a singlet top. The start around the running track in the Sportszentrum was very narrow, but there was little jostling. For the many around us running 78 kilometres it would be a very long day out, so there was little point in wasting precious energy which may be needed in 10 hours' time. Although there were more men than women in the field, the disparity was not as great as in Pattaya, where women running were scarce. There also appeared to be a lot of older runners in the field, with many seemingly over 50.

From the crowded stadium we headed out into the streets of Davos, towards Davos Dorf and past our hotel. We looked at each other. Weren't we headed the wrong way? Yes! But a 180 degree turn soon put us in the direction we thought we'd be heading as we ran down the main street lined with spectators cheering and clapping and ringing cowbells. How Swiss is that? What a buzz as we ran out under the race banners! Many of our co-runners were racing over to family and friends for hugs and wishes of good luck, some even pausing for photographs. We took our fair share but it has bothered O'B ever since that he missed getting a snap of a large, deluxe barbecue labelled 'The Australian' displayed in a shop window.

Soon we were away from the shops and hotels and bitumen and out in the countryside. We were on a narrow trail across a meadow, past barns and small farms. Again we looked at each other quizzically. Was this how the rest of the race might unfold? Was this going to be a trail run? Had we failed to read the fine print? At this stage we were hopeful it might just mean running on soft surface, which after 6 marathons pounding the pavement sounded like a welcome relief. The narrowness of the trail was of some concern though, and we were reduced to walking single file as the grass was too thick, too uneven and too sloping for overtaking, although it was not too steep either uphill or down – yet. This slow pace caused us to look at our fellow runners and shrug our shoulders. Was this event a run or a walk? Even though we spoke different languages we were all saying, 'I thought this was supposed to be a run?' Much to others' disgust, some impatient runners tried to climb up the grassy bank and leapfrog a few positions ahead.

Partnerunning Tip

Travelling to participate in a run, walk or any activity is a lot of fun and very rewarding. It is a great way for friends, couples, families, clubs or people with shared interests to enjoy time together. However, regardless of the event, spending some time planning and researching what is involved is vital to gaining maximum enjoyment and in many cases to being able to complete your undertaking.

Planning is best done early so you can adapt your training to the conditions, find the right clothes and explore the options for what could go wrong. Of course when running in a foreign country where you don't speak the language, try to find an interpreter to help you understand what you are in for. We will – next time!

Planning and Research is:	
Enhanced by	**Hindered by**
• Selecting multiple advisers & sources of information	• No research
• Reading and internet reviews	• Single sources of information
• Checking updates	• Rushed research
• Including everyone involved in the trip	• Out of date information
	• Only one person involved
	• 'Dodgy' suppliers

Our first drink station at approximately 5 kilometres consisted of cups of water only and we really had no idea what would be available in the way of further refreshments. Rivella, one of the chief sponsors, make a variety of fruit and tea drinks and at some following stations their 'iso-tea' was available. O'B stuck to water but I found it tasted okay, slightly sweet, but quite strongly of tea. Other aid stations provided bananas peeled and cut in segments, buns broken into pieces, soup or bouillon, and some delicious muesli bars cut into bite sized squares. Again we had come equipped with our own energy gels so that we wouldn't have to rely on the food provided by the race. Quite a few of the 78 kilometre runners were wearing hydration backpacks filled with their own drink supply, a very good idea due to the absence of frequent electrolyte drink stations.

Our run along the trail showed no signs of returning to the bitumen. A quick check of the footwear of our fellow runners revealed that many were wearing trail shoes. The penny dropped! This was why at the expo quite a few stands were selling such shoes. It was a trail marathon! We were going to be running off-road and across the countryside.

This wasn't the only difference. At quite a few of our previous races, particularly in North America, we'd noticed the skirt phenomenon among female runners as the increasing trend in race wear, accompanied by long shorts for the male runners. Here in Davos it was knee-length compression socks for both male and females who were wearing them with bike or running shorts.

As we headed for our second drink stop at Heidboden we encountered our first downhill run. Oh my goodness! Or words to that effect. In front of us was a winding, narrow, treacherous path down the side of steep hill that we had made good progress up. Every step brought a sharp pain to my shin. The path was wide enough for two runners side by side and we were amazed to see pairs of runners chatting happily, with just a cursory glance at the terrain as they strode confidently down the hill, dodging tree roots and loose stones. On the other hand, we were single file, carefully staying a few metres apart so as not to have an unobstructed view of any random obstacles, eyes glued to the ground below us and carefully picking our footfall, quadriceps jarring as we landed. Those comfortable with this surface were literally flying down the hill, taking large strides, landing toes forward and disappearing into the distance. Like sidewinder crabs, we navigated some sections with feet landing sideways to avoid pitching headfirst down the slope. How did they not fall over or trip? We can only suppose that years of practice and correct footwear helped.

Crowds had gathered in these small farming communities to wish the runners well as they passed through, and many children were manning the aid stations calling out 'wasser' for water and 'the' for the iso-tea. Dressed in red t-shirts with the white cross of the Swiss flags, they were a bit thrown by our 'thank you' in English – and a lot thrown by my 'good on ya mate'. Mind, we were quite confused by the cries of 'hop hop'. I thought they were saying 'pop pop' or even 'up up', as we'd heard the expression 'runner up' meaning pick up the pace and get moving. We never did find out exactly what it was all about. 'Super' and 'bravo' were far easier to understand.

With distance markers every 5 kilometres and the very difficult terrain, it was becoming increasingly problematic to determine our pace. Constantly climbing and descending the treacherous paths, sometimes blocked by slower climbers, then making very good progress on flatter, wider paths, we'd been doing about 30 minutes per 5 kilometres on previous races, but here our calculations became increasingly irrelevant. Looking at the contour map before the race we'd discovered that overall we'd be descending 400 metres from start to finish. In our ignorance we had thought we might be in for a downhill doddle on bitumen. Instead, here we were working our way up and down continual undulations along tree-root infested paths, occasionally leaping over small streams, constantly aware of other runners trying to overtake us as they hurtled down the slopes, but then us catching up to them on the ascending climbs and passing them.

The scenery was magnificent and many turns around corners were photo moments as spectacular views of the valleys, streams and small villages came into view, with the huge looming presence of the Alps around them. We were not the only ones stopping to capture it all on film! The sun was still shining weakly, although some misty cloud had blown in with the promise of a cloudier and colder finish to the day. Those competing in the 78 kilometres had a clothing pick-up at about the 40 kilometre mark before they commenced their huge climb up Jakobshorn. Robert, whom we'd met at Comrades, had said that the previous time he did this race it had gotten so cold he thought he was going to get hypothermia as he battled through the snow. But the C42 runners descending into the valley for our finish at Tiefencastel were only getting warmer.

A very warm welcome awaited us at Spina, quite a large village and our third aid station. A huge homemade banner across the road encouraged runners to keep up the good work as a father and his sons played a row of cowbells like a xylophone. The aid station was full of encouraging volunteers and we felt enthused again after the very tough work we had put in to get to this point, including a punishing climb, on bitumen, to actually reach the village. We had been running for almost 2 hours and were only at the 15 kilometre mark with a lot of uncertainty about the course ahead. It began to dawn on us that this was going to be a very long day, even tougher for me as my leg was causing me agony, with every descending step sending spears of pain into my right shin and calf. I had taken more painkillers than advised on the packet with only minimal relief and was concerned about what would happen in the latter stages of the run if the terrain continued to be so punishing. Little did we know that things were about to get even more challenging.

Ups and downs

After leaving Spina we were back on our trail running again, this time slowly ascending along the side of the mountains. It was such a gradual climb we did not notice we were so high up until we emerged into the open to gaze down at villages far below and across to the cascading waterfalls. This area is known as Graubünden, which roughly translates as grey walls, and that is indeed what a lot of these massive mountains looked like. Just as we did not expect a trail marathon, the amount of uphill running was a surprise too, and for both of our sakes once again I was glad I'd pushed for the flatter C42 race rather than the steeper K42.

The first medical station was at Monstein and it was just as well. Around here we encountered a few runners who had presumably taken a tumble as they hurtled down the paths. One had blood streaming from a gash in his forehead, another was limping badly with scrapes across his thighs, and yet another had bleeding scratches and dirt smeared across his shins. We saw only these three, but surely there must have been more … Some had tried to instruct us to just stride out and take big steps, but we didn't think it was the time to practise this, not even with fresh, strong and healthy legs.

We didn't actually climb over Silberberg Mountain, but instead almost circumnavigated it before yet another massive descent that just kept going and going and had both of us dropping some very strong expletives! I could actually visualise sliding down the side of the mountain as I lost my footing and O'B said he imagined his injured leg collapsing beneath him, sending him tumbling downward as well. The loose rocks combined with the small pebbles and sticks that seemed to ricochet into our shoes made for added discomfort, but there was no way we could stop to remedy this lest the torrent of runners behind us ran over the top of us. Some runners had come prepared for this situation and were wearing gaiters. Luckily, neither of us ended up with blisters or foot problems, again thanks to our Injinji socks protecting each toe, although we could have worn the outdoor ones instead of performance socks, had we known! We only stopped once during the entire race to empty our shoes of debris which we thought was pretty good considering the conditions.

This long descent was gruelling and we both were beginning to dread the state of our quads as every step not only required constant bracing and support but also jarred the muscles with the hard landings as our toes shot forward inside our shoes into the toe boxes. Would this ever end? We were alongside a fast flowing river, but still high above it as we continued to scramble downward before mercifully flattening out onto a wide unmade road and a stop at the town of Schmetzboden for a drink, gel and a regroup. Above us was an old stone rail bridge and, with perfect timing, a red local train came by, sounding a whistle, full of spectators travelling to the next stop on the course where with any luck they could catch up with their participant.

As we ran along hoping to catch a glance of the train, we tried to think of some of the more unusual races we had heard of. One, the Puffing Billy race against the steam train, takes place each year in the Dandenong Ranges just outside Melbourne. True novelty races – involving mud, wife carrying, unusual costumes and nude running – seem to take place in Europe or the US.

Our wide pathway continued as we made our way to the major check point at Wiesen Station where we actually crossed the rail tracks. At last we had 'solid' and flat ground under our feet and were able to stride out. O'B's leg really appreciated the respite and he was moving very well considering the pain he was in. Again, I was reluctant to ask for specifics but I could tell by his grimaces and expletives he was suffering hugely. Our pathway moved in and out of tunnels carved into the cliffside, and in and out of the dark – and I do mean dark. At times you had no idea where you were landing, but hopefully not in a puddle and even more hopefully on even ground and not in a pothole. One of the problems associated with long runs is that your ability to correct a loss of footing or a bad landing goes awry and just now we were not feeling at all confident of our ability to make corrections quickly if needed.

This 4 kilometre stretch was simply unique. Weaving in and out of the rocks afforded the official photographers some spectacular shots. Certainly we'd never seen anything like this scenery on a run course before. It was a pleasure to get back on the smooth gravel surface though. The gradient was fairly even and the road wide enough for two abreast so we could chat too. We were almost at the 20 kilometre mark when we heard loudspeakers through the trees. No, we were not imagining it. There was music as well and lots of loud cheering.

Wiesen Station straddled the rail tracks, making it the perfect location for a major reconnaissance point for runners and supporters, hence the carnival-like atmosphere. An announcer welcomed each runner by name as they entered the clearing. So it was 'Und hier ist Sue O'Brien aus Australie und sie läuft mit Ihre Mann Andrew!' ('And here is Sue O'Brien from Australia and she is running with her husband Andrew!')

A quick walk and some energy and fuel on board and, enthused by the crowd, we set off to cross one of the highlights of the course, the Wiesen Viaduct. This amazing structure spans the gorge many metres above the river. A quick glance over the edge made us run even faster. Boy, that was a long way down! Amazing views, although we suspect on this occasion it would have been pretty awesome looking up at the runners as they crossed the bridge too.

Over halfway! What a relief. Time had become irrelevant as we reviewed our race scenarios and adopted a slower pace on account of the tougher conditions and the increased pain in my right leg. We focused on enjoying the scenery and finishing in the healthiest state we could. The road had been easier for a few kilometres and we were hopeful it might remain so. The sun was shining brightly again by now and Sue discarded her long-sleeved top, tying it around her waist. The next milestone would be when the K78s and K31s turned off to the town of Filsur.

Optimistically we thought that we must be descending steadily. However, it did not take long before we again turned off the wide flatter terrain and began another ascent up yet another narrow winding trail, dodging tree roots and trickling streams. We had begun the climb up the side of Muchecca, some 2,623 metres high. How much more climbing did we have to do? As we were discussing this we passed a runner in an orange shirt with the logo 'St Bee's Triers' on her back. In an apologetic tone she explained in a very British accent that this was the last climb for the day and it was all downhill after this. Once we came to the 'squirrel sign' we were there, she said. Was this some cryptic clue? It sounded like a treasure hunt.

We were running through a large national forest called Park Ela. As we tore our gaze away from the path we noticed signs denoting different animals posted on pine trees. Suddenly it clicked! We didn't actually see the squirrel sign but suddenly we were out in the open again. Far below us in the valley we could hear the music and loudspeakers for the end of the K31 at Filsur. Ahead of us were marshals standing next to signposts. The C42 people were to head right, and the K31 and K78 runners were to descend into the town. The majority seemed to be travelling to the left. Suddenly it seemed very quiet on our trail.

The last stage

It felt very weird to be running away from the noise and excitement of Filsur. The trail descended at a comfortable gradient to the valley below and was wide enough for us to run side by side. The surface was good too; loose gravel that seemed as though it had been used for vehicles. There was no aid station at the turn off although next to it was an old water pump that Sue and some other runners had decided to turn into an impromptu aid station. The next aid station was also manned by children and their parents wearing Swiss flag t-shirts, and we were thrilled to discover that they had cups of cold Coca Cola.

This drink really is the endurance runner's friend. It was a great discovery for us – and an even bigger one for me. I can now justify drinking it on extra long runs. As we'd discovered on some of our ultra runs, the caffeine and sugar just seem to give you that 'pick me up' and the bubbles, while causing a burp, can actually settle the stomach. Whatever hit our systems first we don't know but again we had that lift. We had fewer than 10 kilometres to go and while it looked as though it was going to take over 5 hours we were going to finish. With the wide flat track, we were running well and actually striding out. I had taken another couple of painkillers and the caffeine helped them kick in quickly so I was feeling more comfortable than I had all day.

But where were all the other runners? For the next few kilometres we did not see a soul. Luckily the course was extremely well marked with tape and markers on trees because for a while we thought we were alone out there. Suddenly, along the valley floor we came across a golf driving range. Luckily there was a net separating golfers and runners. A blonde haired woman was practising until we ran past. She put down her club and applauded. Such a different response to the previous weekend in Pattaya where the runners were pretty much ignored by the locals as they went about their business. Sue recalled the time during the LA Marathon when she went into a McDonalds to use the restroom and the diners stopped eating to give her a hearty round of applause before she returned to the course.

Golf driving ranges often mean a golf course nearby and sure enough, we found ourselves running beside one, detouring past the 16th green as a buggy pulled alongside. This whole area was a big recreational park and we soon were facing the new obstacles of mountain bike riders and walkers with daypacks and sticks. We even ran through the middle of a camping ground, between tents and fireplaces.

We could feel the heat in the sun and were chatting happily as we finally came upon – and passed – a few struggling C42 runners, smiling and nodding encouragement to each other as we came to the last aid station at a town called Surava. It was time to enjoy the last few kilometres.

Or was it? We were a bit flabbergasted that we were climbing again as the path began to wind its way among farmhouses and gardens. One old farmer was sitting in his garden, smoking a pipe and calling encouragement as we went by. Acting as a marshal, he had donned a fluoro orange vest but didn't quite look official as he sat there in his deckchair soaking up the sun. Although the terrain was not treacherous our legs were really complaining about this challenging climb up to the finish at the village of Tiefencastel.

Other runners appeared in front of us. Four of the downhill experts who had flown past us earlier in the day – including one Danish couple dressed in matching outfits and working together in true Partnerunning style – had slowed considerably on the flatter and uphill sections. It was a tribute to our cardio endurance that even after the previous 6 weeks we could still finish strongly. We decided to zoom past these runners, not merely catch up to them. So with a surge of power we pushed past them and on through the back streets of Tiefencastel.

The map had showed we finished at the Mistail Church but then we heard other runners speaking of catching the train from Tiefencastel. We were a bit confused. Was the church in Tiefencastel? We could see a church in the distance on a rise above the village. Perhaps we ran up there and then returned to the village? Having mentally prepared for the finish to be close it really sucked to a see a sign on the roadside saying 40 kilometres. Runners in the distance were working their way up a major road with a significant gradient before again heading off-road around the side of a hill. It really was a case of head down and one foot after the other up this last long climb. Suddenly we emerged from the trees to see a van next to a shed.

'We're at the finish!' I exclaimed.

But we were not sure and kept going until an official jumped in front of us holding up his hands and saying 'Halt, halt'. Which we did.

Our time of a few minutes over five hours was our slowest ever for a marathon but, given the difficult terrain and the injuries we were running with, it was one of our best ever finishes. Just like that the Swiss Alpine C42 was over. Quickly grabbing hands, we ran to the results table, not exactly sure when our timing chips had sounded or if we had actually crossed the line. Sue was quite flabbergasted. Where was the Mistail Church? Surely not the shed? Other runners were sitting in the sun, many with shoes off and drinking the sparkling apple juice that was the sponsor's post race refreshment. Officials were buzzing around taking off timing chips from shoes, tearing a strip off our bibs to denote we'd finished. But where were the medals, our finishers shirts and clothing bags we'd handed in at the start? Back at Tiefencastel, the officials told us. A shuttle bus would be arriving soon.

222 Couple on the Run

A tight squeeze

'You're joking,' I said.

There were over 50 runners waiting for the small silver van, and from the looks of things many had been there quite a while. We were fairly far back in the queue and guessed we might make the third trip down. It was going to take forever to get to the recovery area. We considered walking back, even though we didn't know where we needed to go.

How many runners can you squeeze in a van? Legally eight. But reminiscent of *Guinness Book of Records* attempts for numbers of people in a Mini Cooper, the driver kept waving more and more runners in, before lifting the luggage compartment door open and beckoning us to enter. A total of 25 sore, tired runners were jammed into the van, with seven alone in the back, including us!

We don't know whether the driver thought he was Michael Schumacher, but it felt like it. We swayed from side to side as he swung around corners and revved the engine on the straights. Maybe he took a perverse pleasure in our groans as we fell against each other and the walls of the van when he swerved. There was a collective sigh of relief when he pulled up, though crouched on the floor we had no idea where we actually were. After unfolding ourselves we discovered we were at a large community centre with medals, finishers shirts, our gear bags and more refreshments. There were also showers for those who had brought towels. After a few more photos one question remained: how do we get to the station to get back to Davos? Right on cue our minivan driver arrived with another load from the finish; he was doing a two-part shuttle. We decided the walk would do our legs good!

It was a feeling of déjà vu as we walked out of the centre onto the same road we'd run up earlier, and past that 40 kilometre sign again on the way to the station. Gee it was hard work. We were very glad that the train pulled in almost as soon as we got there. Unfortunately the platform was full of other runners so we couldn't get a seat, although judging by the groans as runners hoisted themselves up when the time came to disembark …

The train journey took us back over parts of the course that we had run. Those close to windows pointed out to family members sections they had run through, but there were few runners out there now.

After a change of trains for passengers connecting to places other than Davos there were even fewer of us. Getting seats at last, we struck up a conversation with a Dutchman whose daughter lived in Australia. He was a schoolteacher in his late 50s and planned his races around school terms. He was hoping to make it to the Gold Coast Marathon in the near future and recommended we run a marathon in the Netherlands, where he said the events were well run, frequent and over very flat courses. At this point in the day, that did sound appealing! He and his wife were camping and had driven to the race. How amazing for Europeans to be able to drive through three countries in one day, making the possibilities for marathoners so bountiful.

We decided to get off at Davos Platz and maybe get a massage before returning to the hotel. Judging by the calibre of athletes running past us, we must have just missed the leaders of the K78 coming through, and the K21. The male winner of the K78, Jonas Buud from Sweden, took 6 hours and 26 seconds to complete the race, over the terrain we had covered, then up the massive Jakobshorn, through snow and back to the stadium finish at Davos. The female winner, Jasmin Nunig, from Davos Platz, won in 7 hours and 36 seconds. We later found out that the majority of the field came in between 9 and 11 hours, but what an accomplishment! Despite the difficulty we both said we would love to come back some day, prepared and fresh for the K78. It really seems an amazing event.

The line for massage was nonexistent but unfortunately no-one was able to have a massage until they had showered. What? We'd never encountered that at a marathon before. Usually you just throw your sweaty body on the table as soon as you can. We had thought it strange that there were 'Dusche' signs up at both the finish area and here. Disappointed, we decided to walk the few kilometres to our hotel and try again later. The massage facilities would be open for many hours yet waiting for all the K78s to finish.

Post race

It's amazing how a shower freshens you up and we felt pretty happy with ourselves as we caught the bus back to the sportsground, although O'B's leg was causing him a great deal of pain. We were very concerned as to what damage he'd actually done to the muscles, tendons or both during the run. He'd had to draw very deeply from within himself to get through the day and now the adrenalin had been withdrawn the pain had intensified. He'd been amazingly brave during this marathon, rarely complaining and pushing himself to go on when it was obviously so tough. For both of us our muscles were at this stage fatigued, but we were dreading the pain that we knew would intensify over the next 48 hours as the DOMS (delayed onset muscle soreness) kicked in.

The massage queue was still small so we took a seat and chatted to some of the English-speaking runners. The German guy had run the K78 three times and the event had become part of his annual race calendar. Sitting opposite us was a Kiwi who had just moved from Sydney to Luxembourg for work and had driven from there with his family to run the K42. As a group of Italians took a seat near us, once again we became aware of the truly international flavour of this event.

Modesty is not a European trait! Post shower runners were stripping down to their Y-fronts without a qualm. Even the girls were down to their G-strings without a worry. But a very pleasant massage it was, and O'B particularly seemed to enjoy having one attractive young masseuse for each leg. There were plenty of tables at this time of the day but a system of closures as the field finished would mean by 7.30pm there would only be a few tables operational.

The Sportszentrum had taken on a carnival-like atmosphere as the announcer got into the spirit of the occasion and music pumped from the loudspeakers. It was still warm and sunny, with clouds increasing though, and the sponsors' huge inflatable displays were bouncing in the breeze. Children waiting for parents were running everywhere kicking soccer balls, holding balloons and grabbing as many product samples as they could. Family groups had set up camp to picnic on the artificial grass surface.

A quick check of the time revealed that it was about 30 minutes from the cut-off time for the K78 at the 12 hour mark. After the drama of the Comrades finish we were intrigued to see whether the organisers were as strict as those in South Africa. Before the start I'd chatted to a young woman doing her second K78 and discovered that yes, there was a strict cut-off and you were not allowed to finish beyond this point. So arriving back at the Sportszentrum for the fourth time that day, we took up a position on the hoardings. The last runners entered the stadium to a rousing reception from the still quite large crowd and a personalised greeting from the announcer once he could read the number on each runner's bib.

It was wonderfully emotional to see these guys finish! Some had run as partners all day, husbands and wives embracing as they crossed the line. Others from different countries had paired up to support each other and held hands, raising them in a victory salute. Some individuals grabbed their supporters as they ran into the stadium and completed the last lap as a group; a wife would run out to greet her husband or a child would jog in with their mum or dad. The most unusual finisher's photo would be that of the runner who picked up the leash of his waiting Dalmatian and crossed the line as man and dog!

The announcer kept repeating something about Rolling Stones but I could not understand exactly what it was all about. Then at 8.00pm Mick Jagger sounded out across the stadium with 'Satisfaction'. The crowd started to sing and clap as a solo runner, an old guy, entered the arena. As he made his slow progress around the last lap, a young blonde woman on a bicycle came onto the track behind him, following closely.

Just before 8.06pm he made it to the finish, arms raised in the air as the crowd cheered wildly. We waited for another runner, O'B using his zoom lens to focus on the entry gate at the far end of the track. But after a short pause the woman on the cycle made her way around the track. As she passed our position 20 metres from the finish line we noticed she had a straw broom strapped to her back. Cute, real cute – unless you are out on the course behind her. Once the sweep moves in front of you, you know you have missed the cut-off and will be unable to finish the race.

What a day! My huge fears of altitude effects had proved to be groundless. With the diversion of running cross country and O'B's distressing leg pain I had barely considered the thinness of the air and certainly never felt any tightness in my chest or experienced difficulty breathing or an erratic heartbeat. I slept well again, despite my aversion to the European duvets, but O'B was still in a lot of pain; even our strongest painkillers were providing little relief.

I was relieved when the 5am alarm went off. Time for some work before catching the train to Zurich airport and our next flight.

The day after
Sunday 27 July

We left Davos on Sunday morning, catching an early train to Zurich, then another to Zurich airport to take our Thai Airlines flight to Bangkok. We'd sent our luggage ahead the night before on the train, and with typical Swiss efficiency it was waiting for us at the Zurich airport train station. This turned out to be a brilliant plan; we had only 6 minutes to transfer trains and we weren't sure whether the luggage man (O'B) would be able to move 100 kilograms of bags that quickly, particularly with his leg injury. And nothing could have prepared us for the pain that we woke up with!

Koh Samui
Monday 28 and Tuesday 29 July

Cumulative flying distance:	**90,878 kilometres**
Cumulative flying time:	**124 hours and 40 minutes**
Cumulative total travel time:	**261 hours and 40 minutes**

We had decided to spend a few days relaxing on the island of Koh Samui in the hope of really resting up before returning to Australia and in a way coming back to reality. It was somewhat ironic that while we were looking forward to coming home, particularly to see the kids, we were prolonging our journey by taking a few days out in Thailand. But we'd reasoned that the flight from Europe to Australia would be a killer and to break the journey was going to assist our recovery, rather than wipe us out with jet lag and fatigue. Besides, we'd been to Koh Samui before so it wasn't a venture into the unknown. It would provide us with the opportunity to reflect on our journey so far and what we had learned.

About 1 hour's flight from Bangkok, Koh Samui has lovely wide, white sandy beaches overhung with palm trees and the beachfront is lined with resorts, restaurants and massage studios. We've visited at various times of the year and always found the water to be warm, the beach clean and the atmosphere tranquil. Huge tides and large sandbars mean that at certain times of the day you will see fishing boats marooned on the sand or couples wandering metres out to sea, still only thigh deep in the water. And I do mean couples! We think Koh Samui must be the honeymoon destination for people from all over the world. Our resort, Kandaburi, and others along the beach were full of couples, both young and old enjoying the warm, sunny weather, lying about or wading in the tepid ocean during the day, sharing candlelit dinners on the beach at night or walking hand-in-hand along the shoreline festooned with fairy lights.

We, however, were in agony! When we first arrived and had to carry our hand luggage off the plane and walk across the runway, I was in so much pain that the airport official carried my bag and assisted me to the transportation shuttle! Sue was complaining that her quads felt like useless lumps as they were doing very little to assist muscle function and movement.

Even the slightest downhill slope caused us to almost lose our balance and exclaim in pain. As for the stairs! Why do Thai resorts have so many? We'd stayed at Kandaburi before, but on that occasion were not 2 days out from what both of us considered to be one of the most difficult marathons we'd ever completed. We found ourselves clutching at handrails and delicately lowering ourselves, sideways, one leg at a time, to make it to the beachfront. Our room on the fourth floor provided wonderful views, but when the elevator only reached the third our agony was compounded! Sue said she'd never been so sore after a race, or for as long, including Comrades. I was inclined to agree, although the added problem of my right shin may have affected my judgement.

Our recovery sessions included gentle walks in the water and along the beach, massage of course, and ice packs for my shin. Our challenges were firstly the 30 minute walk into town for our late afternoon shop and evening meal and secondly – and most significantly –the scaling of some 200 steps to reach the resort's breakfast restaurant. For this we needed to allow an extra 15 minutes, although we both agreed the descent was the more painful. We're not sure what the local Thai staff thought we'd been up to, but there was a lot of giggling behind hands.

By the second day it was more comfortable to walk, but our quadriceps were still almost too sore to touch. Even the most gentle of Thai massages caused us to wince, grimace or in my case groan. Was it a good pain? Often tourists fall asleep being massaged at these beachside studios with the warm temperatures, the gentle sea breeze and the magic hands of the Thai masseuses completely relaxing them. Not us! We were trying to restrain ourselves from writhing around and I was worried I might kick one of the masseuses as my leg reflexes reacted. So, there it was. Even by day 4 after Davos we were still the walking wounded, and again very thankful that we'd planned an 8 day break between our last two marathons.

It was with some regret that we said goodbye to Koh Samui although our departure was not without incident. Finally we were hit with a surcharge for excess baggage! Not much we could do about it, and luckily 50,000 baht turned out to be only about $20. But it's definitely a trap for the unwary traveller; many domestic airlines have much lower luggage allowances than the international ones originally booked with!

On the flight back to Bangkok, we were both thoughtful, quieter than at other times during the trip, slightly sad that our adventure was almost over, yet elated at the thought of completing our challenge. We were both hoping that the joy and excitement of catching up with the family would give us a boost in adrenalin for marathon number 8 in Townsville.

Australia bound
Wednesday 30 July

Sore is not a strong enough word to describe the way our quads had been feeling. Even sleeping in the compression tights for 2 days in a row did nothing to alleviate the pain. Getting up or moving around the plane, indeed trying to get comfortable in our seats, was very difficult.

We were still struggling to accept our slower times in the most recent marathons but realised that running every weekend was bound to take a toll. Nonetheless, we were really looking forward to the Townsville Running Festival, having heard so many good things about it and the community who organises the event. We expected a great weekend and a wonderful end to our 8–8–8 trip.

There was no doubt that we ended up with a challenging series of races and without major hills, rough trails, altitude and language problems we were expecting Townsville to be more like the type of marathon course we were used to running. With this in mind, we hoped to slip in under the 4 hour mark for the first time in a while. But given the current condition of our legs, we suspected we may be kidding ourselves and would be happy just to enjoy running in Australia again and soaking up the atmosphere.

We had a few media commitments lined up and as well as the local Townsville media we hoped to do some radio in most of the Australian capital cities – it was likely to be our last chance before the 2008 Olympics started to promote our fundraising for Oxfam

Australia, and the benefits of exercising with a partner and working on successful relationships in all aspects of our lives. The emails continued and we really enjoyed one that said, 'You do realise of course that most people never run a marathon. When you finish on Sunday in Townsville you will have run about 387 Ks in 49 days at about 7.9 Ks per day. But then again you've probably trained on most of the off days. Now this is getting really scary.'

REST AND RECOVERY

Status report

We were in our worst shape of the trip. The Swiss Alps had really punished our legs, especially our quads, and Sue was also struggling to walk. O'B's right calf and shin were in a very bad way and we were hoping he could make it around the course one more time.

PROGRESS

Lesson for life

Follow the plan.
Develop strategy, plan and act.

Our Swiss Alpine Marathon experience highlighted the value of considering multiple scenarios and then developing strategies to deal with the possibilities. When presented with very different circumstances to what we expected, we did not have to stop and think about what to do, but were able to activate the required plan and act accordingly.

The run home:
Townsville, Australia

'There will come a time when you believe everything is finished. That will be the beginning.'

Louis L'Amour

Cumulative flying distance:	**101,055 kilometres**
Cumulative flying time:	**137 hours and 10 minutes**
Cumulative total travel time:	**291 hours and 10 minutes**

The British Airways flight crew treated us like minor celebrities and we felt very pampered as we flew back into Australia. In Sydney we connected with a domestic flight to Cairns and arrived to a gorgeous Queensland day. Clear blue sky, sunny, slight cool breeze and the temperature in the mid 20s. It was amazing to be finally back, hearing the Aussie accent, and having our colloquialisms understood. We were really looking forward to seeing Anthony and Shelley. Over the past 8 weeks we'd done our best to catch up via Skype calls, emails, texts and the occasional phone call but it would be wonderful to see and speak to them in the flesh.

When we picked up our hire car there was some hesitation on both our parts. Which side of the car did we go to? The last time I was a passenger it was the right. O'B always does a magnificent job driving in whichever country we find ourselves, but as 'navigator' all I can say is satellite navigation is a wonderful marital aid!

We had decided to stay the night in Port Douglas, as neither of us had been that far up the eastern coast and quite a few of our friends had recommended it as a holiday destination. Our legs were still not feeling great, particularly the quads and the problem area in O'B's right calf, and considering it was now Thursday afternoon, this was becoming more serious. Thank goodness the Swiss Alpine Marathon had been on a Saturday and we had that extra day for recovery! Every second was going to be needed to get back in shape. All we could do was rest our legs, stretch and self-massage them, and hope they would improve. The short training runs we'd taken between our early marathons in London, Rio and Calgary were well and truly a thing of the past.

After about an hour along a winding road, we arrived at Port Douglas. Along the way we'd passed the Skyrail cable cars taking passengers up into the rainforest. Then the road hugged the coast and we caught glimpses of quiet, secluded beaches, some with only a handful of sunbathers. Past the turnoffs to Trinity Beach, Palm Cove and other Cairns beaches before finally reaching our destination. Despite its growing popularity, Port Douglas still retains a lot of charm with its traditional Northern Queensland architecture. Many large old hotels and buildings have been renovated, yet the wide verandahs and latticework have been kept.

Our phones had been running hot with requests from both local and national media, and after our overnight flight and the drive to Port Douglas we were ready for a big night's sleep before driving back to Cairns airport to pick up the kids from their flight up from Melbourne. After almost 8 weeks away I was getting very emotional just thinking about seeing them.

The emails kept coming. 'Inspirational!' one exclaimed. 'Good S*#T you guys!' We suspect the writer is now very skilled in the 140 characters required by Twitter! At the time it gave us a really nice boost.

A few cross words
Friday 1 August

We returned to our room after breakfast in time for Sue to do a radio interview on 4TO FM. Then it was back to Cairns airport. We'd checked on the internet and discovered that the kids' plane was almost an hour late, so we made the most of our time writing blogs and catching up on emails.

At the heart of our 8–8–8 journey had been the aim of pushing ourselves out of our comfort zone to see what we could learn. We figured 8 weeks with us away from home also meant learning experiences for Anthony and Shelley, and we were keen to hear of their exploits. They too had been placed in an unusual situation but, unlike us, not one of their choosing. On previous trips away from home we'd paid bills, left stocks of food supplies, made sure there was an adequate supply of clothes and so forth, in order to keep the home running in our absence. But this had not been the case this time and we fully expected some changes in our 18 and 20 year old university students – but felt confident the changes would be mostly positive ones as we moved closer to becoming empty nesters.

I dropped Sue outside the terminal and did a few laps of the carpark before heading back to the 1 minute waiting zone. I was scheduled for a 1.10pm interview with Rod and Alex on 4BC and was just about to park when the call came from Brisbane. I told the story of my nipples' near miss with Deep Heat in Pattaya and at the end of the interview Alex told listeners the story of her friend who accidentally cleaned her teeth with the same product!

Driving down to Townsville gave us a chance to catch up with the kids and find out some local and national news. The trip took much longer than we had anticipated due to the traffic, roadwork, the single lane highway and the radio interviews that each of us did on the way. We needed to be very careful to maintain mobile phone reception for the interviews as some of the areas we were driving through were notoriously inconsistent. We've often been asked since our return about how we got along during this trip and I must admit it was mobile phone coverage in Northern Queensland that caused our only exchange of cross words the whole time we were away. I was searching the internet for mobile phone coverage maps when Sue appeared over my shoulder suggesting an alternative search approach. All I need to say is that we found the information and Sue made a hasty retreat. Thankfully we rarely argue but on the odd occasion when one of us does snap at the other we move on quickly and never allow any altercation to escalate or carry forward.

Anyway, the Tourist Information Office had been very friendly in showing us which areas had poor mobile reception, which was a great help. Keeping what they'd told us in mind, we decided to drive to Innisfail for our next scheduled interview. Sue was to appear on the ABC radio program 'Afternoons with Ingrid Just' at 2.50pm. We arrived with just 10 minutes to spare, found a quiet street and tested the phone reception in readiness for the call from Ingrid's producer Scott. In a quick chat with Ingrid during a song, Sue discovered that she was training for the Melbourne Marathon and her enthusiasm for encouraging others was evident.

It was good to have some new 'minds' to chat with and get a little more diversity in our conversation. We'd travelled with each other for so long that although we'd become very focused we were also very 'comfortable' with each other and it was nice to explore some new topics and consider other perspectives. We arrived into Townsville at dusk, just in time to see the massive Castle Hill which seemed to dominate the town. Then a quick catch up for a photo from the local *Townsville Bulletin* before checking in at the City Oasis Inn, our home for the next few nights. Unfortunately our slow drive down meant we missed Katie and Brendan who had been so helpful in finding us accommodation for the weekend. But we were made to feel very welcome indeed. It seemed that every room in Townsville was taken for the weekend. Apart from the marathon, the Oceania Masters Games were in full swing, there was a massive conference on at the Jupiter's Casino, the Toyota Cowboys Rugby team was playing a home game and there was also an annual bike race and a car rally. Phew! We felt so lucky that the City Oasis, one of the Running Festival's sponsors, had managed to find us rooms.

Time for food, so on the receptionist Lizzie's recommendation we headed to Frank's Pizza Napoli. What an amazing place! Open brickwork, lots of tables jammed together, chock-a-block with patrons, and a flurry of waitresses rushing everywhere. We had a fantastic meal. Anthony's giant schnitzel, a massive piece of tender veal with crisp golden crumbs, was exactly what I'd been searching for the week before in Switzerland. Maybe it could be my post Townsville Marathon treat?

A scenic course
Saturday 2 August

Daylight heralded another brilliant North Queensland winter's day and a chance to have a look around the city and check out the marathon and 10.5 kilometres courses. (Shelley was running the 10.5 kilometres event.) By 8.00am we were driving up Castle Hill to get a view from the lookout over Magnetic Island and the hinterland. It was Saturday morning and the road up was full of walkers, and the occasional jogger taking their constitutional up to the top, around the carpark and then back down. All ages and sizes, some solo and some in pairs, we got the feeling this was a regular workout for most. It looked tough work too, and many who were pushing the pace were covered in sweat. Straightaway it occurred to us what good training it would be for Comrades. How many repeats could you do, we wondered.

Then it was on to drive over the marathon course and see what we were in for the next day. It looked to be a very scenic course along the Strand. Runners would complete two city loops before heading out to Pallarenda Road for one long loop. It was easy to work out both the course and where the drink and refreshment stops would be as the instructions and map provided were very clear and concise – and in English! In complete contrast to last week, our course would be extremely flat, on sealed road the whole way, and at sea level. For most competitors the Townsville Marathon would provide a great opportunity for a personal best time. We thought it would be interesting to be approaching this race with fresh legs and reckoned it would be possible to record a fast time.

We breakfasted along the Strand, which was delightful. This area has a sandy beach and views of Magnetic Island on one side of the road, and Castle Hill and lots of apartments and cafés on the other. We walked across to the rock pool and decided this was where we would spend a few hours in the afternoon after registering for the marathon. The rock pool is a large, man-made, open air bathing facility. With varying water levels it's suitable for bathing or swimming. Filled with seawater, it is about 50 metres in diameter, with rocks and a pathway around one side and a café and restaurant with a large outdoor dining deck on the other. A large grassy bank with barbecue and picnic areas provide plenty of space for sunbathers and others just wanting to soak up the atmosphere. Perfect! We took a short walk through the Botanical Gardens before grabbing our bathers and heading back to the pool to relax a bit and let the pale Melbourne university students feel some warmth on their skins.

It's difficult to judge how much time to spend in the sun the day before a marathon. Too much and you end up dehydrated, although hopefully not sunburnt, and move into holiday not race mode. Staying indoors keeps up the fluids and taking it easy is probably the optimal approach, but so hard to do in places like Honolulu, the Gold Coast and Townsville if the sun is shining and the location picturesque. We try to strike a balance. Besides, getting outdoors for a few hours helps us to acclimatise to the conditions, particularly if it is going to be humid, or we have come from winter into the tropics.

We bought some lunch from the Rock Pool Café, carbohydrate based of course, and were looking forward to a quick swim. But two rogue stingrays put an end to our plans! The rock pool was closed until the two escapees could be captured and returned to their ocean home on the other side of the rock wall, and that was proving to be a very frustrating and time consuming task. There'd be no swimming in the pool for us.

Back at our hotel we received a phone call from O'B's friend and business partner in Melbourne, Gary. I asked him what the weather was like and was perplexed when he said it was warm and sunny. 'Where are you?' I asked, imagining Perth, where he had been last week for work.

His answer of 'Outside room 121' had all of us running into the corridor! Gary had decided to surprise us and run the marathon as well. He'd managed to coordinate with event organisers to keep his entry secret, so our online check of entrants did not reveal his name! Very clever and what a wonderful gesture on his part – and on that of his patient wife Michelle who was at home alone with their four young children.

Our friend Jane was also up from Melbourne. Having run with us in Comrades for our first step along the 8-8-8 path she had felt it fitting that she was there for the last step too. It felt very special having friends and family there to see us finish what we had begun two months ago.

After Jane arrived it was time for another pasta or pizza meal to prepare for the race tomorrow. We sat outside at a local restaurant then headed back to make our final preparations and gear check. Shelley had been able to bring up a fresh supply of Injinji socks, but Gary had forgotten his singlet top, not realising it would be quite so warm. Hat, sunglasses (which would not be needed at the 5.30am start and could therefore easily be forgotten!), anti-chafe balm to stop the chafing during the sweaty conditions, and sun cream for later in the day when the sun rose. (Gary also forgot this and ended up with very pink shoulders.) All done, it was time to set the alarm for 4.00am for marathoners and a much more civilised 6.45am for the 10.5 kilometres runners.

O'B was booked in to do an interview with Sport 927 for the late night show 'NightMoves' hosted by Grant Boyden. We made sure we were ready in plenty of time which was lucky as Grant had certainly done his research and the interview went on for 30 minutes.

Record numbers

It was the 10th anniversary of the McDonald's Townsville Running Festival and record numbers were expected. As well, elite senior runners were participating in the half marathon as part of the Oceania Masters Games. Subsequently there was quite an international flavour at registration and we spotted New Zealand, New Caledonian and Fijian entrants at the tables. The organisers were really hoping that their race continued to grow and pick up international recognition. With few marathons on in the Northern Hemisphere summer and southern states of Australia shivering at this time of year, the Townsville Road Runners have every right to believe that their fast scenic course will appeal to increasing numbers of runners. They had gone to great lengths to ensure that the course itself was certified and accurate with the 'blue line' road markings indicating the precise 42.295 mile distance.

There were approximately 80 entrants in the 2008 marathon, with over 200 in both the half marathon and the 10.5 kilometre distances. A 5 kilometre Adult Run/Walk, a 5 kilometre Junior Run/Walk and a Corporate Run/Walk rounded out the competitors to over 1,200. This made for very small queues at the marathon table and much longer ones at the others, a common feature of just about all the running festivals that we have participated in. A few big races around the world – like Chicago, Boston, New York, London and Paris – only have marathon distance runs, but with multi-distance events come a much greater participation and a bigger boost to race numbers. The wide spread of distances means so many more can participate, and quite often running partners and families who train together can plan a holiday or event that everyone can enjoy, even though they are all taking part in different distance runs or walks.

At the merchandise tent, a volunteer asked if I had entered the 'big person's' event. Often known as the Clydesdale, the title I prefer, this category refers to a division for males over 86 kilograms in weight. In the US this group have been around for a while as it's generally recognised how difficult it is in many ways – for instance, the forces that go through the joints as the distance is covered – for runners to complete a marathon carrying extra size and/or weight. While we'd seen the Clydesdales in the US, this was the first time we'd come across this division in Australia. The US Clydesdales have their own website and compare notes on various races. The female equivalent is the Athena or Filly, but Clydesdales are more common due to the height of some male competitors; the ideal weight for my height is 86 kilograms and there are often men taller than me running, but rarely do you see 6 feet 3 inch women on a marathon course.

A set of scales was eventually produced and it was established that yes, I was in the Clydesdales. (Mind you, it was a real thrill for me that someone thought I could be under 86 kilograms; I am sure they were serious and not just being nice!). Sue decided to check her weight too, which established what we'd suspected: we had both put on about 2 to 3 kilograms over the past few weeks. Even though we'd been running a marathon each week, the other days had been spent recovering and then resting for the next run. We'd also ensured that we were eating well, not skipping meals and carbo loading too. Overall, we'd been exercising less over the total week than we normally would, but were pretty confident that we'd lose the weight with a return to our normal exercise and running regimen so were not too concerned. After all, we were enjoying every moment of our adventure and intended enjoying Townsville most of all.

Off and running
Sunday 3 August

All our alarms and both mobile phones went off simultaneously at 4.00am! We each had a quick shower and dressed, before applying the anti-chafe balm and hoeing into our by now fairly monotonous breakfast of electrolyte drink and a protein bar. I couldn't wait to have a 'normal' breakfast next Sunday! Then with Jane and Gary we walked the 10 minutes down to the start, passing jovial partygoers on the way home from a big night out, before arriving at Tobruk Pool where officials were preparing for the start.

We checked in our gear bag although we anticipated that it would not be needed. The balmy warmth of the pre-dawn had been predicted to evolve into a sunny tropical day. It was so pleasant at the start that the trusty gar-bags were not even needed, which worried O'B in particular, as this usually means there's going to be a big rise in temperature during the race. Comfort at the start translates into discomfort by the end!

Partnerunning Tip

ENJOYMENT

If you want to sustain your health, fitness and relationships you need to enjoy your running. The Partnerunning approach, including the use of common goals and ground rules, is designed to create satisfying experiences. For some enjoyment is about fun; for others it is certain achievements. Whether applying Partnerunning techniques at work or in personal or family relationships, enjoyment can be about delivering great results.

Enjoyment is:	
Enhanced by	**Hindered by**
• Defining success/enjoyment	• Lack of clarity on success
• Agreeing on expectations in advance	• Conflicting expectations
• Making genuine commitments	• False agreements
• Selecting realistic activities and goals	• Selecting one-sided activities
• Being present and fully attentive	• Not being present or distracted

Just after 5.30am and we were off and running – and we do mean running! These Townsville marathoners took off fast. Surely this pace couldn't last! We don't think we're exactly slow starters, but for that first kilometre as we headed along the Strand and out towards the Jupiter's Casino complex in the darkness the pace was furious. At this early hour there was little traffic on the road, but with over

3,000 Jehovah's Witnesses conference delegates arriving by 8.00am we thought the roads could get a little messy later in the day, so were pleased to see that there were plenty of marshals along the course to help with any traffic problems.

The volunteers on any marathon course do a great job and it can be a very long day for them in sometimes very unpleasant weather conditions. Not only do they have the elements to contend with, sometimes they are subject to abuse from disgruntled motorists who've been redirected or even runners who try to short cut the course. The least we can do is say thanks to them for coming out for the day! Special mention should be made of the Scottish marshal at the turn to the marina who had donned a Tam O'Shanter and red wig for the occasion! He was the first course official we had seen who had dressed for the occasion.

Heading around the Casino for the first of two loops, we assessed our physical condition. How were we feeling? How were our legs? O'B was in quite a lot of pain and, as in previous weeks, it was proving difficult for him to get started and get into a rhythm. His whole right leg had turned out slightly to compensate for the calf and his running action had modified considerably from his normal gait. With fresh eyes, Gary had noticed his dragging running style.

My legs felt very heavy and the quadriceps which had taken such a pounding in the Swiss Alps just didn't feel ready for another marathon. In addition to leaden quads, my heel and plantar fascia pain (which had been dormant for almost two months due to the cortisone injections) had returned with a vengeance. So it was with some trepidation that we contemplated the kilometres ahead of us.

But we were having lots of fun. Gary was darting around us taking photos and shooting some video footage. After doing the camera work ourselves for the last seven weeks it was a relief to sit back, enjoy the run, soak in the atmosphere and relish the scenery. The loop nature of the course meant doubling back in parts so we had the chance to talk to Jane, who was a few minutes behind us, as we passed each other.

Running back from the Casino complex, we headed into the nightclub district of King Street and Flinders Street East and received more enthusiastic support from other clubbers on their way home.

'Been to bed yet?' we called out.

'Nah, not yet!'

Further along the Strand we came across one clubber/marathon fan who had decided to prop himself against a wall but had fallen asleep, head tilted sideways and mouth agape. Not sure how much of the action he missed, but by our second lap he had moved on.

Turning back onto the Strand we headed out to Kissing Point and past the rock pool and corner café where we'd breakfasted on Saturday morning. Then past the Jezzine Barracks and around the back streets to the Esplanade that would take us to our turnaround at Primrose Street in front of the Seagulls Resort. The sun was just starting to lift above the horizon. A group still partying on their front lawn were extremely enthusiastic and supportive as we ran by.

We were on the pedestrian walkway, close to the sea and on our return to complete our first 10 kilometre loop, when we were treated to a glorious sunrise over the water. Passing the start area for the first time we received cheers and claps from the officials and supporters and noticed quite a lot of half marathoners arriving for their race start at 7.10am. Beginning our second loop was almost as if we were starting a different race. It was now light and we could see much more of our surroundings: the beautiful yachts in the marina, Magnetic Island out across Cleveland Bay and the palm trees lining the route.

How were we feeling? By now we'd settled into our running rhythm, injuries were being managed and we were motoring along, completing the first 10 kilometres in about 57 minutes. Sue was complaining that this was the worst she'd felt in any of the 8 marathons, but I was feeling the best that I had since Mauritius.

The painkillers seemed to be managing my injury. We did seem to be see-sawing in our fitness but the flat course meant that at least there were no geographical obstacles to contend with, and provided the breeze stayed slight there would be little headwind resistance either.

Heading out again we tried to keep the conversation going with some jokes and light banter to distract ourselves from the creeping fatigue and increasing muscle pain. Loop courses can be hard if you're struggling and retreading the same path with 10 kilometres of tiredness in your legs can be disheartening. Many runners were checking their watches regularly to monitor splits; loop courses do let you check your progress.

We developed a nodding and chatting acquaintance with a few of the runners as we kept turning on the course and seeing the same faces, calling out encouragement and one-line jokes as we passed. This was our way of monitoring our steady pace as we started to close the gap between some of them and ourselves, and eventually passed them as our by now finely tuned endurance engines motored along.

The weather was warming up and with the high humidity our shirts were saturated with sweat. For us, having recently been in climates much warmer and more humid than Townsville, the conditions were pleasant, indeed nearly perfect. Our friends up from Melbourne felt the heat a bit, however, in spite of the cool ocean breeze fanning the course.

On our second loop there were many more spectators. We were also seeing runners' supporters, the same faces over again. One group supporting Rob had a huge banner proclaiming 'GO ROB' which they rushed from location to location to spur him on. After seeing it about four times we turned to the runner behind us.

'Are you Rob?'

He was! We ricocheted in front and behind him a few times when we stopped for walk breaks, 1 minute every 20, before he slowed in the second half. We all had a bit of a laugh the time his enthusiastic followers had the banner backwards so it read 'BOR OG.'

Our second loop was also a solid pace and we were maintaining our 20:1 run/walk ratio, and taking water and Endura (the local electrolyte drink) whenever it was available as we were mindful of the warm weather and the need to keep our hydration levels up. We received lots of positive comments from walkers on the Strand; even if you are feeling lousy it's nice to hear that you are looking good! A rousing welcome met us as we ran past the finishing area for the second last time. Gary had run ahead to take photos, and Anthony was also there to capture this moment on film. It was such a great boost to hear the welcome, see our family and friends as we set out on this second half of our 8th marathon. It was a relief to think that the next time we came through here it would be for the finish. There was never any doubt that we'd get there but it now looked hopeful that we'd finish strongly too.

By the time we ran past the Casino complex again, the Jehovah's Witnesses conference delegates were starting to arrive at the convention hall adjacent to the Casino, but the incomplete road closure seemed to be working without too much inconvenience – to runners anyway! The night clubbers had all gone by the time we returned to King Street and Flinders Street East, but that threatening looking giant spider sculpture was still hovering above us, although it didn't look quite as sinister as it had when it was still dark.

We had hoped we might turn the corner back onto the Strand just as Shelley began her 10.5 kilometre run at 7.45am but we just missed seeing her, although we did spot the rest of the group head off just in front of us. All these coordinated multi-distance events made for a very interesting time as we all tried to catch a glimpse of friends and family members, and admire the pace and form of the leaders. The organisers had done a wonderful job with this and there was minimal interference between the competitors in the different events, from our perspective anyway.

After passing the front lawn party animals for the third time and watching Lisa Jane Weightman (an Australian marathon runner who was competing in the Beijing Olympics) fly past us as she ran on to win the 10.5 kilometres, it was off into uncharted territory along Pallarenda Road. This loop was 21.098 kilometres in distance and again hugged the coastline. Despite the man-made walking track, the landscape along here was natural bush, with gum trees and native plants, quite a contrast to the manicured grass and palm trees of the Strand. After running two loops of the previous part of the course, it was refreshing to only be going out and back once. I was really struggling both mentally and physically by now and each step felt like a huge effort. Was it muscular fatigue or pain in my foot? Or perhaps the realisation that our wonderful adventure was coming to an end?

The road was very flat in a sweeping arc, which meant that we could see some distance in front but not the elusive turning point we were hankering after. 'Where is the turn?' we kept asking ourselves and each other.

With every sweep of road we encouraged each other – 'I think it's just up near that car' – only to have to rethink our landmark. We could see runners heading back on the path close to the shore and were watching the distance markers tick over with glee, but still no turn! By now we were saying, 'It must be soon'. It would be fantastic to finally turn around and head triumphantly back towards the finish.

Pallarenda Road was mentally challenging but we enjoyed catching glimpses of half marathoners who were on this part of the course and who we began to see in great numbers. Many were, of course, Oceania Masters Games competitors, wearing their nation's colours proudly and running great times as they battled for medals.

On the return along Pallarenda Road we saw Jane, moving along very smoothly and looking comfortable as she clocked up her umpteenth marathon for the year. We also managed to take in some magnificent views back to the city of Townsville from the Soroptomist Park viewing point. In the meantime a light cloud had misted over, keeping temperatures down just as they had the potential to make conditions tough for competitors from the southern states. Although the humidity was high, we didn't feel uncomfortable, and both Jane and Gary told us later that at no stage did they feel heat distressed during the run either.

Perhaps it was the adrenalin rush of nearing the finish but O'B was still feeling good physically as we headed down the Strand for the last time. My heel was sore but I was moving well too, with the heaviness and pain of the last kilometres forgotten. Our cardio systems were strong as we contemplated a finish under 4 hours. Physically it was possible – but it would take a mighty effort. Wanting to have the last few metres captured on film, we slowed our pace a bit to let Gary and Anthony get to the finish before us.

There were so many thoughts running through our heads as we ran those last few kilometres – elation that the finish was in sight and we were going to make it, relief that we had as good as completed our massive challenge, sadness that our adventure was drawing to a close. But the last stretch gave us a chance to reflect the weeks just past, and set in motion thoughts and ideas that we'd continue to mull over in the days and weeks ahead. For the moment, however, it was time to bask in our achievements. The crowd along the Strand became very thick with both vocal supporters and runners with medals already around their necks, some from the marathon but mostly from the half marathon and 10.5 kilometre events.

The sun was shining brightly again as we passed the Picnic Bay Surf Lifesaving Club where the post marathon party was taking place. The water adventure playground was already busy. We loved watching the huge bucket of water slowly fill and then up-end, releasing a deluge of water on the delighted kids beneath! The path was crowded with walkers by now too, some three and four abreast, with prams and strollers as well. Surely this wasn't usual for a Sunday morning. Then we realised! We'd come back into the pack of 5 kilometre corporate/ fun walkers. After dodging around them onto the grass a few times, Sue decided a more direct 'runners coming through' approach was required. She must have said it with some attitude because each time she called out there was a dramatic parting of the crowd.

Finally the finish, with walkers heading left and runners to the right for the timing chute. Gary had run on and was filming behind the finish line. Shelley was waiting at the back and Anthony was on the side with his camera as the announcer began to wind up the crowd for our arrival. In one of those unusual twists of serendipity, we came to the line at the same time as some of the City Oasis Inn team in their green shirts. Lisa and Katie (who had been such a help to all of us) were picking up their pace to get past some corporate opposition in the 5 kilometres and we almost bowled each other over. Approaching the finish will do that to you!

To rousing applause, holding hands of course, we finally crossed the finish line for the last time in our 8 week journey. A hug and a kiss for each other and an embrace for Shelley, Anthony and Gary in the finishing area before receiving our medals and having our timing chips removed from our shoes. We stayed there for a long time, taking photos of each other and chatting to other runners and the media. When Brendan and Katie from the Oasis Inn came up to congratulate us it started to sink in. We had done it! We had actually run 8 marathons in 8 countries in 8 weeks! After all the travelling, hauling suitcases, waiting at airports, catching sleep where and when we could our journey was complete.

Meeting Ronald

After talking to Channel 7 and the *Townsville Bulletin* we met George, a McDonald's franchise owner and big supporter of the Townsville

Running Festival. We'd been very lucky in many of the cities and towns on our marathon tour to meet people who were successful in their business and community lives and who contributed to supporting community fitness programs, including running and marathon events. Without the commitment and expertise of such people, participants would not have the opportunities to enjoy the challenge and fitness benefits of the events they organise.

George was joined in the post race crowd by Ronald McDonald who had completed the 5 kilometre run, a mighty achievement given his big red shoes. Our photo collection of the characters we'd met along the journey would not have been complete without a picture with Ronald and we were grateful he agreed to pose for a couple of snaps with us before we moved on to try for a post race massage.

Post race Massage

It had been tough going, there was no doubt about it. My legs comprised sore areas, very sore areas and extremely sore areas. One of the frustrations of my injured right leg was the incredible pain I suffered when running and walking but no obvious sore point to ice or massage. With lots of tight areas and fatigued muscles to work on, my masseuse did a very skilful job on a jumpy and tender subject who, despite all best efforts, struggled to relax. With no marathon to run next weekend, recovery this week would be all about being able to walk relatively pain free as soon as possible, and then begin the rest and then recovery period proper.

We'd been missing our usual training – running shorter distances, indoor cycling, walking, weights and our core strength program – and after a couple of days' rest it would be good to start regaining the fitness we'd lost in recent weeks. Usually in the week after a marathon we do a lot of walking, often as much as 25 kilometres a day, but with the weekly marathon schedule and my inability to walk very far, from Monday to Friday each week we'd done very little, hoping to save our legs and deal with injury. At least this week we'd be able to walk as much as we could, no longer having to save our energy for a 42.2 kilometre run.

Jane wins

A real thrill for us was Jane Sturzaker coming first in her age group in the marathon. Jane had been a wonderful help to us in preparing for the Comrades Marathon in South Africa. She'd completed her 3rd Comrades in June and it was great to finish the 8 marathon tour with someone we'd shared our first race with. Having run marathons and ultra marathons all over the world, Jane has a wealth of running knowledge, and in December, as our 'return' event, we planned to run the Honolulu Marathon with her.

A surprise presentation

With the presentations over we decided to walk slowly back to our hotel for an overdue shower, some fresh clothes and something to eat. As we gathered our belongings the MC announced there was one more presentation to be made. As he continued we realised we were the final presentation. What a wonderful surprise!

It took us a few moments to make our way to the stage. Caught up in the moment as we were, neither of us can recall too much of what was said as we accepted a trophy recognising our 8-8-8 achievement. But we do remember how absolutely thrilled we were, and the warm applause. It was a tremendous way for us to finish our running tour which was best described in an email we received via the blog which simply said, 'What an amazing 8 weeks!"

Status report

Tired, sore and very happy was the best way to describe our condition. We were both keen to find out what was wrong with O'B's leg and he was pleased to be rid of the painkillers, having always been concerned that one way or another they contributed to his Chronic Fatigue Syndrome. Sue was thrilled to have survived the ordeal and was looking forward to a few days' rest before returning to her group fitness instructor routine.

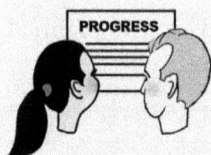

Lesson for life

Enjoy the achievements of others.
Make your partner's success your success.

Focusing on helping your partner cross the finish line has become a guiding principle in our relationship and with everyone we work with. We have discovered that when you truly enjoy the success of others they take you along with them and you win far more than you can when you focus just on your own. Besides, there is something special about enabling others to be successful and fulfil their potential.

Postscript

'To the person who does not know where s/he wants to go there is no favourable wind.'

Seneca

Cumulative flying distance:	103,351 kilometres
Cumulative flying time:	140 hours and 40 minutes
Cumulative total travel time:	335 hours and minutes

It was a stress fracture!

Peter Thomas our trusty physiotherapist diagnosed O'B's leg immediately as a stress fracture. After a frustrating two weeks of tests including an x-ray and ultrasound which showed the leg was fine, a bone scan finally confirmed our worst fears, a severe stress fracture of the right tibia. No wonder he had been in such pain during so many of our marathons.

O'B struggled on crutches for 3 weeks as he discovered the difficulties of day to day activities. Carrying a cup of coffee to his desk with both hands holding the crutches was almost impossible (a thermos flask in a run bottle belt was his solution on day 2). Working in Sydney, Adelaide and Darwin he also found airports extremely challenging. Travelling alone he was unable to pull his wheel on bag he struggled to hobble as short distances took on marathon proportions.

Whether it was the leg and associated frustration or the let down after the 8-8-8 trip O'B was miserable and I was worried about him.

Advice from the specialist that his leg would mend and be stronger than ever did little to improve his mood and when his return to running was delayed from 6 to 8 and then 10 weeks he threw himself into work. We both wondered how long it would take before we could run along our favourite home trail again.

Partnerunning Tip

Learning and improvement are ingrained in Partnerunning and we encourage you to regularly ask questions.
What was meant to happen?
What happened?
Why did it happen?
What will we do differently next time?
The Partnerunning approach has helped us identify 'what we want to happen' which in turn enables us to learn and improve.

Review is:	
Enhanced by	**Hindered by**
• Training diaries and blogs	• Not allocating time to review
• Allocating time	
• After action learning reviews	• Asking closed questions
• Documenting reviews	• Not listening
• Systems thinking techniques	• Not looking for cause and effect and patterns
• Researching alternatives	
	• Not documenting learning

The sports medicine experts told us O'B should not have been able to run 6 marathons with a stress fracture and we both realised how fortunate we were to have been told along the way that it was only a strain. I have no doubt O'B was selective in the answers he provided to the sports therapists we met along the way as he remained adamant until the day we returned home that his leg was not fractured. In the absence of a firm diagnosis he was determined to keep on running and make our vision a reality.

What an adventure!

While in Townsville I booked an appointment with the physiotherapist. Peter has done an amazing job keeping me running as I have now enjoyed more than 50 marathons since I was told never to run again due to very bad arthritis in my right hip. After dropping Sue and the luggage at home I found myself hobbling into Peter's Cheltenham clinic on the morning of the 8th of the 8th 2008 having just run 8 marathons in 8 countries in 8 weeks. Wow, I was keen to thank Peter for all his help but at the same time nervous about what he would diagnose.

After a bunch of questions followed by Peter shaking his head and then a series of prods and pokes, each one accompanied by 'does that hurt?' or 'what about that?' Peter said, 'how many marathons did you run?' Another shake of the head was followed by another shake of the head and then the verdict. 'I am as certain as I can be you have a stress fracture and have had for the last six weeks, how did you deal with the pain?'

I left Peter to pick up my new set of crutches. 'Keep off the leg until the tests are done and absolutely no running' were Peter's last words. I could not bring myself to tell him my next stop was to meet Sue and a television news crew at the local beach trail for an interview and to film us running for the evening news. It was to be my last run for some time.

It felt like the news reporter and cameraman knew of my fracture as they asked us to run up and down the cliffs and I was reminded of the pain from the Swiss Alps. This time it was without pain killers and boy did it hurt! The video showed just how lame I was. When Mark Howard from Channel 10 News asked me how did I feel about what I had done I was at first lost for words, then realised I had the answer to Peter's question about how I dealt with the pain.

From the moment I committed to Sue to run the 8-8-8 challenge I stopped thinking in terms of 'I' or 'me' and it was all about 'we' and 'us'. I had not stopped to think about how 'I' felt as all our conversation and thinking was shared and was about how 'we' felt. Prompted to think about how 'I' felt it dawned on me I felt proud of what we had done and had subconsciously dealt with the pain and difficulty by doing everything I could to help Sue be successful. I realised I felt really good about supporting my partner and being unconditionally committed to her success. Who would have thought a news story would have provided another opportunity for learning about what we had been through?

Mixing with the elite

Road running is very special in the way it enables people of all abilities to compete in the same event and experience 'the roar of the crowd'. It also gives us licence to talk about our experiences. In 6 months in 2008 we participated in the same events as two of the greatest distance runners of all time. First, we finished our Comrades run ahead of Comrades Great Bruce Fordyce (the 9 time winner was reported to be enjoying a social Comrades by running with friends but the record shows O'Brien S and A were faster on the day).

Our next outing against a running legend was more true to form and ability. After I recovered from my fractured leg, we resumed event running in the Great Australian Run (Melbourne, Australia) which was won by marathon world record holder Haile Gebrselassie. Sue was very thrilled to hear him describe her uncle Ron Clarke as his running hero as we watched him give a radio interview from a live broadcast at the event.

2009

We returned to marathon running with the Honolulu Marathon in December 2008 and started 2009 with the Hobart Marathon in Tasmania, Australia in January. March saw us run our second Oxfam in as many years teaming with Trailwalker legends Ty Goldsworthy and Matt Bowker. We were excited to be the first mixed team to finish the 100 kilometre event. Our time was 13 hours and 45 minutes, and Sue was the first woman to cross the line. O'B still can't believe he has made the journey from smoking 100 cigarettes in a day to running 100km in less than 14 hours.

April was more training and another long held goal completed when we ran the London Marathon after a disaster running the Vienna Marathon when for the first – and hopefully only time ever – we lost each other at the 6 kilometre mark. We ran the rest of that race frantically searching for one another! We used this experience to refine our Partnerunning technique for NOT getting separated during a race.

May 2009 saw us go back to South Africa to 'do it all again' and we earned our cherished back-to-back Comrades medals for completing an 'up' run and a 'down' run in consecutive years. At 89 kilometres, with many ups to complement the overall downs, we found up easier. Sue struggled towards the end with plantar fasciitis but we finished in 10 hours and 45 minutes. (Back in our rightful place behind the great Bruce Fordyce to make it one all over the distance). A highlight of 2009 Comrades experience was acting as the hosts for the Travelling Fit touring party as we enjoyed the role of assisting new and returning Comrades runners enjoy their time in South Africa.

Our Comrades trip provided one of the best experiences of our lives as restrictions on flights meant we had a few days to spare. Somewhat reluctantly, we visited the Kruger National Park. It was a fascinating experience to see the African animals up close and once again we discovered the power of trying new things. For years we'd said we were not interested in a safari and our closed minds had prevented us from seeing the possibilities. If not for our shared commitment to running, seeing the wonders of the African Jungle would have been another life experience to pass us by.

2010

In 2010 we decided to stick to marathon running and spare our bodies the challenge of ultra distance running. Instead we focused on writing, speaking, business activities and developing the online community for partnerunning (www.partnerunningcommunity. com). The year started badly with O'B rushed to hospital where he spent the first few days of the year battling a mystery virus, just making it out of bed in time to catch a plane to run one of our favourite events, the Rock n Roll Arizona Marathon.

Our goal to run 10 in 10 in 2010 saw us run marathons in New Zealand, Adelaide, Sydney, Gold Coast, Miami, Venice, Traralgon, and Shepparton. Returning to run the Townsville Marathon without a stress fracture and enjoying the wonderful atmosphere was another highlight.

On the 10th of the 10th 2010 we returned to Chicago to run our 50th Marathon together. This was the celebration and 10 year anniversary of two important milestones, our first marathon together and the beginning of Partnerunning. Three weeks later we joined the Travelling Fit Tour Group for a much bigger celebration as we ran the Athens Marathon to celebrate the 2,500th anniversary of the marathon. This event followed the footsteps of the messenger Pheidippides as he ran from Marathon to Athens 2500 years ago and runners from all over the world had arrived to participate. Running into the Olympic stadium to cross the finish line was truly remarkable and unexpectedly we both shed a few tears, overcome with emotion by the atmosphere.

Our last marathon for 2010 was in New York where the crowd and organisation are truly fantastic. It felt like the crowd of more than a million people were cheering just for us! We are reluctant to tell others what to do, however we really do think everyone should run the New York Marathon at least once in their life. (Then maybe the rest of the other BIG 5 – London, Chicago, Boston and Berlin Marathons).

The big lesson

As we celebrated crossing the marathon finish line hand in hand for the 50th time the number one question we were asked was 'How many marathons do you plan to run together?' This prompted some serious reflection about our running as with the exception of the few months before we hit fifty we had never thought about numbers. We don't run for numbers. We run to be fit to do whatever else we want to do in life.

Thinking back to the first time someone said to us 'you are so lucky to run together' we were fortunate it set off a chain of events that led to the development of Partnerunning. In doing so we came to realise that life can be complex and tricky. Yet an easy to understand and implement set of principles like those comprising Partnerunning can be adopted for success in our personal and professional lives as well as in exercising with a partner.

Running together has been wonderful for our relationship but applying the principles to everything we do has transformed it. Our big lesson has been that by using the Partnerunning approach we have gained the confidence to support each other in taking on new challenges and discovering what is possible. No longer content to avoid challenges and fear failure we are motivated by the idea 'What if we succeed?'

What next?

Continuing to run, walk and/or exercise together to be fit and healthy is well established as a vital aspect of our relationship. The response we received from people during our 8-8-8 challenge convinced us the Partnerunning approach is worth sharing. It might not be for everyone but increasing numbers of people are already enjoying the benefits.

Professional speaking, writing books, publishing, developing websites, filming videos, creating Partnerunning workshops and online courses and growing an online community have become our new tools of the trade. Like the journey from walking a 100 metres to running the Comrades our focus on becoming world class speakers and educators is daunting. Our Partnerunning approach is proving invaluable as we venture into new territory. Running together continues to provide a break from work pressure. It provides the time to focus on what matters and to solve the problems of the day.

We love spreading the word and encouraging as many people as we can to enhance their relationships, health and fitness. It is also very satisfying as people share their stories of improved performance and quality of life at work, at home and on the run. Whether it be for couples, friends, teams, work colleagues or families there are so many ways to benefit from Partnerunning.

We would love to help in any way we can and look forward to hearing from you.

See you down the road somewhere. We wish you all the best in making the most of the power of partnership and the success it brings today and in the long run.

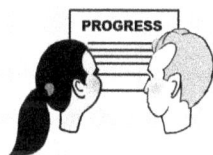

Lesson for life

Create your desired future.
Develop a shared vision worthy of your full commitment.

We have no doubt that our clarity about a desired future made all the difference and allowed us to run the 8 marathons in spite of a series of gruelling challenges along the way. Our constant focus on wanting to encourage others to give Partnerunning and partner exercise a go, and the way we connected our 8 marathon challenge to this long term objective, was vital in keeping us going every step of the way from the beginning of our training until now and beyond.

Afterword

There is a special chemistry when two or more people run together. The positive feelings from a run together are almost always better than those received from running alone. Every week I hear the stories of those who trained for or finished a race with a relative, friend or co-worker and discovered aspects about the person that they had not noticed before. Many spouses have told me that their runs together, or training for a special event together, enhanced their marriage more than any other activity. As you have seen in this book Andrew and Sue have made a wonderful contribution to fitness, friendship and relationship-building and I am honoured to write the afterword. It is also an honour to 'close' a book that was 'opened' by Ron Clarke — who inspired me to be the best I could be, when I was a young runner.

I've noticed that couples who value running together tend to have a strong relationship. I'm very pleased to have helped many partners do this, through my run-walk-run method. By setting the right ratio, those of different abilities can stay together as they run. In fact, it was after a clinic on my run-walk-run method that I first met the O'Briens. From the start I knew that they were a special couple — they disclosed that in a 3 week period, they had successfully used run-walk-run to run Boston, Albuquerque and Big Sur. That was just the beginning. Later they ran 8 marathons in 8 countries in 8 weeks. Shortly afterward, Andrew attended one of my running schools where I encouraged him to write a book. It is a joy to see the finished product — a great job!

My wife Barbara and I met through running. During the first 15 years of our marriage we ran at different paces. But over the past 20 years I have learned the joy of running with her as we do most of our runs together. Currently, we run 7 marathons each year — mostly side-by-side. Even if we have been together all day long, we find ourselves talking about things not covered before, as running activates some areas of our brain and improves vitality — on practically every run. I also appreciate just being with her.

I have run every edition of the Walt Disney World Marathon. At first we came so that our young boys could enjoy the Magic Kingdom. Now, almost every year, all of us Galloways return to Disney for this weekend, but now Brennan and Westin run far faster than we. It is a joy to share the race experiences and the glow of achievement together. The Disney events (Princess Half, Epcot Wine and Dine, Disneyland Half) attract thousands of couples and family groups. Even if the kids don't run, they can be rewarded for not seeing as much of Mom and/or Dad during the months of training.

As mentioned above, good things can happen when two people train together. Elite couples push one another to better quality. Beginners reinforce one another in establishing the habit of fitness and celebrate the improvements together. There's a lot of information in this book that relates to runners at all levels of ability.

Couple on the Run is a valuable contribution, not just because of the running, the achievement, the travel and the story of Andrew and Sue working together. It is the tips and insights into running with a partner that enables the reader to move from inspiration to action and go further together. Congratulations to the O'Briens and I am sure that Partnerunning will enhance the lives of people around the world.

Now it's your turn to take the things you have learned and help other couples enjoy this experience.

Jeff Galloway
US Olympian

www.RunInjuryFree.com

Glossary

AFL: Australian Football League: The premier professional competition for Australian Rules Football. The AFL was formed in 1990 when the former Victorian Football League (VFL) expanded to become a national competition. The VFL has since been reborn and is a Victorian competition once more.

Anti-chafe balm: A product that looks like a roll-on deodorant and is designed to avoid chafing during exercise. Often applied to underarms, thighs, neck, chest and other areas where rubbing of material on skin damages the skin.

Desired Futures: An approach developed by Andrew as a result of his doctoral research and corporate work with organisations, teams and individuals. The Desired Futures approach assists individuals, couples, teams, business and community organisations determine the future they wish to create and then to work together to achieve it.

Energy gel: A mix of complex carbohydrates and glucose specially designed for consumption during endurance events to provide energy and sustenance. Provided in a small, easy to open packages, energy gels are easy to carry when running.

Essendon: Football club in the AFL for which Sue's father, Jack Clarke played.

Flash to bang ratio: The flash to bang ratio is calculated by starting counting on the lightning flash and stopping counting when the associated thunder is heard. You then divide this number (in seconds) by 5 to determine the distance (in miles) to the lightning flash. For example, if the time in seconds between the lightning being spotted and the thunder being heard is equal to 30, divide that by 5, and you get 6 (30/5 = 6). Therefore, that lightning flash was approximately 6 miles away from the observer.

Gel: Short for energy gel.

GU: An energy gel used during endurance events.

Half marathon: A footrace over 21.0975 kilometres or 13.1 miles.

Jack Clarke: Sue's father, an architect and elite Australian Rules Footballer, who went on to represent Australia in Triathlon. Jack played 263 games for the Essendon Football Club, was captain from 1958 to 1964, played in the 1962 and 1965 premiership teams and was a three times All Australian who also coached Essendon from 1968 to 1970. Jack died tragically of a rare form of cancer in 2001.

Jeff Galloway: See About Contributors.

Kilometre: A metric measure of distance comprising 1,000 metres and equal to 0.621 miles. The kilometre is used on road signs throughout the world except in the United States and the United Kingdom.

Marathon: A foot race over 42.195 kilometres or 26.2 miles.

Mile: An imperial measure of distance comprising 1,760 yards equal to 1.609344 kilometres. The mile is used on road (and marathon) signs in the United States and United Kingdom.

Pace group: A group of runners aiming to complete a running or walking event in a designated time. The group is led by an experienced runner or walker who often carries a flag, sign or balloons and wears a shirt displaying the target time. Participants sign up to join the group before the event but anyone can join in during the run or walk.

Partnerships that Matter: Parent company for our business activities. Details at www.coupleontherun.com, www.Partnerunning.com, www.partnerunningcommunity.com and for Desired Futures at www.andrewob.com.

Partnerunning: The term describes running with a partner and includes a set of tools to support a successful partnership. Partnerunning is a registered trademark used under licence by Couple on the Run and Partnerships that Matter.

Plantar fascia: The thick band of tissue which supports the arch of the foot. In layman's terms it runs along the bottom of the foot from the heel to the ball of the foot.

Plantar fasciitis: A painful inflammatory injury normally due to excessive wear to the plantar fascia. People who spend a lot of work time on their feet, such as retail workers and nurses, as well as runners are susceptible to this condition.

Ron Clarke MBE: See About Contributors.

Shin splints: The term used to describe a painful condition in the shin often due to running or jumping.

Soleus: A strong muscle in the back part of the lower leg known to most of us as the calf.

St Kilda: Football Club in the AFL for which Sue's father, Jack Clarke, was an assistant coach.

Stress fracture: Also known as a hairline fracture; a crack in the bone due to repeated impact.

Taper: A period before an endurance event where training is reduced in order to rest and recover so as to improve race performance.

Travelling Fit: A leading travel company specialising in providing packages to the worlds greatest half-marathon, marathon, ultra marathon and other running events. See www.travellingfit.com for more information.

Ultra marathon: A footrace longer than 42.195 kilometres.

Ultra marathoner: A person who participates in ultramarathons.

Vision that Matters: A process developed by Andrew as a result of his doctoral research and CEO work. It is a key aspect of his work on desired futures for individuals, partners, teams and organisations.

About Sue and Andrew O'Brien

Sue O'Brien

Sue is a sought-after speaker and workshop presenter, and is recognised as a leading fitness expert who is a living example of what is possible when you put your expertise into practice. She loves her profession and has worked in the fitness industry for more than 25 years, regularly teaching 15 to 20 indoor cycle, aerobics and core strength classes each week while working with individual clients and developing Partnerunning.

Sue is a mother of two who many years ago started running with her father, former Essendon great Jack Clarke, and brother Ian. Before taking up marathon running Sue was a regular winner of state and national age group triathlons and twice represented Australia at the world triathlon championships. Sue has a Bachelor of Education and is a regular contributor to her own learning as well as to the learning of others.

> *'Shared joy is a double joy;*
> *shared sorrow is half a sorrow.'*
> Swedish Proverb

Andrew O'Brien

Andrew took up running in his 30s in order to improve his health and fitness after living an unhealthy lifestyle during his 20s. It was during this effort to regain his health that Andrew met Sue and before too long decided to run a marathon as a goal for recovering from illness. In 2004 Andrew was the Customer Service Institute of Australia's Victorian CEO of the Year and has worked in industries including retail, food service, sport and fitness, facility management and higher education.

Andrew works with executive leaders to engage teams, staff and customers in effective strategy, successful partnerships and desired results. Andrew is the author of the Desired Futures series and shares the stage with Sue as well as speaking alone on his areas of expertise which include vision, strategy, performance and thought leadership.

Andrew's doctorate, focusing on organisational performance through shared vision and collaboration, is from Swinburne University of Technology where he also completed a Master of Business Administration. Andrew also has a Master of Management degree from Monash University and a Master of Financial Planning from the University of the Sunshine Coast. He combines more than 20 years' CEO work with the latest management and partnering thinking to act as an executive adviser and Thought Leaders Mentor.

'I like her because she smiles at me
and means it.'

Anonymous

About the Contributors

Ron Clarke (Foreword)

Ron grew up in the Melbourne suburb of Essendon and spent as much time as possible playing sport and running with Sue's father, Jack Clarke. Olympian Ron Clarke is a running legend, successful businessman, bestselling author and in 2010 was serving his 2nd term as Mayor of the Gold Coast in Australia. Ron was the first athlete to break 13 minutes for the 3 miles and 28 minutes for the 10,000 metres. Ron set 19 world track records and 36 Australian records. From 1968 to 1972 Ron held every world record for distances between two miles and 20,000 metres. Ron has mentored Sue and Andrew in their running and writing endeavours.

Jeff Galloway (Afterword)

Olympian Jeff Galloway is based in Atlanta, Georgia, USA and has worked with tens of thousands of runners all around the world to help them stay motivated, enjoy running with fewer aches and pains and to increase their enjoyment. Jeff is the author of the best selling running book in North America, an inspirational speaker and *Runners World* columnist. Jeff represented the USA at the 1972 Olympics and has completed more than 100 marathons. Andrew and Sue are fortunate to count Jeff Galloway as one of their mentors.

Jock Macneish (Illustrations)

Jock was born in Trinidad and went to school in Scotland. He studied Architecture in London and in Melbourne and has worked in many parts of the world. His work covers Architecture, Acoustic Consultancy, Illustrations and Cartooning. Jock now runs a company that creates images designed to carry ideas. He calls them "Strategic Images." He lives in the hills near Melbourne where, if he heard a hooter, he'd assume there was a bushfire rather than the start of a marathon.

Acknowledgements

We are particularly grateful to the following people for their support and encouragement:

Ron and Helen Clarke have been a constant source of encouragement and support and we are very grateful to Ron for writing the foreword.

Jeff Galloway was also very encouraging and his tips and techniques for sustainable running have been invaluable.

Jock Macneish brings ideas to life and communicates them in a way we can all talk about. Jock is wonderful to work with and an ongoing source of inspiration and guidance. A special thanks to Jock and Di for all their encouragement and understanding.

The Comrades Marathon Association provided permission to quote from their website and program guide whilst Deane Riddick provided permission to use the photograph on the front cover. We did our best to do justice to their words and picture respectively.

Oxfam Australia provided great support and made life easier by handling the receipt of donations via the Oxfam website.

Every weekend race officials, volunteers, and a seemingly endless supply of supporters make it possible for people like us to run in organised events. You are our heroes and we can't thank you enough. Also worthy of great thanks are our fellow runners. Many faster and more experienced than us who provide tips, suggestions and encouragement to help others enjoy the challenge. A special mention to all the partner and couple runners who provide us with great inspiration.

Gary and Michelle Ryan, our business partners and friends, continue to offer great support and we look forward to 'Going Further Together' in the years ahead.

Peter Thomas, our dedicated physiotherapist, has been keeping us on the road since our first marathon together and we are forever grateful for his advice, knowledge and ability to help us mostly avoid and from time to time overcome injury.

Paul Ramler AM has been a longstanding friend and mentor, providing an ongoing source of advice and belief in what is possible.

Friends Jane and Robert Sturzaker and Chris and Leanne Sutcliffe helped immensely with extra encouragement and assistance for our training for Oxfam Trailwalker and the Comrades Marathon.

Brooke Alexander has been fantastic in managing the *Couple on the Run* book project and helping us through the publishing maze while accommodating our slower than ideal work on the manuscript. Thanks also to Dr Janet Hutchinson who did a mighty job in editing our manuscript and to Gillian Smith who provided valuable editorial advice during the writing of the book.

Matt Church has provided a timely reminder that our message is worth sharing while mentoring us in bringing our story to life on stage as we embark on the speaking and presentation aspect of encouraging people to go further together.

Gihan Perera is a master at helping us take our passion online with his outstanding strategic thinking, technical knowledge, service and enthusiasm.

Justine Bloome as our marketing adviser has been a wonderful addition to our world as we continue to discover how much we have to learn about connecting with people.

Gary Rothville, Chelsey Nash, Geoff Macdonald, Helen McDonald, Nigel Collin, Ana Roman, Sharon Hoar, Brett Perozzi, Craig Bulmer, Tyson Goldsworthy, Matt Bowker, Steve Teleki, Simon Dikkenberg, Malcolm Fielden, Stuart Ingram, Trevor Young, Jaselyn O'Sullivan and the many, many people we have met along the way and who attend Sue's fitness classes and Andrew's business and Desired Futures programs have provided much needed encouragement and we thank them very much.

Finally big thanks to our family – Anthony, Shelley, Estelle, Arnold, Joan, Ian, Harriet, Josh, Alex, Jack, Chris, Janine, Thomas, Kayla and Molly.

Couple on the Run Services

Integral to Andrew and Sue O'Brien's Partnerunning activities is the focus on sharing their learnings, success principles and message with likeminded groups, organisations and companies. Andrew and Sue welcome the opportunity to talk with you about ways they can be of assistance. Opportunities include:

- Keynote speeches to inspire, challenge and create action
- Conference packages for a unique experience
- Partner conferences to enhance relationships
- Theme weaving and facilitation for learning and action
- Workshops to improve performance
- Mentoring for corporate and personal success
- Partnerunning programs for team and individual performance

With combined expertise ranging from senior corporate management through to fitness training, Andrew and Sue work with you to tailor programs and events that deliver results. Whether you are looking to improve individual performance, develop teamwork and collaboration or provide a partner conference with a difference the O'Briens welcome the opportunity to talk about how they can assist you.

Find Couple on the Run online at:
Book and speaking: www.coupleontherun.com
Twitter @coupleontherun
Blog at: www.coupleontherun.info

To discuss your requirements please email:
info@partnerunning.com.

'Those who are ready to join hands can overcome the greatest challenges.'
Nelson Mandela

Also from Couple on the Run

Go Further Together

Combining the partnership lessons from Couple on the Run and Dr O'Brien's executive leadership, corporate strategy, thought leadership and large group facilitation work Go Further Together is presented as:

1. Go Further Together Keynote Presentation for Conferences and Events;
2. Go Further Together Workshop; and,
3. Go Further Together Book.

The 'Go Further Together' Keynote and Workshop are tailored to suit your audience as the principles can be applied to a range of settings including business and community organisations, teams, partnerships, couples and individuals.

Email: info@partnerunning.com for more information.

Find Dr O'Brien's Desired Futures and Thought Leaders at:

www.andrewob.com

www.andrewob.info

Twitter @andrew_ob

www.thoughtleaders.com.au

www.partnerunningcommunity.com

The time has come for Partnerunning as an emerging movement to assist you to achieve your desired success in your personal and professional life.

Life is at its best when we:

- Experience great relationships
- Enjoy our health and fitness
- Achieve and create the future we truly want

The Partnerunning™ principles combine the best of fitness, relationship and management practices to enable members of the Partnerunning community to perform at their best.

With three levels of membership the Partnerunning Online Community is continuing to grow and provide members with :

- Regular webinars on running, partner exercise, training, event, travel and member requested topics;
- Exclusive access to Andrew, Sue and other experts;
- Facilities to create your own Partnerunning blog and personal webpage;
- Training programs and online courses;
- Reviews of events, products and services; and,
- A developing range of run, travel, relationship and Partnerunning goodies.

Connect with the Partnerunners at:
www.partnerunningcommunity.com
Follow us on Twitter @Partnerunning or find out more at
www.partnerunning.com or www.facebook.com/Partnerunning

PARTNERUNNING™

www.ingramcontent.com/pod-product-compliance
Lightning Source LLC
Chambersburg PA
CBHW052031090426
42739CB00010B/1864